INTRODUCING
THE CHURCH OF CHRIST

DISTINCTIVE FEATURES OF THE CHURCH OF CHRIST
DISCUSSED BY OVER FIFTY OF HER MINISTERS

To all those godly souls, past and present, who have earnestly sought for the truth that makes men free, we dedicate this volume. May it contribute in some small way to the realization of that desire for generations now living and yet to come.

ISBN 0-933672-72-1

STAR BIBLE PUBLICATIONS, INC.
P.O. Box 821220
Fort Worth, Texas 76182

FOREWORD

The Bible is the only book that is a safe and sure guide on any and all subjects "pertaining to life and godliness" (2 Peter 1:3). This book is only intended as an incentive to the reader to "search the Scriptures to see whether these things are so" (see Acts 17:11). On the important theme of the church Jesus built, neither the editor nor any writer would want to leave the impression that the chapter he had written about the church constituted any kind of an authority or creed for settling questions or disputes. Rather, he would have the reader to go to the Scriptures and allow God to speak the final word.

If a more extensive study on these matters is desired, the reader may enroll in a Bible course by mail which is described on the back cover of this book. For any good you may derive from our humble efforts in editing, writing and publishing the book, we shall be thankful and shall ascribe unto God all "the glory in the church and in Christ Jesus unto all generations" (Ephesians 3:21).

Alvin Jennings
Director and Managing Editor
Star Bible Publications, Inc.

September 3, 1981
Fort Worth, Texas

First Printing 1981, 88,000
Second Printing 1982, 50,000
Third Printing 1993, 50,000

INTRODUCTION

Institutional church membership is declining. People are turning away from the established churches in great numbers. Why?

In many churches, people went to hear a message from God's word but only heard the Bible discredited and ridiculed.

They went to worship the Lord and the preacher told them God was dead.

They went to learn of Christ, to be saved. They heard him dethroned by teachers who denied his virgin birth, his miracles, his resurrection, his divinity.

They went seeking communion with God and food for their souls, but heard a harangue on politics and social problems.

They took their children to learn God's rules for right living. They were given lectures endorsing situation ethics and civil disobedience. Homosexuality and free love were extolled. The forces of law and order were castigated.

They gave their gifts to God to care for the needy and evangelize the world for Christ. The money was given to radical militants and to political lobbies. It provided worldly, sinful entertainment for their young.

They sought to sing praises unto God, but were forced to listen to the blare of a "spiritual jazz concert."

Does some or all of this sound familiar? Are you going to church more but enjoying it less? What would you give to worship as the first Christians did? You can, you know. There is a group of dedicated Christians near you practicing First Century Christianity. They are a church you can read of in your Bible. They have rejected the corruptions we have referred to. They honor the Bible as God's Holy Word. It is their only guide.

Who are these people? They are the "churches of Christ" (Romans 16:16).

To introduce you to this church and inform you of her beliefs and practices, we have prepared this collection of lessons. We hope you will find time to carefully read each one through checking the Biblical citations.

After you have read the book, do you have other Bible questions for which you seek answers? If so, write us. A carefully researched and Biblically documented answer will be sent.

Would you like to enroll in a free Bible Correspondence Course to further develop your knowledge? Such is available at your request.

Would you want to become a Christian as were Paul, Peter and others of the New Testament? We will be pleased to put you in touch with a non-denominational Christian who will gladly assist you in completing your submission to Jesus by immersing you for forgiveness of sins.

If you would like to worship with a group of New Testament Christians, we will advise you of the church nearest you. If one is not available, we will send you further instructions on how to start a Bible church in your home.

Write us in care of the publisher.

It is our prayer that this book will help you to understand God's will for your life more clearly and will inspire you to follow his precious Son, Jesus.

The Editor

CONTENTS

5

1

The church was
PREDICTED BY THE PROPHETS

By LeRoy R. Durley

There is a common concept that the Lord Jesus Christ came to this earth to set up or establish his kingdom, but being rejected by the Jews, he postponed his kingdom and set up the church instead. Proponents of this doctrine believe that Jesus will set up his kingdom on earth when he returns the second time. This concept relegates the church to the role of a stop-gap measure, a kind of after-thought conceived by Christ to provide something to fill the gap between his return to the Father and his return to the earth. It is also commonly believed that the prophets said nothing about the church. They saw only the first coming of the Christ and his yet to come, earthly kingdom. In this lesson, our aim will be to show that the New Testament church was planned by God and prophesied by the prophets and that these prophecies were fulfilled on the first Pentecost following the resurrection of Jesus Christ.

Was the church predicted by the prophets? In order to arrive at the correct answer, it is imperative that we understand, that in the Bible, the kingdom and the house of the Lord in the prophecy of the Old Testament often refer to the church of the New Testament.

Jesus predicted that he would build his church (Matthew 16:18). He called his church "the kingdom" (Matt. 16:19). Therefore, the church and the kingdom in this sense, are the same. Christ is the head of both the church and the kingdom. The terms of admission are the same. Those in the church are also in the kingdom. The apostle Paul said, that "the house of God is the church of the living God" (1 Timothy 3:15). From these Scriptures, we may conclude that the Lord's house, the kingdom and the church often refer to one and the same thing.

At this juncture, I suggest that you read and consider the seventh chapter of Second Samuel. This chapter reveals that David the king, had purposed to build a house for God. In contrast, God rejected David's proposal but promised to build a house for David and the people. This mission would be accomplished through David's seed after the death of the former. In addition to building his house, his throne would also be established (2 Samuel 7: 12-16). The full accomplishment of this prophecy, related to Jesus Christ who is often called David and the Son of David. He was of the seed of David (Acts 13:23). The promise "I will be his Father and he will be my Son," is expressly applied to Christ by the apostle (Hebrews 1:5). The establishing of his house and his throne, and his kingdom for ever (2 Sam. 7:13 & 16), can be applied to no other than Christ and his kingdom. David's earthly house and kingdom long ago came to an end. Only the kingdom of Christ is everlasting. On the day of Pentecost, the apostle Peter said that God had sworn unto David that he would raise up Christ to sit on his throne (Acts 2:30). The announcement of the reign of Christ was given on the day of Pentecost. See Acts chapter two.

The first prophecy we will consider was recorded by Isaiah. "The word that Isaiah the son of Amoz saw concerning Judah and Jerusalem. And it shall come to pass in the last days, that the mountain of the Lord's house shall be established in the top of the mountains, and shall be exalted above the hills; and all nations shall flow unto it. And many people shall go and say, Come ye, and let us go up to the mountain of the Lord, to the house of the

8

God of Jacob; and he will teach us of his ways, and we will walk in his paths; for out of Zion shall go forth the law, and the word of the LORD from Jerusalem (Isaiah 2:1-3). This Scripture prophesied of the church which was to be established on the top of the mountains or above all other governments. Isaiah also stated three fundamental facts, namely:

1. The prophecy would be fulfilled in *The Last Days*.
2. *All Nations* would flow unto it.
3. It would have its *Beginning In Jerusalem*.

After interpreting the dream of Nebuchadnezzar, king of Babylon, Daniel predicted that the God of heaven would set up a kingdom which would never be destroyed. This kingdom would not be left to other people, but would break in pieces and consume all the other kingdoms and would stand for ever (Daniel 2:44).

When John the Baptist came preaching in the wilderness of Judea, his message was, "Repent ye: for the kingdom of heaven is at hand" (Matt. 3:1). To be "at hand" meant "to be near," denoting that the kingdom was not in actual existence in the days of John. This prophecy of the kingdom was a prophecy of the church.

Others who preached the kingdom as near but yet in the future was Jesus (Matt. 4:17) and his disciples who preached it to the lost sheep of the house of Israel (Matt. 10:5-7). The seventy disciples preached it also (Luke 10:1-9). Each of these Scripture references point to the kingdom to be established in the future.

Again, let us recall that Jesus said that he would build his church (according to Matthew 16:18), and he called his church "the kingdom" in verse 19. Since the kingdom was predicted, therefore, the church also, was predicted.

Jesus gave another prophecy when he said, "Verily, I say unto you, that there be some of them that stand here, which shall not taste of death, till they have seen the kingdom of God come with power" (Mark 9:1). Here we can see that some of the people standing there with Jesus would not die until they had seen the kingdom

9

come with power. Now we ask the question. What is the power predicted to come?

After his resurrection, Jesus said to his disciples: "Thus it is written and thus it behooved Christ to suffer, and to rise from the dead the third day: And that repentance and remission of sins should be preached in his name among all nations, beginning at Jerusalem (Luke 24:46-47). In this prediction, the prophecy of *all nations* and *beginning in Jerusalem,* spoken of by Isaiah, is about to be fulfilled. Now we must check to see if it occurred during the *last days.*

Shortly, before Jesus ascended back to heaven, the disciples asked him if he would restore again the kingdom to Israel. (Acts 1:6). Jesus said unto them, "It is not for you to know the times or the seasons, which the Father hath put in his own power. But ye shall receive power, after that the Holy Ghost is come upon you" (Acts 1:7-8). The Lord made it known that power would come with the Holy Ghost. When we establish the time of the coming of the Holy Ghost, we will know when the power came and also, when the kingdom, which is the church, had its beginning.

On the day of Pentecost, the Holy Spirit came and filled the apostles. They spoke with new tongues or languages as the Spirit gave them utterance (Acts 2:1-4). They were charged with being drunk or filled with new wine (Acts 2:13). Peter denied the charge and stated that what the people were seeing and hearing was that which was spoken by the prophet Joel, "And it shall come to pass in the last days, saith God, I will pour out my Spirit upon all flesh . . ." (Acts 2:16-17). Here we may learn that the events of Pentecost transpired during the last days. The three fundamental facts of Isaiah's prophecy were fulfilled on Pentecost. They took place in the last days; all nations were assembled there; and these events had their beginning in Jerusalem.

You will remember that Jesus said that the kingdom would come with power. The power came with the Holy Spirit. Since the Holy Spirit came on Pentecost, we conclude that the kingdom, the church, came on Pentecost as was prophesied. On Pentecost, the people heard and obeyed the gospel. The Lord added to the church those who were being saved (Acts 2:47). No one was added to the church before Pentecost. Therefore, the church had its beginning on the day of Pentecost.

The church was also according to the plan or purpose of God. This purpose was a mystery or secret. Paul said that he was less than the least of all saints but God called him to preach to the Gentiles, and to explain to all people the meaning of the secret. God kept this secret to himself from the beginning of the world. What was his reason for this? To show to all the rulers how perfectly wise he is when all his family — Jews and Gentiles alike — are seen united together in the church, in just the way he had planned through Jesus Christ our Lord (Ephesians 3:7-11).

The actual historical formation of the church occurred in Jerusalem on the day of Pentecost. On that day the Spirit was poured out upon the disciples to form the body of Christ, the church. Peter referred to that as the beginning (Acts 11:15-16). The beginning can only refer to Pentecost, thus identifying it as the time of the "baptism with the Holy Ghost." Pentecost marks not only the beginning of the church as the spiritual reality of the body of Christ, but also the visible church.

QUESTIONS

Was the church of the New Testament planned by God and predicted by his prophets?

What Scriptures in the Old Testament show the prophecy of the church?

What Scriptures in the New Testament show the fulfillment of the prophecies?

Does this church exist today?

Are you a member in this church?

2

The church was
FOUNDED BY JESUS
AND ON HIM

By Hugh Fulford

T he church of Christ is correctly called the church of Christ for several reasons. Such designation is not a denominational name nor the only exclusive name by which the Bible refers to the church. But because Christ founded the church and because he is the very foundation of the church it is very appropriately called the church of Christ.

THE CHURCH'S FOUNDER

In Matthew 16:18 Jesus said to Simon Peter, "And I say also unto thee, that thou art Peter, and upon this rock I will build my church; and the gates of hell shall not prevail against it." From this passage it is very obvious that Christ is the builder or founder of the New Testament church and that he calls this church his church. Any church founded by someone other than Christ is not Christ's church. David, in the Old Testament, announced a great truth when he said, "Except the Lord build the house, they labour in vain that build it" (Psalm 127:1). In the New Testament we learn that the "house of God is the church of the living God" (1 Timothy 3:15). If the Lord did not build the house (church) those who did build it labored in vain. Jesus declared, "Every plant which my heavenly Father hath not planted, shall be

12

rooted up" (Matthew 15:13). No one should be a member of any spiritual household, religious plant, or church which man was responsible for starting. One should be a member of the church Christ established!

CHRIST THE FOUNDATION

Not only is Christ the founder of the church but he is also the foundation of the church. In that same statement to Simon Peter cited earlier Christ said, "Upon this rock I will build my church" (Matt. 16:18). What was or is the rock on which the church of Christ is established? It is the bed-rock foundation fact that Peter had just acknowledged — namely, that Jesus is the Christ, the Son of the living God. In Matthew 16:16 Peter said to Jesus, "Thou art the Christ, the Son of the living God." Following this statement Jesus said that upon this rock he would build his church. The rock was not the apostle Peter or any other man; rather it was Christ and his divine relationship to God — the fact that he is God's Son. The apostle Paul makes this abundantly clear when he states, "For other foundation can no man lay than that is laid, which is Jesus Christ" (1 Corinthians 3:11). Any church built on a man or some special religious doctrine or some form of church government is built on the wrong foundation and will not stand. The church our Lord established is built on him — on the fact that he is God's Son. That is why every person who becomes a member of the church must confess his faith in Christ as the Son of God (Acts 8:37). The church is said to be a spiritual house made up of lively or living stones. Before a person can be placed on Christ the foundation and made a stone in that house he must believe that Jesus is the Son of God (1 Peter 2:5, 6).

FOUNDED IN JERUSALEM

The church Christ established and which is founded on him was started in the city of Jerusalem on the first day of Pentecost following the resurrection of Christ (Acts 2). The prophets had long predicted the coming kingdom of the Messiah (Isaiah 2:2-4; Daniel 2:44). This kingdom was not a physical kingdom but a spiritual one (John 18:36) and was realized in the founding of the church by Christ.

After his resurrection Christ appeared to his apostles and said, "Thus it is written, and thus it behooved Christ to suffer, and to rise from the dead the third day: and that repentance and remission of sins should be preached in my name among all nations, beginning at Jerusalem" (Luke 24:46,47). Then in Acts 1:8, just before he ascended back to heaven, Christ said to the apostles, "But ye shall receive power, after that the Holy Ghost is come upon you: and ye shall be witnesses unto me both in Jerusalem, and in all Judea, and in Samaria, and unto the uttermost part of the earth." Observe in this statement that Jesus said the apostles would receive power (power to preach the gospel in all its fullness, resulting in the coming of the kingdom or church) when the Holy Ghost came upon them. In Acts 2:1-4 we find the Holy Ghost coming upon the apostles and their being empowered to preach the gospel in the languages of the people gathered in Jerusalem for Pentecost. As a result of the apostles' preaching, people were pricked in their heart and asked what to do to be forgiven of their sins (Acts 2:37). They were instructed, "Repent, and be baptized every one of you in the name of Jesus Christ for the remission of sins, and ye shall receive the gift of the Holy Ghost" (Acts 2:38). "Then they that gladly received his word were baptized: and the same day there were added unto them about three thousand souls" (Acts 2: 41). Thus, the kingdom or church of our Lord came with power (Mark 9:1). It was established in the city of Jerusalem in the year 33 A.D. by Christ upon the bedrock foundation truth that he is the Son of God. On every occasion thereafter when people heard of Christ, believed in him, repented of their sins, confessed Christ to be the Son of God, and were baptized for the remission of their sins, the Lord added them to his church. "And the Lord added to the church daily such as should be saved" (Acts 2:47).

A GREAT PRIVILEGE
TO BE IN CHRIST'S CHURCH

It is a great privilege to be a member of the church Christ established and of which he is the foundation. By being a faithful member of that church one can have eternal life in heaven when his life here on earth is over. On the other hand, it is dangerous to be a member of any church not founded by Christ and not established on him. There is no promise of eternal salvation by being a member of a church devised and established by man! Why take a chance with your soul?

QUESTIONS

Is it scriptural to refer to the church as the church of Christ? Why?

Who is the founder of the church?

How many churches did Christ promise to build?

What will happen to plants (churches) not planted by the heavenly Father?

Is the New Testament church founded on some man, religious doctrine, religious practice, or form of church government?

What is the foundation of the church of Christ?

Can one become a member of the Lord's church without confessing that Jesus Christ is the Son of God?

Where was the church of Christ established? When?

What does the Lord do with a person who hears the gospel, believes on Christ, repents of his sins, confesses faith in Christ, and is baptized for the remission of sins?

3

There is but
ONE
TRUE CHURCH OF CHRIST

By Dale R. Larsen

An observing person, concerned about God, truth and eternity has reason to be perplexed. Why is Christendom fragmented? Are some churches right, and some wrong? Does it make a difference?

A FEW THOUGHTS COME INTO FOCUS

Most every denominational organization and sect that claims a Christian purpose calls itself a "church." In spite of all their diversity, that common term stands out. Where did the idea come from? The Bible introduces the church, but also clearly depicts it to be a single, unified organism. The Bible, which traces the Divine church through prophecy and its founding, should also be the one authority for the church's organization, pattern of worship and doctrine today.

Just listening to the many radio and television programs on a given Sunday morning presents another enigma. The plans of salvation they preach do not agree. A few of these groups may, on the surface, seem to be preaching doctrines that are about alike, but the teachings of some are in direct opposition to those of others. Two opposites, each claiming to be truth, cannot both be correct.

16

The existence of so many varied denominations, most claiming to be the church, testifies to the fact that, somewhere, there is, or was a true original. Even counterfeit money is evidence there is a real thing — and that it is valuable.

WHAT DOES THE BIBLE SAY?

There is only one place to go for answers about the church. The Bible, the word of God, tells all about God's church, and it clearly presents *one* church! From the very first of the Bible we find God's oneness stressed, and the unity of His followers taught. The harmony of God's creation is revealed in Genesis 1:31 ". . . it was very good." God is not a God of confusion (1 Corinthians 14:33). Deuteronomy 6:4 is one of many passages which teach the oneness of God. Genesis 2:24 reveals the beginning of marriage and says the man and wife ". . . shall be one flesh." An inspired apostle, Paul, uses the Divine institution of marriage to illustrate the nature of the church, which is his body (Ephesians 1:22,23; Colossians 1:18). The figures of the body and the oneness of husband and wife carry through many verses of Ephesians 5. Paul culminates the comparison by saying, ". . . I speak in regard of Christ and of the church" (Eph. 5:32). The Bible says "There is *one body*, . . . one spirit, . . . one hope, . . . one Lord, . . . one faith, . . . one baptism, . . . one God . . ." (Eph. 4:4-6). Jesus prayed for unity of his people, "that they may all be *one*" (John 17:21).

For further identification of that one church we look briefly to Old Testament prophecies: Both Isaiah and Micah speak of a special kingdom (future) and describe it as "the mountain of Jehovah's house" (Isaiah 2:2, 3; Micah 4:1,2). These predictions designated the beginning place as Zion, or Jerusalem, and a message called "the word of Jehovah." Jesus said the Kingdom would come during his generation, and that it would come with power (Mark 9:1). The great Pentecost occasion recorded in Acts 2, fulfills all of these predictions, and from that time forward the New Testament speaks of the church as being in existence (Acts 2:46,47; 20:28; 1 Cor. 16:19). Matthew 16:18,19 and Acts 20:25-28 use interchangeably

17

the terms "kingdom" and "church." The first letter to Timothy (3:15) calls the church "the house of God."

None would deny God's relationship to the church, but in a very special sense it is Christ's church. Jesus said, ". . . I will build my church;" (Matt. 16:18). The word "church" is singular. The passage in Acts 20:28 says the Lord purchased the church "with his own blood," and Ephesians 1:23 calls it "his body." The church is a living organism with Christ the head and Christians members of that body.

So undenominational was that original church that it was sometimes spoken of simply as "the Way" (Acts 9:2). The basic meaning of the original Geek word for church was "the called out ones." The New Testament pictures one universal church with one common message: "And he said unto them, Go ye into all the world, and preach the gospel to the whole creation. He that believeth and is baptized shall be saved; but he that disbelieveth shall be condemned" (Mark 16:15,16). The members of this one body, or way, were scattered everywhere and as they met in their respective geographic locations they were called, in a local congregational sense, "churches of Christ" (Romans 16:16).

HOW DID DIVISIONS ORIGINATE?

Nowhere in the New Testament is there a record of Roman Catholicism or any of the numerous Protestant denominations. How did the variety of present-day "churches" come into existence? The church always has been made up of human individuals, susceptible to human error. Paul warned the church at Corinth (1 Cor. 1:10-13) not to follow men — not even good men — instead of Christ. In that very passage he asks, "Is Christ divided?" Implied is his answer, "No!" Division comes from humans and their views, and especially so when we look to men rather than to the Bible for our authority.

The Roman Catholic system of religion evolved as men departed from and altered the original pattern. Examples of such unauthorized additions are: holy water; penance; Latin mass; extreme unction and purgatory.

These practices came too late to be apostolic or "original." Perhaps the greatest departure came in the area of organization, and over a period of a few hundred years the traditional Roman Catholic hierarchy emerged, about 606 A.D., with an unscriptural leader (pope) called Boniface III.

Protestants began as protestors. A denomination (of anything) is a division. Early leaders of protestant movements were Catholics: Peter Waldo; Martin Luther; Ulrich Zwingli; etc. Their intention was to reform a church which had become full of abuses and errors. Instead, many of these leaders were excommunicated and their efforts crystalized into new organizations. These were established too late to be the church of the New Testament, and they were founded by someone other than the one who spoke in Matthew 16:18. Many teachings and practices of Protestant denominations are additions to, or subtractions from, the New Testament pattern, and several are retained from the Catholic church. Throughout the years still more denominations with new doctrines have continued to arise.

WE MUST BE IN CHRIST'S CHURCH

What is wrong with selecting a "church" of one's choice? As free, moral agents we do have the capacity to choose, but our "choosing" can be wrong. In the case of the church, Christ built it, purchased it, and is its head. Those who respond to *his* invitation, on *his* terms, will be added to *his* church (Acts 2:41). Acts 2:47 states that the Lord added those that were being saved. He is the author of eternal salvation ". . . unto all them that obey him" (Hebrews 5:9). He is the savior of the body, his church (Eph. 5:23).Proverbs 14:12 warns: "There is a way which seemeth right unto a man; but the end thereof are the ways of death." Jesus himself said there would be those who professed the name of the Lord and who did works in his name, who would be lost.He said those who did the will of his Father who is in heaven would enter heaven (Matt. 7:21-23).

A will, or testament, of man is strictly honored by the courts. As we prepare for final judgment and eternal life

19

we must make certain we are members of Christ's church (the one described in the New Testament) having complied with *his* will, and having been obedient to *his* commands! On this basis we shall be judged (John 12:48).

QUESTIONS

Why do so many people accept, with little or no questioning, the religion of their parents?

Discuss how religious division contributes to skepticism, and even unbelief.

What is the difference between unity and tolerance of differences?

Discuss various religious doctrines common in denominations today and show how they differ from Bible teaching.

Examine the subject of authority and show how basic this is to religious unity.

4

Christ's church is
NOT A DENOMINATION

By Wendell Winkler

O ur currency system is divided into various denominations: five dollar, ten dollar, etc. Our political system is also denominated: i.e., the Republican party, the Democratic party. We can see from these illustrations that the word "denomination" signifies a division or a segment; thus, in the religious sense, a sect or a party. A denomination is larger than any local church, but smaller than the redeemed as a whole. Yet, the New Testament speaks only of local congregations (1 Corinthians 1:2) or the church embracing all of the saved (Ephesians 1:22, 23). Hence the New Testament church cannot be fitted into any denominational mold.

THE CHURCH OF CHRIST IS THE
NEW TESTAMENT CHURCH OF THE
FIRST CENTURY

(1) *An observation.* Let us kindly observe that the church of Christ (a) *is not a Jewish synagogue.* The Old Testament, the foundation of Judaism, has been done away (Rom. 7:1-4; Colossians 2:14,17; Hebrews 8:8-13). Furthermore, (b) the church of Christ *is not a Protestant denomination.* All the denominations of our day were established by men, hundreds of years after the church of our Lord was established on Pentecost, Acts 2, A.D. 33 (Mark 9:1; Acts 1:8; Acts 2:1-4, 47). Denominational earmarks are conspicuously absent in the church of

Christ: prayer altars, voting on baptismal candidates, mechanical instruments of music in worship, universal and territorial organizations, etc. (c) The church of Christ *is not the Catholic Church.* The Roman Catholic church did not come into existence in a fullgrown state until 606 A.D., nearly 600 years after the Lord's church was established in 33 A.D. as previously observed. The cardinal doctrines of Catholicism are not in harmony with biblical teaching, as can be scripturally observed in many of the chapters composing this volume.

(2) *The church defined.* The word "church" is from the Greek word *ecclesia,* and means "the called out." Thus, the church is that body of people who have been called out of the world by the gospel (2 Thessalonians 2:14), by obedience thereto (2 Thess. 1:7-9). Christ rules as the singular head of the church (Colossians 1:18), and the Spirit dwells within her (Ephesians 2:22, 23).

(3) *The church is singular in number.* There is one fold (John 10:16). The church is that fold (Acts 20:28). There is one body (Ephesians 4:4); that body is the church (Ephesians 1:22,23). The Lord taught the monogamy of marriage (Romans 7:1-4) and the church is his bride (Ephesians 5:22-33).

The church of Christ is that one, true New Testament church which existed in the first century. Such can be seen by the fact that it possesses the same identifying features.

THE FIRST CENTURY CHURCH	THE CHURCH OF CHRIST IN THE 20TH CENTURY
(a) *Designations:* church of Christ (Romans 16:16), church of God (1 Cor. 1:2), church of the Lord (Acts 20:28 ASV).	(a) The church of Christ is designated as just that, the church of Christ, etc.
(b) *Organization:* elders, deacons, evangelists and members in the local congregation (Philippians 1:1).	(b) The church of Christ is organized with elders, deacons, evangelists, members.

(c) *Worship:* met on first day of each week (1 Cor. 16:2), and engaged in acapella singing, praying, teaching, the Lord's supper and giving (Acts 2:42, 47; 1 Cor. 14:15; 16:2; Acts 20:7).

(c) The church of Christ meets upon the first day of each week and engages in acapella singing, praying, teaching, the Lord's supper, and giving.

(d) *Guide:* the apostles' doctrine was their sole rule of faith and practice (Acts 2:42; Gal. 1:6-9; Rev. 22:19).

(d) The church of Christ is guided solely by the apostles' doctrine, the New Testament.

(e) *Terms of entrance:* believed, repented, confessed Christ and were baptized (Acts 8:26-40).

(e) The church of Christ is entered by people believing, repenting, confessing and being baptized.

(f) *Mission:* to support the truth (1 Tim. 3:15).

(f) The church of Christ engages in the support of the truth.

NOTE: A thing is composed of the sum of its parts. Accordingly, it can be seen that the church of Christ is not one among the many; but, rather, it is the one, true New Testament church.

OUR LORD WAS UNDENOMINATIONAL SO MUST HIS CHURCH BE

(1) *Our Lord did not align himself with any party or division during his earthly pilgrimage.* While our Lord lived upon the earth, there were four principle divisions among the Jews: the Pharisees, the Sadducees, the Herodians, and the Essenes. Though each of these advocated some truth, our Lord identified himself with none of them. This is most significant.

(2) *Additionally, let us note:* (a) Our Lord *prayed* for unity, the antithesis of denominationalism (John 17:20, 21); (b) our Lord *paid* for unity, the antithesis of denominationalism (Eph. 2:16); (c) our Lord *pleaded* for unity, the antithesis of denominationalism (1 Cor. 1:10); and (d) our Lord *planned* for unity, the antithesis of denominationalism (Eph. 4:1-6). Therefore, our Lord was unde-

nominational and anti-denominational. Thus, must his church be!

A TWO-FOLD CONTRAST

THE CHURCH OF THE NEW TESTAMENT	DENOMINATIONALISM
(1) *Divine in origin.* (Matt. 16:18; Daniel 2:44).	(1) *Manmade, without divine origin.* The Lord is not the author of confusion nor denominationalism (1 Cor. 14:33). Our Lord did not work against his own prayer for unity by establishing conflicting and contradictory denominations (John 17:20,21).
(2) *Will last forever.* (Dan. 2:44; Heb. 12:28, 29).	(2) *Will be rooted up.* (Matt. 15: 13).
(3) *Designated by Bible names.* (Rom. 16:16; Acts 20:28; 1 Cor. 1:2).	(3) *Named after men, forms of church government, virtues, days "ordinances," etc.* Yet, we are to speak as the oracles of God (1 Pet. 4:11).
(4) *First century in origin.* (Acts 2:47).	(4) *Catholicism had its beginning in the 7th century and Protestantism had its beginning in the 16th century.*
(5) *Heavenly headquarters.* (Eph. 1:22,23; 1 Pet. 3:22).	(5) *Earthly headquarters.* Some in Rome, or Salt Lake City, or Independence, Missouri, or Cleveland, Tennessee, etc.
(6) *Bible only* (Acts 2:42; 1 Pet. 4:11; Gal. 1:6-9; Rev. 22:18, 19; Jude 3).	(6) *Creeds, manuals, disciplines, confessions of faith, catechisms.* Such reflects upon the all-sufficiency of the word of God (2 Tim. 3:16,17).
(7) *Added to* (Acts 2:47).	(7) *Join.* You do not join the family of God; rather, you are added thereto (1 Tim. 3:15).
(8) *Essential to salvation* (Eph. 5:23; Acts 20:28).	(8) *Can be saved and never be a member of a given denomination.* Thus, denominationalism stands self-condemned as being unnecessary and nonrelated to salvation.

24

THE CHURCH OF THE NEW TESTAMENT	DENOMINATIONALISM
(9) *Calvary-purchased* (Acts 20: 28; Eph. 5:25).	(9) *No such price paid.*
(10) *The apostles were members of this church* (Acts 2:41).	(10) *There was no apostolic membership in human denominations. After all, they were not even in existence!*
(11) *The church of Christ's choice* (Matt. 16:18,19; Col. 1:24).	(11) *The church of man's choice.* Now, read Psalm 127:1.
(12) *Entered by believing, repenting confessing and being baptized* (Acts 2:36-47; 8:26-40).	(12) *Human laws of induction. One man, being told he must have an experience of grace before he could be considered as a candidate for membership in a given denomination, fabricated a story. Whereupon this denomination voted and accepted him. Later, his conscience bothered him because of the lie. Accordingly, he returned, stating the same, resulting in his expulsion from this denomination. He succinctly observed,* "They voted me in for telling a lie, and they voted me out for telling the truth!"
(13) *Jerusalem the birthplace* (Zechariah 1:16; Isaiah 2:1-4; Mark 9:1; Luke 24:46; Acts 1:1-4).	(13) *Varied places of beginning, with Jerusalem not being the place of beginning for a single one.*

VARIOUS REASONS WHY THE CHURCH OF CHRIST IS NOT A DENOMINATION

1. Denominationalism is contrary to the Lord's prayer (John 17:20, 21).

2. Denominationalism is a fruitful cause of infidelity (John 17: 20, 21).

3. Denominationalism is wrong because Christ is not divided (1 Cor. 1:11-13).

4. Denominationalism is wrong because the body of Christ is one, not many (1 Cor. 12:13,20; Eph. 4:4; Col. 3:15).

5. Denominationalism is contrary to one of the basic purposes of Calvary's cross (Eph. 2:15, 16).

6. Denominationalism is a vain attempt to serve God (Matt. 15:9; Psalm 127:1).

7. Denominationalism divides homes, when God wants homes united (Joshua 24:15; Amos 3:3; Mark 3:25).

8. Denominationalism is contrary to Paul's plea for unity, for undenominational Christianity (1 Cor. 1:10).

9. Denominationalism is contrary to the apostles' doctrine (Rom. 16:17, 18).

10. Denominationalism is a sin that God hates (Proverbs 6:6-19).

11. Denominationalism implies that God is the author of confusion (1 Cor. 14:33).

12. Denominationalism is not apostolic.

13. Denominationalism is destined for destruction (Mark 3:24, 25).

THE CURE FOR DENOMINATIONALISM

We must have an unreserved commitment to the Bible as the sole, objective standard in religion. If three people differ as to the time of day, they can settle their differences by consulting the objective time standard, the naval observatory time. Such settles the matter, and produces unity. If a man goes to three different post offices, he will be given the same postage for mailing of his package. Why? Because each postal clerk consults the same guide book. Unity exists because of allegiance to a single objective authority. In like manner, when all men will lay down their creeds, disciplines, manuals, confessions of faith, catechisms, think-so's, maybe's, and subjective feelings and each with an unprejudiced and receptive heart turns to the word of God, then, and only then, will unity result. Such will constitute the death knell to denominationalism. We must be committed to being nothing, calling ourselves nothing, obeying nothing, and saying nothing except that which is authorized by the word of God. Only then will we have "the unity of the spirit" of Ephesians 4:1-6: one body — unity of organization; one Spirit — unity of guidance; one hope — unity of aspiration; one faith — unity of message; one Lord — unity of authority; one baptism — unity of practice; and, one God — unity of worship.

To look at it another way, one of God's immutable laws is that seed bears after its kind (Genesis 1:12). Accordingly, if we preach only the gospel, it will produce in our day the one, true New Testament church that it produced in the days of the apostles, when no denominations existed. To believe otherwise, is to repudiate one of God's immutable laws!

The church of Christ is not a denomination. If she were, she would surrender her right to exist (Matt. 15: 13). Our Lord was undenominational and antidenominational. His church cannot afford to be otherwise. Her plea is for pure, New Testament, undenominational Christianity. And, how encouraging it is that many are being attracted thereto.

QUESTIONS

Define "denomination" in its temporal and religious senses.

What meanings does the Bible give to the word church?

Give three New Testament examples that illustrate the oneness of the Lord's church.

State four reasons why Jesus' church is not a denomination.

What is the cure for denominational division?

5

She has
JESUS AS HER ONLY HEAD

By Howard Winters

In Colossians, chapter 1, Paul depicts Christ as the redeemer (14), the creator (15-17), and the head of the church (18). He concludes, "That in all things he might have the preeminence. For it pleased the Father that in him should all fullness dwell" (18, 19).

Other Scriptures also make clear the fact that Christ is the head of the church (Ephesians 1:22,23; 4:15; 5:23; Colossians 2:10). This means that he is the source of her life (all things are from him) and that he rules over her with divine authority. For this reason, every member of the body must be in subjection to him (Col. 2:19). To make application of this grand fact, let us notice:

A DIVINE HEAD

The church has a divine head, Jesus Christ her Lord. This simply means that Christ rules over her. The church is not a monstrosity — it is not a many-headed body. It is one body with one head. Christ does not share his rule or authority with man. This being true, it follows then with all the force that reason, logic, and Scripture can have, that the church has no human head. Any man who claims to be the head of the church, either in heaven or on earth, makes a false claim and seizes for himself a prerogative that belongs to Christ alone. Christ is not only the divine head of the church, he is her only head.

A DIVINE BODY

Christ is the head of the church, which is his body

(Col. 1:18; Eph. 1:22-23). It would be an incongruity for a human body to have a divine head, or vice versa. The conclusion is therefore inevitable that the church is a divine institution. The church is divine because she was conceived in the mind of God (Eph. 3:10, 11), foretold by the prophets (Isaiah 2:2-4), built by Jesus (Matthew 16: 16-18), purchased with his blood (Acts 20:28), and constructed under the immediate direction of the Holy Spirit working through the apostles of Christ (Acts 2). This divine institution is made up of all the saved (Acts 2:47); has for her mission the salvation of lost souls (Mark 16: 15-16); and God's divine law, as revealed in the New Testament, is her only rule of conduct (2 Timothy 3:16, 17). Every member of the Lord's church is a member of a divine institution.

This should be contrasted with modern denominations, which are human in origin, name, doctrine, organization, and practice, have human heads, and are ruled by human laws.

DIVINE AUTHORITY

Because she has but one head, the church of Christ is subject to only one source of authority. Jesus said, "All power (authority, ASV) is given unto me in heaven and in earth" (Matt. 28:18). His authority is exercised through his word. Thus when one obeys the word of God he is submitting to divine authority, the only voice of authority known by the New Testament church.

By authority we mean the power or right to command. In America we are accustomed to a balance of authority between the branches of government. Legislative authority resides in Congress, executive in the President, and judicial in the courts. But in the church there is only one source of authority, Jesus Christ, the Lord.

A DIVINE PRACTICE

Since the church follows only the instructions given by her divine head (through his divine word), all her practices are divine. The way of God is far above the ways of man (Isa. 55:8, 9) and it is not in man to direct his own steps (Jeremiah 10:23). This means that every action

29

must be directed by the Scriptures — every act must be an authorized act (Col. 3:17). Paul stated this principle clearly when he said, "Prove all things; hold fast that which is good" (1 Thessalonians 5:21). This simply means that if a thing cannot be proven (by the Scriptures), it cannot be practiced. If one holds fast only proven things, then it necessarily follows that he must reject everything not proven. All directions must come from the head.

No council, synod, convention, or creed of men can establish the standard for the Lord's church. To recognize Jesus as head is to follow his directions; and to follow his directions results in divine practice.

DIVINE PERPETUITY

"Jesus Christ the same yesterday, and today, and for ever" (Hebrews 13:8). The church therefore never changes heads. She functions under the same head, the same authority, century after century. When Pope John XXIII died, I wrote the following four lines for our weekly church bulletin:

> Pope John Twenty-three is dead
> And the Roman church is without a head;
> But let me say, with all that in me lies,
> The head of the Lord's church never dies.

Poetry that decidely is not; truth it most certainly is.

A DIVINE RELATIONSHIP

Because Christ is the head of the body, which is the church, Christ and the church are inseparably joined together. Christ works through his body and the body does the work of Christ (cf. 1 Corinthians 12:12-27; Eph. 4:11-15; 1 Peter 4:8-11). This makes it impossible to reject the body without also rejecting the head, "From which all the body by joints and bands having nourishment ministered, and knit together, increaseth with the increase of God" (Col. 2:19). Christ cannot be received apart from his body.

CONCLUSION

Christ is the head of the church, her ruler, her authority, her director. If one desires to have Christ as his head he must be in the church, the church which is his body. And he must follow the directions given by the head. If one loves the Lord, if he respects him as the head of the church, why would he want to be in anything else? How could he be in anything else Scripturally? To be in another body would be to have another head.

QUESTIONS

Do the Scriptures teach that Jesus is the head, and the only head, of the church? What is the significance of this?

Why is it vital to have a divine rather than a human head?

How may we know that the church is a divine institution?

Who is the divine source of authority for the church and how does he exercise that authority today?

Why is a divine head (who never dies) superior to a human head?

May one reject the body without rejecting the head?

6

The church is
DESCRIBED
BY MANY FIGURES

By Maxie B. Boren

I n his revelation to us, God described the church of the Lord Jesus Christ in various ways. He obviously did this that we might be able to understand the nature of the church and to perceive its importance. We refer to these various descriptions as "pictures" or "figures." God simply used things with which people were familiar in order to convey great spiritual truths. In this article we want to very briefly notice ten such Divinely given "figures" of the church. The church is described —

(1) As a *family.* God is our Heavenly Father. "Of his own will begat he us with the word of truth" (James 1:18). The apostle Paul, recognizing the greatness and goodness of God in providing salvation for us in Christ, wrote, "For this cause I bow my knees unto the Father . . . of whom the whole family in heaven and earth is named" (Ephesians 3:14-15). People are begotten of God when they believe the gospel, and they are born into his family when they obey the terms of pardon revealed in the gospel. God has promised these, contingent upon their willingness to sanctify themselves, "I will be to you a Father, and ye shall be to me sons and daughters" (2 Corinthians 6:18). As his children, Christians should most assuredly bear the image of the Father. Members of the church have been called into fellowship with Christ

(1 Corinthians 1:9), with the Father, and with one another (See 1 John 1:3-4). Therefore, being brothers and sisters in God's family is a close and wonderful relationship of kindred spirits.

(2) As the *body* of Christ. In a beautiful context of scripture, Paul made a comparison between a physical body, and the spiritual body of Christ. A physical body is composed of many parts, but it is just one body. So also is the church. Composed of many members, yet all of them functioning harmoniously together for the ongoing of the body. Thus, the church must be united for God's design and purpose for it to be realized. "God tempered the body together . . . that there should be no schism in the body; but that the members should have the same care one for another . . . now ye are the body of Christ, and severally members thereof" (1 Cor. 12:24-25, 27). God gave Christ "to be head over all things to the church, which is his body" (Eph. 1:22-23). And Paul made it clear that there is only "one body" (Eph. 4:4). As head, Christ is to have all the preeminence in the church (Colossians 1:18).

(3) As a *bride*. The church is married (spiritually speaking, of course) to Christ. Paul wrote to the church in Corinth and said, "I espoused you to one husband, that I might present you as a pure virgin to Christ" (2 Cor. 11:2). In writing to the Ephesians, he compared the relationship of a husband and his wife to that of Christ and his church. "Husbands, love your wives, even as Christ also loved the church, and gave himself up for it" (Eph. 5:25). Therefore, the church should be a "glorious church, not having spot or wrinkle or any such thing; but that it should be holy and without blemish" (verse 27). Note also Romans 7:4.

(4) As a *kingdom*. The church is in subjection to Jesus Christ, who is the king of his kingdom. Christ's kingdom is a spiritual kingdom. He said, "my kingdom is not of this world" (John 18:36), simply meaning that it was never intended by God to be an earthly, temporal domain, as the one over which Saul, David, and Solomon reigned. Christ's kingdom is a heavenly kingdom, and

33

thus, "our citizenship is in heaven" (Philippians 3:20). And yet, his spiritual kingdom is very definitely in existence upon the earth, as it has been since its establishment in 33 A.D. on the Jewish feast day called Pentecost, as recorded in Acts 2. Paul informed the Christians in Colossae that God "delivered us out of the power of darkness, and translated us into the kingdom of the Son of his love" (Col. 1:13). The evangelist Philip went down to Samaria and preached unto those people "concerning the kingdom of God and the name of Jesus Christ" (Acts 8:12). In about 96 A.D., the apostle John, writing to the seven churches of Asia, expressed that Christ "loved us, and loosed us from our sins by his blood; and he made us to be a kingdom" (Revelation 1:5-6). The kingdom is not something yet to come . . . it has already come! The church and the kingdom are one and the same thing. To be a member of the Lord's church is to be a citizen of his kingdom.

(5) As a *flock*. Jesus Christ is the shepherd of the sheep, and Christians are depicted as sheep. Thus, the church is dependent upon the love and care of the Shepherd. The church heeds his voice, "and the sheep follow him" (John 10:4). The apostle Peter admonished those who were serving as elders in the church to "tend the flock of God which is among you" (1 Peter 5:2), "and when the chief Shepherd shall be manifested, ye shall receive the crown of glory that fadeth not away" (verse 4). As sheep having gone astray, Christians are a people "now returned unto the Shepherd" (1 Pet. 2:25).

(6) As a *house*. The church is not a building made of brick, stone, or wood. It is a spiritual house. The apostle Peter wrote to Christians, and said, "Ye also, as living stones, are built up a spiritual house, to be a holy priesthood, to offer up spiritual sacrifices, acceptable to God through Jesus Christ" (1 Pet. 2:5). Paul wrote to the Christians in Ephesus, and told them they were "built upon the foundation of the apostles and prophets, Christ Jesus himself being the chief corner stone; in whom each several building, fitly framed together, groweth into a holy temple in the Lord" (Eph. 2:20-21). To the church at Corinth, Paul inquired, "Know ye not that ye are a

34

temple of God, and that the Spirit of God dwelleth in you" (1 Cor. 3:16)?

(7) As a *vineyard*. There were many vineyards in Palestine, where our Lord lived and taught during his personal ministry. He used that with which the people of his day were so familiar to illustrate that there is work to be done in service to God. Thus, the kingdom, or church, is compared to a vineyard. Please read Matthew 20:1-16. Paul urged Christians to "be steadfast, unmovable, always abounding in the work of the Lord, forasmuch as ye know that labor is not vain in the Lord" (1 Cor. 15:58). In the context of Matthew 21:28-41 Jesus employed the figure of the vineyard to give even more insight into the nature of the kingdom.

(8) As a *pearl*. Jesus said, "the kingdom of heaven is like unto a man that is a merchant seeking goodly pearls: and having found one pearl of great price, he went and sold all that he had, and bought it" (Matt. 13:45-46). In giving this parable, Jesus masterfully taught the incomparable value of the kingdom, and all that is entailed in that word. Involved, in understanding this, is salvation from sin and participation in all the spiritual blessings God has so graciously provided in Christ. "Blessed be the God and Father of our Lord Jesus Christ, who hath blessed us with *all* spiritual blessings in heavenly places in Christ" (Eph. 1:3). This, then, is the pearl of great price! No amount of earthly wealth . . . in fact, the whole world . . . can be compared to the value of a person's soul being saved! Jesus asked, "For what shall a man be profited, if he shall gain the whole world, and lose his own soul" (Matt. 16:26)? People who receive these teachings of Christ into their hearts with perceptive understanding will make whatever sacrifices are necessary in order to possess the kingdom and its blessings as a reality in this life. To be a member of the Lord's church, dear reader, is the greatest blessing and joy a person can experience!

(9) As an *army*. Certainly the church is "at war" with the forces of evil. But the warfare is not a carnal warfare, with planes, tanks, guns, and bombs. Paul wrote to Christians, "For though we walk in the flesh, we do

not war according to the flesh (for the weapons of our warfare are not of the flesh, but mighty before God to the casting down of strongholds); casting down imaginations, and every high thing that is exalted against the knowledge of God" (2 Cor. 10:3-4). He urged Timothy to "suffer hardship with me, as a good soldier of Christ Jesus" (2 Tim. 2:3). And he wrote to the Ephesian Christians, exhorting them to "be strong in the Lord, and in the strength of his might. Put on the whole armor of God, that ye may be able to stand against the wiles of the devil" (Please read the context of Eph. 6:10-17).

(10) As a *candlestick*. In the second and third chapters of Revelation, the Lord wrote through John, letters to the seven churches which were located in what is now the westernmost part of the country of Turkey. And in the symbolic language that introduces these letters, Jesus used candlesticks to refer to those seven congregations. "The seven candlesticks are seven churches" (Rev. 1:20). Jesus said to his disciples, "Ye are the light of the world. A city set on a hill cannot be hid. Neither do men light a lamp, and put it under the bushel, but on the stand; and it shineth to all that are in the house. Even so let your light shine before men; that they may see your good works, and glorify your Father who is in heaven" (Matt. 5:14-16). Paul wrote to the church in Philippi, instructing them to be "harmless and blameless, children of God without blemish in the midst of a crooked and perverse generation, among whom ye are seen as lights in the world, holding forth the word of life" (Phil. 2:15-16).

Friend, I conclude this brief article, by suggesting to your mind that God used these "figures" in Holy Writ to give you insight and understanding into the nature of the church, and what it means to be a Christian. Please reflect upon these ten Divinely given descriptions of the church prayerfully and carefully. I pray that in so doing you will be able to see the undenominational nature of the church, and the unique character of it. The church is God designed. The pattern for it is in the New Testament. Those saved by the gospel are added to it. We all need to gain as much knowledge of God's eternal purpose which he purposed in Christ and which was made known through the church (see Eph. 3:8-11), as we possibly can.

QUESTIONS

Why did God reveal various "pictures" or "figures" of the church to us?

Is the kingdom of the Lord something altogether different than his church? Or are they the same thing?

When and where was the church of Christ established? Where in the Bible can you read about its beginning?

Who is the head of the church? How much authority does the head have? (On this latter question, please read Matt. 28:18 and Eph. 1:20-23).

What kind of relationship should be maintained among members of the church?

Do you think that when Christ comes to receive his bride unto himself that he will be pleased if she is all contaminated with sinful practices and polluted with false doctrines? How does he want to receive her?

Do sheep heed voices other than that of the shepherd?

How valuable is the kingdom anyway? What does it mean to a person to be a member of Christ's church?

Is there work to be done by Christians? If so, discuss the work and who is to do it.

In view of the "figure" of the lighted candlestick, what should that tell us about our influence? Do you think that worldliness in the church is destroying the influence of many Christians? What can be done about it?

7

The New Testament is her only
STANDARD OF AUTHORITY

By E. Claude Gardner

What are the dimensions of the room where you are? How many feet wide and long is it? By taking a 12-inch ruler or a yardstick you can get an accurate measurement. Likewise if ten others used the same measuring stick, they would report exactly the same figures as you found. If in religion everyone accepts one common standard of authority, then this should result in the same faith and practice. Confusion and frustration are experienced because different standards of authority are accepted. Good people are mystified by all the conflicting doctrines that are preached.

Our plea that is both scriptural and sensible is this: The New Testament is our only rule of faith and practice. We call all men back to the word of God to guide us in all matters of our lives — spiritual, worship, personal, family and business. We earnestly plead that we should "speak where the Bible speaks and remain silent where the Bible is silent; we should call Bible things by Bible names and do Bible things in the Bible way."

Christ and his teaching must govern us. We acknowledge him as Lord and Savior. We bow to him as "Lord of lords and King of kings" (Revelation 17:14). He is the head of the church and therefore controls our lives and authorizes how we are to worship. Paul wrote about the headship of Jesus when he said, "And hath put all things under his feet, and gave him to be the head over all things to the church" (Ephesians 1:22). The risen Christ made a

38

bold and sweeping claim, "All power is given unto me in heaven and in earth" (Matthew 28:18).

God, our Creator, has revealed himself through Christ who has spoken to us through the New Testament. "God, who at sundry times and in divers manners spake in time past unto the fathers by the prophets, Hath in these last days spoken unto us by his Son, whom he hath appointed heir of all things, by whom also he made the worlds" (Hebrews 1:1-2).

Jesus does not speak to us audibly, nor "through a still small voice," nor by the conscience, but through his Word revealed to the apostles as given in the New Testament. To the apostles (and not to us today) he promised, "the Comforter, which is the Holy Ghost, whom the Father will send in my name, he shall teach you all things, and bring all things to your remembrance, whatsoever I have said unto you" (John 14:26). The Lord also assured them of guidance into all truth so that their message is inerrant (Cf. John 15:26; 16:13). We conclude that the New Testament is an expression of our Savior's divine will and way and it is, thererefore, our authority. It is the "one faith" (Eph. 4:5). It is the only book to determine our faith, conduct, and worship; by it we should live and by it we should die; on it we should build our homes and our businesses or professions.

Jesus is the "mediator of the new covenant" (Heb. 12:24). He is our Savior through the new covenant or testament. Sin has separated us from God (Isaiah 59:1-2) and Christ is our "go between" (mediator) through the new covenant.

The Word of God furnishes us completely and hence, we need nothing more. Paul asserted, "All scripture is given by inspiration of God, and is profitable for doctrine, for reproof, for correction, for instruction in righteousness: That the man of God may be perfect, thoroughly furnished unto all good works" (2 Timothy 3:16-17).

The New Testament is powerful enough to save us from sin. We must receive the implanted word that is able "to save your souls" (James 1:21). It is described as "quick" (living) and "powerful." "For the word of God is quick, and powerful, and sharper than any two-edged sword, piercing even to the dividing asunder of soul and spirit, and of the joints and marrow, and is a descerner of the thoughts and intents of the heart" (Heb. 4:12).

The New Testament is not a "dead letter." It is *not* essential for the Holy Spirit to "come into one's heart" in a direct and mysterious way in order to quicken the word in the heart. The reason is clear — it is living. The only power God is using for our salvation is the New Testament for Paul taught, "I am not ashamed of the gospel of Christ: for it is the power of God unto salvation to every one that believeth; to the Jew first, and also to the Greek" (Romans 1:16). It is this truth that sets us free. "And ye shall know the truth, and the truth shall make you free" (John 8:32).

Because Jehovah is mindful of his creation, he has supplied all of our needs. This is one of the precious promises of the New Testament, for Peter wrote, "According as his divine power hath given unto us all things that pertain unto life and godliness, through the knowledge of him that hath called us to glory and virtue: Whereby are given unto us exceeding great and precious promises" (2 Peter 1:3-4). We cannot look to the Old Testament, books of philosophy, nor creeds of men to grant us spiritual life. Hence, we must contend earnestly for this faith. "Beloved, when I gave all diligence to write unto you of the common salvation, it was needful for me to write unto you, and exhort you that ye should earnestly contend for the faith which was once delivered unto the saints" (Jude 3).

We repudiate all human creeds, confessions of faith, manuals and church disciplines because the New Testament is our guide. Also, numerous instances can be cited to show how they contradict the Word of God. They are also subject to frequent changes. A sensible motto rightly states: "If a human creed contains more than the Bible it contains too much; if it contains less than the Bible it contains too little; but if it contains the same thing as the Bible we do not need it anyway."

We earnestly plead that all men come back to the New Testament and to Christ as supreme authority in religion. May we all require a "thus saith the Lord" in all that we believe and practice. The voice from heaven said at the transfiguration, "This is my beloved Son in whom I am well pleased; hear ye him" (Matt. 17:5).

QUESTIONS

Measure the dimensions of your room or an object with a 12-inch ruler and then ask another to do the same. What is the implication of this test?

What is the basis of so much confusion or religious teachings?

What is the significance of Christ being the "head" of the church? Does this leave room for a pope or any human being or human creed?

How does God speak to man today?

What are three chief objections to human creeds and confessions of faith?

Show by the scriptures that the New Testament is the only standard of authority.

8

The Old Testament is
FOR HER LEARNING, BUT NOT HER LAW

By William Woodson

A s a people of the Book, members of the church of Christ have profound respect for the inspired writings of the Bible. All scripture is profitable for doctrine, reproof, correction, and instruction in righteousness (2 Timothy 3:16-17).

One matter of concern, however, is the relation of the Old Testament to the church today. This article will discuss this point both negatively and positively.

I. The Old Testament is not the law for the church.

Jewish sympathizers sought to bind the Old Testament on the church in the days of Paul (Galatians 5:1-4), but this effort was vigorously resisted (Acts 15:1-29; Galatians 2:1-5). Modern day religious groups seek to bind parts of the Old Testament on Christians, i.e., Seventh Day Adventists, etc. Various people have lingering questions and concerns about the matter of how we relate to the Old Testament.

The following truths make it clear that the people of God are not under the authority of the Old Testament today.

1. The Old Testament law was given to a specific group of people, the Jews, and was never said to have been given to anyone else, Christians included. God said to Moses, "... I have made a covenant with thee, and

with Israel" (Exodus 34:27). The "children of Israel" were "to observe the sabbath throughout their generations" as a sign between "me (God) and the children of Israel forever" (Ex. 31:16-17). God made the Mosaic covenant with the Jews of Moses' day, not with others (Deuteronomy 5:1-3; Nehemiah 9:13-14).

2. The Old Testament law was only temporary and was, consequently, to come to an end. Jeremiah foretold this fact and the Hebrew writer declared its fulfillment (Jer. 31:31-34; Heb. 8:6-13). God indicated that a new covenant, different from the covenant through Moses, was to be given; the Hebrew writer set forth its accomplishment. He then explained that in his day the old was "ready to vanish away" (Heb. 8:13) and that indeed "there is made of necessity a change of the law" (Heb. 7:12).

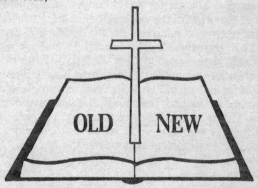

3. The Old Testament law was nailed to the cross of Christ and thereby was brought to an end as a law to guide God's people. Paul declared that Christians are "dead to the law by the body of Christ" and that this law was the law which said, "Thou shalt not covet", i.e. the ten commandments law (Romans 7:4,7). Elsewhere, Paul indicated that the veil which was "untaken away in the reading of the Old Testament . . . is done away in Christ," the reason being it was "done away" (2 Corinthians 3:14, 11). Christ "abolished in his flesh . . . the law of commandments by the cross' (Ephesians 2:15-16). In fact he was said to have removed the "handwriting of ordinances

43

by nailing it to his cross" (Colossians 2:14).

The result is, then, that the Old Testament as a law for God's people was removed by the death of Christ. Christians, therefore, are not to observe the Old Testament as the law for God's service today.

II. The Old Testament, though not the regulative will of God today, is still of much practical value for the Christian.

Two valuable passages on the usefulness of the Old Testament are Romans 15:4 and 1 Corinthians 10:11. These verses show that the Old Testament has value for our "learning," "admonition," and "patience and comfort."

1. The Old Testament supplies much material for our learning. This relates to: (a) Fundamental questions such as the origin of the world (Genesis 1:1; Psalm 33:6, 9), the origin and nature of man (Genesis 2:7, Zechariah 12:1), the origin of sin (Gen. 3:1-6) and the beginning of the Hebrew nation (Gen. 12:1-3); (b) Essential information for the understanding of the New Testament such as the history of the Jewish people from Abraham to the end of the Old Testament; the understanding of Jewish events and activities mentioned in the New Testament, i.e., Passover, Pentecost, Sabbath, shedding of blood, etc; biographical allusions in the N.T. to O.T. people i.e., Elijah (Matthew 17:1-9), Moses (John 1:17), Adam and Eve (1 Timothy 2:12-15), etc.; and background for geographical allusions such as Jerusalem, Jordan, Samaria, etc. These bits and pieces of Old Testament allusion in the New Testament are better understood by a knowledge of the Old Testament. (c) Important information about Jesus and his way of life such as his genealogy (Matt. 1; Luke 3), the prophecies which pointed to his coming (Psalm 16:8-10; Isaiah 53, etc.), the failure of the blood of bulls and goats to take away sins (Heb. 10:1-2), and various essential words such as sin, righteousness, holiness, prayer, etc. Thus, the understanding of Jesus and his way is aided by the "learning" of the Old Testament.

2. The Old Testament supplies many admonitions

for guiding and warning man. These include: (a) Admonitions concerning man's weakness such as the control of the heart (Proverbs 4:23), the danger of jealousy (Prov. 6:34-35) and of covetousness (Ex. 20:17; Joshua 7:1ff), and the "deadly sins" (Prov. 6:16-19). (b) Admonitions which show the need to obey God such as the examples of obedience in Hebrews 11, Joshua at Jericho, Naaman, Noah, etc. (c) Admonitions concerning the meaning and punishment of unrighteousness such as the sin of David (2 Samuel 11; Psalm 51), of Saul (1 Sam. 15), of Nadab and Abihu (Leviticus 10), and of Balaam (Numbers 22). These admonitions, by precept and example, show the need of proper service and character for God's people.

3. The Old Testament provides for our patience and comfort in various ways. There are excellent readings which tell of God's care and keeping of his people (Psalm 23; 27; 103; 121, etc.). Also, there are examples of his keeping of his servants such as Job (Book of Job), David (Psalm 37:25-26), and Joshua (Josh. 1:5-9). In addition, the care God provided for the Jewish nation, in spite of its frequent failings and sins, serves to show his interest and provision for us today.

The Old Testament, then, should not be regarded as the law of God's people today since as a law it served its purpose, was fulfilled, and removed from authoritativeness by the death of Christ. The Old Testament, however, should be treasured as an inspired book from God which supplies means of our learning, admonition, patience and comfort.

QUESTIONS

Name a group which maintains that the Old Testament, in whole or in part, is binding on Christians today.

True or False. The Sabbath commandment, as well as the Old Testament law in general, was given only to the Jews?

True or False. The writer of Hebrews stated that the Old Testament law was still binding?

The New Testament teaches that the Old Testament law was nailed to the _____ of Jesus.

How can the Old Testament be used for our admonition?

9

Like the early Christians
SHE WORSHIPS IN SONG

By James M. Tolle

I n rejecting the use of instrumental music in worship, churches of Christ do not do so just to be peculiar nor because of any expense involved. To them it is a matter of principle rather than of expediency. They have sought out the correct answer to the all-important question: *Does Jesus Christ authorize the use of instruments of music in the worship of God?* From their investigation of the divine word, they have concluded that there is neither command, precept, nor example for this practice. See Matthew 17:5; 28:18; John 14:26; 1 John 4:6. Every single New Testament reference to music in divine worship pertains to singing only: Acts 16:25; Romans 15:9; 1 Corinthians 14:15; Ephesians 5:19; Colossians 3:16; Hebrews 2:12; James 5:13.

LAW OF WORSHIP

The New Testament law of worship is set forth in John 4:24, "God is a Spirit: and they that worship him must worship in spirit and truth." No worship, according to this utterance of Jesus, can be right unless it is done in spirit and truth. What is the truth? "Sanctify them in the truth: thy word is truth" (John 17:17). Where does God's word expressed in the New Testament advocate the use of instrumental music in worship? Not anywhere; therefore this practice cannot be done in truth, for the "word is truth." We thus conclude that instrumental music in worship violates the law of worship expressed in John 4:24.

The opposite of true worship is *vain* worship. All forms of worship unauthorized by the New Testament are vain — void and useless. Jesus said in Matthew 15:9, "But in vain do they worship me, teaching as their doctrines the precepts of men." In the context of this statement, the Pharisees had remonstrated with the Lord because his disciples did not wash their hands before eating. The Pharisees taught that this practice was a direct service rendered to God and that those who failed to so act were spiritually defiled and displeasing to God. But, in fact, God had never commanded men to wash their hands before eating. This act was merely a precept of men, and the failure to practice it did no spiritual harm to the individual. See Matthew 15:20. Jesus Christ condemned this doctrine, along with all other man-made religious precepts, when he described it as "vain worship." Instrumental music in worship is vain because it originated with man and not with God.

But one may ask, "Is there anything really wrong with washing one's hands before he eats?" Morally, no; religiously, yes. An activity can be morally right and yet religiously wrong. Consider the following examples: (1) It is morally right to eat ham and eggs, but it is wrong to do so as a religious rite, as an act of worship. (2) It is morally right to apply water to an infant's body for the purpose of bathing it, but it is wrong to do so as a religious rite. (3) It is morally right to play on instruments of music for recreation and entertainmnet, but it is wrong to do so in the worship of God.

NOT AUTHORIZED
BY OLD TESTAMENT EXAMPLES

Old Testament examples of instrumental music in worship do not advocate its use in the Lord's church. The Old Testament is no longer binding on men as a system of religious doctrines and practices. It has been nailed to the cross in order that the New Testament might come into force (Heb. 10:9,10; Col. 2:14). Christ is the supreme authority in religion for the church, not Moses (John 1:17; Heb. 8:6). Christ gives no authority for the use of instrumental music in worship, and faithful Christians reject this practice because of their respect for the Lord's will expressed in the New Testament.

The apostle Paul said, "Tell me, ye that desire to be under the law, do ye not hear the law?" (Galatians 4:21). If one appeals to the Old Testament to justify the use of instrumental music in worship, to be consistent he is obligated to accept all the other forms of worship found therein: burning of incense, offering of animal sacrifices, etc. But churches of Christ reject *all* these practices for the simple reason that they are not included in the teachings of the New Testament, the authority of Christ.

HISTORICAL INFORMATION

There is not a solitary reference to the use of instrumental music in any congregation of the Lord's people during the entirety of the apostolic age.

The first appearance of instrumental music in worship was about the sixth century A.D. The exact date of its introduction varied in different locations. But we can safely conclude that it was not generally practiced until after the eighth century. The best of historical scholarship agrees that singing only, was the apostolic practice.

"Many centuries were to pass before instruments accompanied the sung melodies."[1]

"Only singing, however, and no playing of instruments, was permitted in the early church."[2]

"There can be no doubt that originally the music of the divine service was everywhere entirely of a vocal nature."[3]

"At first church music was simple, artless, recitative. But the rivalry of heretics forced the orthodox church to pay greater attention to the requirements of art. Chrysostom had to declaim against the secularization of church music. More lasting was the opposition to the introduction of instrumental accompaniment."[4]

"All the music employed in the services of the early Christians was vocal."[5]

"Ambrose expresses his scorn for those who would play with the lyre and psaltery instead of singing hymns and psalms; and Augustine adjures believers not to turn their heart to theatrical instruments. The religious guides of the early Christians felt that there would be an incongruity, and even profanity, in the use of the sensuous nerve-exciting effects of instrumental sound in their mystical, spiritual worship. Their high religious and moral enthusiasm needed no aid from external stimulus; the pure vocal utterance was the more proper expression of their faith."[6]

"Music in churches is as ancient as the apostles, but instrumental music not so. The use of the instrument, indeed is much more ancient, but not in church service."[7]

CONCLUSION

With all the evidence at hand, the conclusion is inescapable: instumental music in worship was never practiced by the primitive church. Churches of Christ today worship in song as the early Christians did. This is scriptural. This is safe. In everything we do in the worship of God, may we always explicitly follow the divine plan as set forth in the New Testament.

---

[1] Kurt Pahlen, *Music of the World,* p. 27.

[2] Hugo Leichtentritt, *Music, History and Ideas,* p. 34.

[3] Emil Nauman, *The History of Music,* Vol. I, p. 177.

[4] John Kurtz, *Church History,* Vol. I, p. 376.

[5] Frank Landon Humphreys, *Evolution of Church Music,* p. 42.

[6] Edward Dickinson, *Music in the History of the Western Church,* p. 55.

[7] Joseph Bingham, *Works,* London Edition, Vol. II, p. 482.

QUESTIONS

What should be the determining factor in the kind of music we use to worship God: what we want or what the Lord wants?

What kind of music in divine worship does the New Testament advocate?

What testimony do competent historians give concerning the music used in the church during apostolic times?

Discuss the significance and importance of Christians today worshipping as the early Christians did.

How does instrumental music in worship violate the law of worship?

10

The Scriptures Direct Her To
LAY BY IN STORE

By James Pilgrim

Churches of Christ seek to restore the New Testament pattern in giving. We are to do "all in the name of the Lord Jesus" (Colossians 3:17), that is, at his direction, because he told us to do so. We must neither add to nor subtract from his word (Compare Revelation 22:18,19). Let us therefore see what Jesus has directed us to do with our goods.

PURPOSE TO GIVE

The church of God in Corinth (2 Corinthians 1:1) was told to purpose in their hearts to give (2 Corinthians 9:7). *Strong's Exhaustive Concordance*, p. 820, says the word "purposeth" means "to *choose* for oneself, *before* another thing (*prefer*), i.e. (by impl.) to *propose* (intend)." To purpose therefore is to willingly pre-determine what we will give, rather than haphazardly giving.

EACH ONE WHO PROSPERS

"Every one" who *prospers* is to "lay by him in store" (1 Cor. 16:2). The rich, middle class, and poor who prosper are directed by Jesus to give. Each Christian is to carry his/her part of the load (cf. 2 Cor. 8:13-15). Such was the case in Mark 12:41-44, though the poor widow was proportionately carrying the greater part of the load. Jesus praised her.

CHEERFULLY

Those who give are not to give "grudgingly, or of ne-

51

cessity: for God loveth a cheerful giver" (2 Cor. 9:7). "Cheerful" is from the Greek word HILAROS, meaning, ". . . readiness of mind . . . joyousness . . . cheerful (Eng. hilarious) . . . 'to cause to shine' " (Expository Dictionary of New Testament Words, Vol. I, A-D, p. 184). Christians are glad rather than sad to give to the Lord. They are willing contributors rather than reluctant givers who contribute because they are obligated to do so.

AS PROSPERED

The inspired word of God (2 Tim. 3:16, 17) instructs us to give according to our prosperity (1 Cor. 16:1,2). Much is required of those to whom much is given (cf. Luke 12:48). One's giving will vary according to one's salary. The more one makes the more one is required to give. If you are still giving what you did before your last raise(s), and if you were properly giving then, you cannot now be giving according to your prosperity. Giving according to one's prosperity means giving according to the number of pay checks one has received. Fifty-two pay checks means fifty-two contributions, not fifty-one or less. Fewer than fifty-two would be giving less than one had prospered. It would be robbing God (cf. Malachi 3:8-10). Christians are to give bountifully if they expect to reap bountifully (2 Cor. 9:6; Luke 6:38; Matthew 6:33). Those who sow sparingly will reap sparingly. Romans 12:8 says those who give (i.e., impart) are to do so with simplicity (i.e., liberality). Examples of God-approved givers are the Macedonians who gave beyond their power (2 Cor. 8:1-4), and the poor widow of Mark 12:41-44. God gave his only begotten Son (John 3:16). Jesus gave his life a ransom for many (Mark 10:45).

FIRST DAY OF THE WEEK

The order Paul gave the churches of Galatia and the Corinthian Church for the collection was "upon the first day of the week" (1 Cor. 16:1,2). Thus "the first day of the week" is God's pattern for the collection, not daily as some do in revivals, or through suppers, lotteries and rummage sales, or from begging friends and businesses. We also learn that the collection is to be taken EVERY week. "The first day of the week" comes around every week. The language is the same as that in Acts 20:7, and means the same — every week. We understand a banker to mean every month when he uses similar language. For example: He may say, "The note is payable upon the first day of the month." We understand him to mean *each* month. Too, the article "the" before week in 1 Corinthians 16:2 is from the Greek word KATA, meaning and elsewhere translated "every" (cf. Acts 14:23). Those converted on the day of Pentecost continued stedfastly in the "fellowship" (Greek, KOINONIA, also translated "contribution;" cf. Acts 2:42 and Romans 15:26).

SOME "NOTS"

We are not to be covetous (Col. 3:5). Neither are we to lay up treasures upon earth, but in heaven (Matt. 6:19-21). We are not to give to be seen of men, else we will receive no reward (Matt. 6:1-4). We are not to give grudgingly or of necessity (2 Cor. 9:6). We are not to sow sparingly (2 Cor. 9:7). Neither are we to give God the scraps (what is left over), but the firstfruits of our labors (Matt. 6:33). We figure our taxes on our gross income, yet many want to give to God based upon less than their net income, or what is left after taxes, rent, food, and such like have been deducted. That is not giving according to one's prosperity. It is not in harmony with the song we sometimes sing, *GIVE OF YOUR BEST TO THE MASTER.*

CONCLUSION

"It is more blessed to give than to receive" (Acts 20:35). Giving is a grace (2 Cor. 8:1-7), which proves one's love (2 Cor. 8:8,9). It is a sin to know to give, but not do so (James 4:17). Let us be faithful to God to do what he has outlined, and content neither to add to nor subtract from his word. Let us do as God has directed, as did Noah: "According to all that God commanded him, so did he" (Genesis 6:22). May we give liberally so that the saving gospel (good news, Rom. 10:13-14) of Jesus Christ may be preached to the lost of every nation (Mark 16:15,16; Matt. 28:19), taught to the saved (1 Cor. 14:12; Matt. 28:20), and the destitute may be relieved (Gal. 1:2; 6:10).

QUESTIONS

How do we determine what to do in all matters?

What does it mean to purpose?

Who is to lay by him in store?

Discuss the Christian's attitude toward giving.

How much are Christians to give?

When are Christians to give?

What was said negatively about giving?

Where does the Bible teach us to have lotteries, rummage sales, and beg our friends and businesses to raise funds for the Lord's work?

Am I giving as I should in the manner, attitude and amount?

11

Members of the church
COMMUNE
AS CHRIST ORDAINED

By David E. Hanson

Terms such as "The Lord's Supper" (1 Corinthians 11:20); "the breaking of bread" (Acts 2:42); "communion" (1 Cor. 10:16); and "the table of the Lord" (1 Cor. 10:21) are biblical expressions designating an act of worship. "Eucharist," "sacrament" and "church ordinance" are terms invented by men (they are not found in the Bible) to designate the Lord's supper.

Jesus instituted the Lord's supper in an upper room of a house in Jerusalem on the night before his crucifixion. Four accounts of this event are presented in the Bible (Matthew 26:26-29; Mark 14:22-25; Luke 22:17-20; and 1 Cor. 11:23-26). His words were anticipatory. The memorial was established before the event it commemorated took place.

Jesus instituted the Lord's supper immediately after he and his disciples partook of the Passover meal. Because of this close connection, the Passover meal is an important background for understanding the Lord's supper. God instituted the Passover meal as Israel's celebration of deliverance from slavery (Deuteronomy 16: 1-8). The Lord's supper is the Christian's memorial of what it cost God to deliver him from the slavery of sin.

The covenant meals in the Old Testament provide another background for the Lord's supper (Genesis 18 — the renewal of the promise of a son to Abraham; Gen. 31

— a sign that there would be peace between Jacob and his father-in-law; and Isaiah 25:6-10 — descriptions of the coming salvation). After Jesus gave the disciples the fruit of the vine, he said, "For this is my blood of the *New Covenant* . . ." (Matt. 26:28). Subsequently, the Lord's supper is a renewal of the covenant, entered into at baptism, that the Christian has with God.

The Lord's supper is a memorial service. Jesus said, ". . . this do in *remembrance* of me" (Luke 22:19). Jesus left no shrouds, personal relics or statues of himself — only an unpretentious act, the Lord's supper. The Lord's supper is the world's greatest monument commemorating the world's greatest event. As Christians remember Jesus' sacrifice on the cross they become conscious of their past *need* (they were sinners without hope), and their present *responsibility* (to live a life of purity and devotion to God).

To partake in a worthy manner, each participant is to examine his life in light of the terms of the New Covenant (1 Cor. 11:27-28). Although the Christian's self-examination is not restricted to the worship assembly (2 Cor. 13:5), each should thoroughly examine himself just before partaking of the bread and the fruit of the vine. The self-examination is for the purpose of *identifying* and *repenting of* any sin in one's life (Psalm 139:23-24). Proverbs 28:13 says, "He that covereth his sins (not bringing them out in the open by self-examination) shall not prosper: but whoso *confesseth* and *forsaketh* them shall have mercy" (God will accept his worship). When observed in a worthy manner, the Christian leaves the Lord's supper with renewed spiritual strength gained by (1) his reflection on *why Jesus had to die* and by (2) his *renewed determination* to live out the terms of the New Covenant.

The Lord's supper is made up of two elements — the "bread" and the "cup." The bread of the Passover meal was unleavened bread (Exodus 12:17-20; Matt. 26:17-20). The leaven (which is a yeast that causes dough to sour or ferment) was to be removed from the house for a seven-day period (Ex. 12:15, 19). Jesus instituted the supper immediately after he and the disciples observed the Passover meal. To suggest that Jesus had leavened bread in the upper room is to accuse him of violating Exodus 12:15, 19.

Jesus used the word "leaven" in a figurative sense to denote corruption (Matt. 16:6; Luke 12:1 — cf. 1 Cor. 5:6-8; and Galatians 5:9). The unleavened bread is symbolic of Christ's body (Luke 22:19). Therefore, the "bread" is without leaven, even as Christ is without corruption or sin (Hebrews 4:15; 7:26). No leavening agents were present in the Passover meal because it was to be a perpetual reminder to the Hebrew people (Ex. 12:25-27) of the "haste" in which they left Egyptian slavery (Deut. 16:3). Likewise, the absence of "leaven" in the bread of the Lord's supper reminds the Christian of the "haste" in which he left the slavery of sin.

The "cup" contained the "fruit of the vine." The word "wine" (which can mean either unfermented grape juice — Isa. 65:8; John 2:1-11 or fermented grape juice — Prov. 20:1, depending solely on the context) is never used in the Bible to refer to the Lord's supper. Only the terms "fruit of the vine" or "cup" are used. The "fruit of the vine" is symbolic of Christ's shed blood (Mark 14:23-25; Matt. 26:27-29). Because it is pure and wholesome it is a fit symbol of the life-giving blood of Jesus Christ.

Many religious people believe that the "bread" and the "fruit of the vine" become the literal or actual "body" and "blood" of Jesus Christ. Matthew 26:26-28 says, ". . . Take eat; this is my body . . . Drink ye all of it; For this is my blood of the new testament (i.e. covenant) . . ." When Jesus took bread and said, "this is my body" he was living in his earthly body. If the bread became his literal body then he had two literal bodies at the same time. If, as Jesus spoke the words, "this is my body," he had suddenly disappeared, and the apostles had seen nothing but the bread — they would have understood that his body had been miraculously transformed into bread. However, his body was still there, and his blood was still flowing in his veins, proving that Jesus was not teaching a miraculous transubstantiation.

John 6:53 says, ". . . Except ye eat the flesh of the Son

of man, and drink his blood, ye have no life in you." The context shows that Jesus was not talking about the Lord's supper. Verse 60 suggests that the disciples took the statement literally. But Jesus corrected their misconception in verse 63 by showing that his statement referring to the eating of his flesh and drinking of his blood (verses 53-59) was figurative — "It is the spirit that giveth life; *The flesh profiteth nothing*: the words that I have spoken unto you are spirit, and are life." Men eat the flesh and drink the blood of Christ *by accepting his words and bearing them out in their daily living.*

In addition, the Lord's supper is a memorial — ". . . this do in *remembrance* of me" (Luke 22:19). Memorial services are not held for people who are physically present. If the Lord is physically present in the bread, the Lord's supper could not be a "memorial" service.

Immediately after Jesus instituted the Lord's supper he said that he would not partake again until they were in the kingdom (Matt. 26:29). In Luke 22:30 Jesus said, "That ye may eat and drink at my table *in the kingdom* . . ." The kingdom was established 52 days later on the day of Pentecost. The term "kingdom of God" is Old Testament terminology expressing a New Testament concept — namely, the church. The kingdom and the church are one and the same institution (Matt. 16:18-10).

Jesus said that the Lord's table was to be "in the kingdom" (Luke 22:29-30). The Lord's table was in the church at Jerusalem, Troas and Corinth (Acts 2:42; 20:7; 1 Cor. 10 and 11). Therefore, the churches of Christ at Jerusalem, Troas and Corinth were *in the kingdom.* The Lord's supper is authorized only for those who are citizens "in the kingdom" — i.e., members of the Lord's church. Some say that the kingdom is not now in existence. But those not in the kingdom have no authority to eat at the Lord's table.

Do all Christians (those in the kingdom) have a right to partake? The Bible does not use the words "open-communion" or "closed communion." First Corinthians 11:28 says, "But let a man examine *himself* (notice we are not to examine each other), and so let him eat of the

58

bread and drink of the cup" (notice every Christian is to partake of both emblems).

Jesus said, ". . . this *do* in remembrance of me" (Luke 22:19). The frequency was not revealed to the apostles until the kingdom was set up 52 days later on the day of Pentecost. From that time on, Christians observed the Lord's supper on a weekly basis. Acts 20:7 says, "And upon *the first day of the week,* when they were gathered together to break bread . . ." The first day of the week comes 52 times a year. When Christians meet together *"each"* first day of the week, they are meeting on *"the"* first day of the week, according to the example in Acts 20:7.

"Every" first day of the week is conveyed by the use of the definite article — *"the"* first day of the week, not *"a"* first day of the week. Just as the Jews knew the command to observe *"the* sabbath" (Ex. 20:8) meant *"every"* sabbath, so, Christians know the example in Acts 20:7 means *"every"* first day of the week. As a result of this weekly observance, the church at Jerusalem is said to have "continued steadfastly" in the breaking of bread (Acts 2:42); and the church at Corinth observed the Lord's supper "often" (1 Cor. 11:25-26).

The observance of the Lord's supper is the only act of worship that is limited to the Lord's day — "And upon the first day of the week, when the disciples came together to break bread . . ." (Acts 20:7). Not only are Christians to observe the Lord's supper *"every"* first day of the week — they are only authorized to partake *"on"* the first day of the week. It is true that Jesus instituted the Lord's supper on a Thursday, but he said that he would not partake again ". . . *until that day* when I drink it new with you in my Father's kingdom" (Matt. 26:29). The only day that the Lord's supper was observed in the kingdom was *"on"* the first day of the week (Acts 20:7).

Even the apostle Paul did not have the authority to partake on any day other than the first day of the week. In Acts 20 Paul was on an urgent trip, but he delayed his journey to fellowship with the church at Troas in the observance of the Lord's supper (verse 7). Even though this no doubt inconvenienced him, he was not free to observe the Lord's supper on any of the six days preceding the Lord's day. The Lord's supper is a memorial of the Lord's death, and is to be observed only on the Lord's day (Revelation 1:10) — the day Jesus arose from the dead.

God wants those in the kingdom to observe the biblical pattern (Heb. 8:5), regarding the Lord's supper "until" the Lord's return (1 Cor. 11:26). At that time there will be no need of a reminder of Christ because we will be in his presence (Rev. 22:3-5) and ". . . we shall see him as he is" (1 John 3:2).

QUESTIONS

Discuss the merits of this statement: "The annual, semi-annual, quarterly or monthly observance of the Lord's supper is just another attempt by the devil to make Christianity a bloodless religion."

The Bible is a continuous whole. It reveals the progressive unfolding of the redemptive plan of God over a period of hundreds of years. How can a recognition of this fact lead to a fuller understanding of the Lord's supper?

If the kingdom and the church are not just different descriptions of the same institution — then why did the early Christians partake of the Lord's supper? (cf. Luke 22:29-30)

Discuss why the Lord's supper is to be observed "every" Lord's day and "only" on the Lord's day.

12

The Biblical Pattern Is Followed
IN PRAYER

By Alvin Jennings

Members of the church of our Lord are taught to pray. Any Christian who loves God surely will consider prayer to be a most essential evidence of love for God and a right relationship with God. Since there are many abuses of prayer one may pray and still not have assurance that God hears and accepts his or her petitions.

LOVE FOR GOD AND PRAYER

The Pharisees loved to pray, but their prayers were not acceptable to God (Matthew 6:5; 15:7-8). Their long prayers, uttered to be heard and praised by men, received no reward from the heavenly Father. Empty repetitions in prayer do not reach the ears of God; words without thoughts may please men but they are a mockery to God. "God heareth not sinners: but if a man be a worshipper of God, and do his will, him he heareth." There must be proof that we love God before we can pray acceptably (1 John 3:18).

Evidence that we genuinely love God is shown when we believe in Jesus Christ and obey his commandments (1 John 2:1-5). To know Christ and to keep his commandments is not grievous (1 John 5:3). This involves believing (1 John 3:23; 5:1), turning from sin (1 John 3:6), confessing faith in Christ (1 John 4:2, 15), being born again into God's family (John 3:5, Acts 2:38, Romans 6:1-6), and striving to observe all things he commanded until death (Matt. 28:20).

Having evidenced our love for God in obedience, we are cleansed of sin by the blood of Christ, and are added to the family of God, the body, the church of Christ (Acts 2:47; Galatians 3:26-27). After Christ established his church in 33 A.D., there is no record of any man being told to pray until after his sins were washed away through obeying the gospel (see 1 Peter 1:22). For this reason, in churches of Christ no "mourner's bench" or "altar to pray through" will be found. Prayer is a privilege for those in the spiritual family, the church, rather than the means of entrance into it.

PRAY OFTEN

Although sinners are not saved through prayer from their alien sins (those sins of their former lives before they came to Christ), yet they must come in a prayerful, penitent and humble attitude like Saul of Tarsus did (Acts 9:11) when they inquire what they must do to be saved (Acts 2:37-38). After obeying Jesus' commandments for salvation (Mark 16:16), then prayer is a daily essential in the personal life of every Christian (1 Thessalonians 5:17). It is also prominent in the worship assemblies of the saints. Through repentance and prayer, forgiveness of sins is obtained by the child of God — forgiveness for his shortcomings continued from day to day through ignorance, weakness or negligence (Acts 8:14-24).

FOR WHAT DOES THE CHRISTIAN PRAY?

In addition to praying to God for forgiveness (1 John 1:9), members of Christ's church are to pray for "all things" (Philippians 4:6) which would include the following:

1. *Adoration, and Praise of God.* God's holy name is to be hallowed when we pray (Matt. 6:9). We thus

place God where he belongs — far above us, majestic, perfect, sinless, great, pure, ever-present kind and good. "We are dust" (Psalm 103:14) and worthless in relation to the Almighty God, ever-to-be adored.

2. *Thanksgiving.* Thank God for everything! For the gift of the Holy Spirit, for the gift of God's love, for Christ, his church, our Christian brothers and sisters, our families, and all God's innumerable blessings. Many Psalms are outpourings of gratitude in prayer (see Psalms 8, 9, 30, 35, 103, 117 and 118 as examples).

3. *Wisdom.* God will grant wisdom to those who ask (2 Chronicles 1:1-13; James 1:5). We gain knowledge of God's will through a study of the Scriptures (2 Timothy 2:15; 3:16-17; Psalm 111:5), but the ability to discreetly use the knowledge comes through prayer.

4. *Others.* Members of the churches of Christ pray for preachers and teachers of the gospel and for elders (2 Thess. 3:1). They pray for all Christians (Colossians 4:2-3; Hebrews 13:18) as well as for government officials and rulers (1 Timothy 2:1-2). Jesus taught us to love our enemies and to pray for them (Matt. 5:43-45). Christ died for us "while we were yet sinners" (Romans 5:8), so it behooves his disciples to love and pray for all men, including them that persecute you."

5. *Deliverance from Temptation.* Jesus told his disciples to "watch and pray, that ye enter not into temptation; the spirit indeed is willing, but the flesh is weak" (Matt. 26:41). He said further in the model prayer, "And bring us not into temptation, but deliver us from the evil one" (Matt. 6:13). God does not tempt us (James 1:12-16), but he does allow us to be tempted. He will not "suffer you to be tempted above what you are able to bear; but will with the temptation make also the way of escape, that ye may be able to endure it" (1 Corinthians 10:13).

6. *Peace.* The world needs peace today, but it cannot be obtained in the many ways by which man has sought it in the past. Read Philippians 4:6-7 for God's way to obtain a lasting peace.

7. *Unity.* Jesus, the Head and Founder of the true church, prayed that all disciples who believe on him

might be united together with each other, the same as he and his Father are "one" (John 17:20-21). Since the prayer life of Jesus is an example for members of his church, we should pray for all Christians to be one, to be "perfectly joined together" in one mind, in the one body, the church (1 Cor. 1:10-13). Divisions over names and doctrines are sinful and we are commanded to avoid the party spirit within the church. We should therefore pray fervently that denominational divisions be utterly and quickly destroyed. If we "obey God rather than men" (Acts 5:29) and speak only "as the oracles of God" (1 Pet. 4:11) there will be unity in the one body, the church for which Christ died and to which he adds the saved (Acts 20:28; 2:47). Truth and unity constitute a great part of Jesus' prayers to the Father.

GOD ANSWERS PRAYER

When we pray "in faith" and "according to God's will," God will hear us and will answer our prayers (Matt. 7:7-11; 21:22; 1 John 5:14). Some who pray are not heard because they ask for things to gratify their own lust (James 4:1-3). prayers must be honest, sincere (Psa. 17:1; Isaiah 29:13) and humble (Luke 18:14).

CHRIST THE MEDIATOR

There is "one God, and one mediator between God and man, himself man, Christ Jesus" (1 Tim. 2:5). In spite of this plain teaching in the Bible, today the religious world recognizes literally hundreds of mediators. Some say to pray through Mary; othrs say, "No, pray through Mohammed" or some other prophet or man. Friend, there is no priest on earth through whom God is approached. Pray to God through the one he has appointed (Heb. 4:14-16; Col. 3:17; John 14:4).

QUESTIONS

Can you give a biblical example of prayers that were not acceptable to God?

What Bible teaching regarding prayer is violated by praying memorized prayers with (or without) beads?

Does God hear and answer prayers of those who have not obeyed the gospel of Christ, and who are not in the spiritual family, the church?

Can you give any Bible reference for women leading in a public prayer in assemblies when men were present? What does this suggest about church leadership today in the light of such passages as 1 Timothy 2:8-12?

Name some things for which Christians are to pray.

13

Like the Apostles
HER PREACHING IS BIBLICAL

By Richard Powlus

God told Jonah: "Arise, go unto Ninevah, that great city, *and preach unto it the preaching that I bid thee*" (Jonah 3:2). The only kind of preaching that pleases God is preaching the things he bids us to preach. Unfortunately, in the denominational world today, this kind of preaching is not commonly found. Preachers are often more concerned with pleasing their audience than with pleasing God. First century preachers were only concerned with pleasing God in their preaching (see Acts 4:20 and Galatians 1:10). Preachers in the churches of Christ depend upon God's Word as the source and power of their preaching. Our concern is the saving of souls, not the "tickling of ears."

Ray Hawk, now a preacher in the church of Christ, was a licensed preacher in a denominational church prior to his conversion. In a series of articles he wrote entitled, "Are We Preaching Damnable Doctrine," he states: "If I rejected the (Methodist) Discipline, it meant I would have to leave the Methodist church. *My license to preach stated that I was appointed a Methodist preacher to 'preach the gospel according to the Discipline of the Methodist church.'* I could no longer do so, for the Methodist Discipline would not allow me to preach simple Bible truths." Most denominational preachers are in this position today. They are committed to their church creeds more than to the Bible as the source of their teaching.

Even more astonishing is the attitude many denominational preachers have toward the Holy Scriptures. *Christianity Today* (October 13, 1967), reported the results of a poll taken among 7,441 Protestant preachers in the U.S. In this poll 89% of Episcopal priests, 82% of Methodist preachers, 81% of Presbyterian preachers and 57% of American Lutheran preachers rejected a literal interpretation of the Bible when asked if they believed the Bible is the inspired word of God. *Time* magazine (December 30, 1974) in an article entitled, "The Bible: The Believer Gains," discusses this same unbelief in the literal inspiration of the Bible among denominational leaders and teachers.

Now let us examine the attitude of preachers in the New Testament church toward the Bible.

They studied the word of God. In 1 Timothy 4:13, Paul instructed Timothy to, ". . . give heed to reading . . ." It is obvious from the context as well as from 2 Timothy 2:15 that the word of God was the subject of that reading. They knew that they must handle the word of God properly in order to present themselves as approved workmen unto God. This requires diligent study! In Hebrews 5:12-14, we learn that those who study and use the word of God are able to understand it and to teach others. In 2 Peter 3:15-16, we have an obvious reference to the apostle Peter studying the letters of Paul. Preachers in the church of Christ must give diligence in studying God's word in order that they can proclaim it effectively.

They used proof-texts from the Bible to support their preaching. In his sermon on Pentecost, Peter used Joel 2:28 to prove that their speech was from God, not wine. He used Psalm 16:8 to prove that David had looked forward to Christ's coming and his resurrection. He used 2 Samuel 7:12 and Psalm 132:11 to prove Jesus was now on his throne in heaven. Stephen used the Old Testament scriptures to prove the hard-hearted rejection of truth by the Jewish leaders in Acts 7. When Philip taught the Ethiopian eunuch about Christ and the plan of salvation Acts 8:35 says, ". . . and beginning from this scripture (Isaiah 53), preached unto him Jesus." In Acts 18:28, it is said of Apollos' preaching, "for he powerfully refuted the Jews, and that publicly, showing by the Scriptures that Jesus was the Christ." It is written of Paul and Barnabas, that they, ". . . tarried in Antioch, teaching and preaching the word of the Lord, with many others also" (Acts 15:35).

They believed the Scriptures alone were sufficient. They had no need of creedbooks, in fact, they condemned the creeds and doctrines of men (Galatians 1:6-9; 1 Tim. 1:6-7; 4:1-3; 2 Tim. 2:16-18; 3:5-9; Titus 1:9-11). In 2 Timothy 3:16-17, Paul (by inspiration from the Holy Spirit) makes it very clear that New Testament preaching relied upon the Scriptures as *all sufficient* to make us complete and furnish us "to every good work." It is even said that we should learn in them, ". . . not to go beyond the things that are written" (1 Cor. 4:6). Of those who feel that we need more than Christ has given in his doctrine, it is said that they, have not God. "He that abideth in the teaching, the same hath both the Father and the Son" (2 John 9). Jesus promised to guide the apostles into all truth (John 16:13). In 2 Peter 1:3 that apostle said, "seeing that his divine power both granted unto us all things that pertain unto life and godliness, through the knowledge of him that called us . . ." In 1 John 4:6, that apostle said, "We are of God: he that knoweth God heareth us; he who is not of God heareth us not. By this we know the spirit of truth and the spirit of error." You can mark it down that anyone or any group who is *not* content with the sufficiency of the Scriptures and not willing to "contend earnestly for the faith once for all delivered to the saints" (Jude 3), is not representing God's church.

How different the attitude and preaching of the New Testament church was from the preaching in denominational churches today. The church of Christ patterns her preaching from the example of these New Testament preachers. The power of their preaching was derived from the Scriptures.

Many preachers depend on wisdom of words to give their preaching power. Philosophy is required in many schools training preachers. Some preachers depend on theatrical methods to entertain their audience. Some resort to extreme emotionalism to stir up their audience and thus feel they have preached powerfully.

New Testament preachers relied upon the gospel as their source of power in preaching. "For Christ sent me . . . to preach the gospel: *not* in wisdom of words, lest the cross of Christ should be made void. For the word of the cross is to them that perish foolishness; but unto us who are saved, it is the power of God" (1 Cor. 1:17-18). One should read Romans 1:15-17, which also declares the power of the gospel. Paul said, ". . . when I came unto you, (I) came not with excellency of speech or of wisdom, proclaiming unto you the testimony of God" (1 Cor. 2:1). Yet he was successful in converting the lost to Christ and in building strong churches. He succeeded because he relied upon God's power through his word. "Which things also we speak, not in words which man's wisdom teacheth, but which the Spirit teacheth; combining spiritual things with spiritual words" (1 Cor. 2:13).

The power of apostolic preaching was their willingness to declare the "whole counsel of God" (Acts 20:27). Preaching that does not include scripture falls short of declaring the whole counsel of God. Teaching only part of the gospel has no more power to save than teaching error.

The power of their preaching was also their willingness to declare unto their audience everything that was profitable (Acts 20:20). That is, whatever the church or the lost *needed* to hear, was what they preached. We need preachers with the same courage today! Too many today are like those Paul describes in 2 Timothy 4:3-4. How sad it is that so many profess godliness today while at the same time they deny the power thereof (2 Tim. 3:5).

CONCLUSION

The result of this kind of preaching is given also. "Take heed to thyself and to thy teaching. Continue in these things; for in doing this thou shalt save both thyself and them that hear thee" (1 Tim. 4:16). May God help us to always pattern our preaching after the example of New Testament preachers.

69

QUESTIONS

What kind of preaching pleases God?

Discuss the attitude of many denominational preachers toward the Bible and how this would affect their preaching.

Why must preachers and teachers study the word of God?

How can we know the spirit of truth and the spirit of error in preaching?

What was the power of New Testament preaching?

When preachers preach after the New Testament pattern, what will the result be?

14

Each local church is
SELF - GOVERNING
UNDER CHRIST

By Wallace Alexander

W hen Jesus called his disciples together in Caesarea Philippi to inquire about whom the people considered him to be, he made a solemn promise to build his church (Matthew 16:13-16). His later commission to the apostles to take the gospel into "all the world" (Mark 16:15) affirms the universality of the church. The scriptures frequently refer to the church in a *universal* sense, encompassing the entire family of God throughout the world.

The New Testament also frequently refers to the church in a *local* sense. Many of Paul's letters were directed to the church in a particular city (Romans 1:7; 1 Corinthians 1:2; Philippians 1:1), or region (Galatians 1:2).

NO UNIVERSAL ORGANIZATION

Christ's church may well be described as a monarchy. Other than Jesus, the absolute monarch and head of the church (Ephesians 1:20-23), who possesses all legislative authority (Matt. 28:18), the New Testament authorizes no organization for the universal church. In the absence of any Biblical authority for organizing the church universal, any assumption of authority beyond the local congregation constitutes a government not sanctioned by the scriptures.

71

In his divine wisdom, God did not permit ambitious men to wield undue influence on the church universal. Jesus emphasized humility and service to others as character traits of those great in his kingdom. Ambitious men seeking power over others through an organizational structure greater than the local church runs contrary to greatness as God sees it.

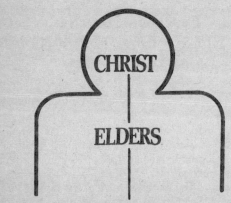

LOCAL ORGANIZATION

The scriptures, however, do present God's plan for the organization of the local church. That all things might be done decently and in order, he commands the selection of a plurality of men in each congregation to serve as shepherds of the flock. These men are scripturally described as elders (1 Peter 5:1), bishops (Phil. 1:1; 1 Timothy 3:1), the presbytery (1 Tim. 4:14), overseers (Acts 20:28, KJV), or pastors (Eph. 4:11).

The divine wisdom of God was demonstrated in making each local church self-governing under Christ. Each was to have its own leaders. In Acts 20, Luke records Paul's meeting with the elders of the church in Ephesus (v. 17). Paul gave these men the solemn charge to "Take heed unto yourselves and to all the flock, in which the

Holy Spirit hath made you bishops . . ." (v. 28). When writing to the church in Philippi, Paul addressed his letter "to all the saints in Christ Jesus that are at Philippi, with the bishops and deacons" (Phil. 1:1). To Titus, Paul said, "For this cause left I thee in Crete, that thou shouldest set in order the things that were wanting, and appoint elders in every city, as I gave thee charge" (Titus 1:5). Each church had its own elders.

The elders in each locality had specific responsibilities to teach, oversee, rule, and be examples to the flock of God under their care. Each congregation functioned with a plurality of elders. The elders in one city, or congregation, had no responsibility or authority in another city. Likewise, all elders in a congregation had equal responsibility and authority in that congregation.

The organization God planned for his church was simple. A plurality of men qualified by character and experience (1 Tim. 3:1-7) were to be chosen (Titus 1:5). The plan did not include a modern "single pastor" system. It did not include any individual with authority and responsibility beyond his own congregation. It did not include a "bishop" elevated above the other elders or bishops.

Other forms of government such as are now practiced by many religious organizations with their synods, general assemblies, councils, conferences, presbyteries and the like did not develop suddenly. The departure from the New Testament pattern in organization began early in the history of the church and has gradually evolved into the many forms of organization used today. However, any deviation from the New Testament pattern must be rejected for what it is — a deviation.

AN EARLY DEPARTURE

One of the first departures from the New Testament pattern was the development of the monarchal bishop. One man from among the elders accepted the title of bishop (a term scripturally referring to an elder) and was elevated above the rest. He became "chairman of the elders." One by one, monarchal bishops were ordained

73

until around 150 A.D. it became a generally accepted practice.

The position of "bishop" continued to gain prominence as churches evangelized their surrounding areas. The church in a large city, such as Rome, Antioch, or Alexandria, would begin a church in a smaller city and, with a sense of paternal responsibility, the bishop accepted the oversight of the new congregation. It was natural that the monarchal bishops in the larger cities wielded a great influence. The gradual development of synods resulted. Ultimately, religious authority emanated from Rome, perhaps partially because Rome was the seat of political power.

With the establishment of monarchal bishops, these men met in councils as representatives of their respective congregations to consider their common interests. It was not long, however, until the bishops saw themselves, not as representatives, but as authorities to dictate to the churches. The bishops' conclaves were described as councils or synods and the resulting regulations were known as canons or rules. Late in the second century there were attempts to establish a succession of bishops back to the apostles. This attempt shows the undue authority the bishops were accepting. To trace their lineage back to the apostles had the effect of placing them on an equality with the apostles.

RESULTS OF DEPARTURE

The selection of monarchal bishops was far more than an insignificant deviation from the pattern. It became the beginning of an organizational system which eventually evolved into the hierarchal form of government seen in Catholicism today. The ultimate assumption of power came in 1870 when the Vatican Council declared the doctrine of papal infallibility.

When the courageous reformation leaders came on the scene seeking to reform the apostate church, the result came to be known as Protestantism. Many of the Protestant groups were influenced by the Roman hierarchy and retained various elements of its polity after they broke away. Others, preferring different organizational structures, adopted forms of government which seemed good to them. The result is the diverse methods of organization seen in the religious world — many of which cater to the pride and ambition of men but do not resemble the simple command of Paul to "ordain elders in every city" (Titus 1:5).

TODAY'S PLEA

Churches of Christ today plead for a return to the organization of the church of the New Testament. Jesus Christ is the absolute monarch and sole legislator. A plurality of elders with equal authority and responsibility in each congregation and with no authority beyond their local congregation oversee the affairs of the local church under Jesus, the chief Shepherd (1 Peter 5:4). All children of God throughout the world are brothers and sisters in Christ — with no clergy or laity distinctions — but each congregation must be autonomous, working within the framework of the simple organization described in the New Testament.

QUESTIONS

The term "church" is used in what two ways in the New Testament?

To what extent is the universal church organized?

To what extent is the local church organized?

Where does legislative power in the church reside?

To what did the term "bishop" originally refer? How was it changed?

Who is the Chief Shepherd?

15

Each Congregation is
OVERSEEN
BY BIBLICAL ELDERS

By Rex A. Turner

With the passing of the apostles from the scene of action, the direction of the church was left under the oversight of men who were variously designated as elders, bishops, overseers, pastors or shepherds, and teachers. Each church was to be governed and supervised by a plurality of such men, not by one man that wears the title, "the Pastor."

PURPOSE FOR TITLES AND DESIGNATIONS

Several titles or designations — such as, elders, bishops, overseers, pastors, shepherds, teachers — are used to shed greater light on the duties and responsibilities of these men of God. They are called elders because they are to be men of advanced age and of superior wisdom and experience. They are called bishops, or overseers, because they are to watch over and superintend all matters pertaining to their respective church. They are called pastors, or shepherds, because they are to assume the responsibility for the spiritual care and well-being of every soul. They are called teachers because they are to teach, instruct, and direct all of the members in the way of sound doctrine.

The New Testament passages which bear directly upon the office, work, and qualifications of the men who are responsible for the direction or oversight of God's heritage are as follows: Acts 20:28-30; 1 Timothy 3:1-7; 5:17-19; Titus 1:5-16; and 1 Peter 5:1-4. The specifications contained in these passages may be divided into two categories; namely, Qualifications of Elders and Duties of Elders,

QUALIFICATIONS OF ELDERS

The qualifications of elders naturally fall into two classifications. There are negative qualifications and positive qualifications.

The negative qualifications of an elder are as follows:

1. He must not be a novice — or he must not be a new convert or a beginner.

2. He must not be soon angry — or he must not be a vengeful, hotheaded, or an impetuous person.

3. He must not be self-willed — or he must not be a haughty, imperious, and an arrogant person.

4. He must not be given to wine — or he must not be one who drinks wine and other intoxicating beverages.

5. He must not be a brawler — or he must not be one who is given to strife and debate, or disposed to fight in a figurative sense.

6. He must not be a striker — or he must not be one who is quarrelsome, pugnacious, and disposed to physical combat or encounter.

7. He must not be greedy of filthy lucre — or he must not be one who gets money by base and dishonorable means.

8. He must not be covetous — or he must not be one who is inordinately desirous of wealth, or not one who is of an avaricious spirit.

The positive qualifications of an elder are as follows:

1. He must be the husband of one wife — that is, he must be a married man, but not unlawfully divorced or a polygamist.

2. He must have children that believe and who are not accused of riot or unruly — that is, they must be old enough to be Christians on the one hand, and they must be faithful Christians on the other hand.

3. He must be of good behavior — that is, he must be court-

77

eous and considerate of others, and not uncouth or boorish.

4. He must be vigilant — that is, he must be watchful, attentive and protective and not indifferent, unobserving, insensitive, and sluggish.

5. He must be sober — that is, he must be thoughtful and well balanced in judgment, and not frivolous, impulsive, worldly, and given to extremes.

6. He must be patient — that is, he must be forebearing toward others, and not fretful, complaining, or murmuring even in the face of provocations.

7. He must be temperate — that is, he must be marked by moderation and restraint in all areas of his life, and not intemperate in desires, habits, and language.

8. He must be just — that is, he must be committed to that which is right, fair, and reasonable, and not unjust or given to prejudice and passion in dealing with others.

9. He must be gentle — that is, he must be kind, sympathetic, and gentle by nature, and not bitter, unfair, harsh, or inequitable.

10. He must be holy — that is he must be godly, spiritually pure, and committed to the principle of the righteousness of God, and not lacking in full dedication and consecration to Jehovah.

11. He must be a lover of good men — that is, he must have an appreciation for good men and a strong desire to see them persevere and succeed in their good works, and not an admirer of or a participant with evil men.

12. He must be given to hospitality — that is, he must be keen to the needs and welfare of others, particularly strangers, and not unsocial or unresponsive to others.

13. He must be qualified to teach — that is, he must have extensive knowledge of God's Word coupled with the ability and desire to teach it, and thus not lacking in natural ability or Bible knowledge.

14. He must be able to exhort and convince the gainsayers — that is, he must have sufficient knowledge and ability to defend the truth against the gainsayer, and not one so ignorant of the sound doctrine as to be impotent in the protection of the flock against false teachers who teach for gain.

15. He must be blameless — that is, he must be one of unquestioned and upright character, and not one against whom evil reports continue to circulate.

78

16. He must be of good report among them without — that is, he must have a good moral reputation for honesty and integrity of character, and not one who is of evil report and sharp criticism from those who are not Christians.

DUTIES OF ELDERS

Whereas the qualifications for the Christian elder or bishop naturally divide into two categories — negative qualifications and positive qualifications — the specifications relative to the duties of elders also divide naturally into two categories. The two categories of duties are the primary duties and the secondary duties. The primary duties are those duties which relate to the elder himself. The secondary duties are those duties that the elder must fulfill for the welfare of the church.

The primary duties of elders are:

1. The elder must take heed to himself. He must be humble, dedicated, prayerful, gentle, and Christlike.

2. The elder must rule well his own house. Here lies an acid test for "If a man knows not how to rule his own house, how shall he take care of the church of God?"

3. The elder must have believing children.

4. The elder must have his children in subjection. Unruly children, regardless of unfortunate or nullifying sinister influences, will prevent any man from serving successfully as an elder in the church.

5. The elder must hold fast the faithful word. He must respect the word, teach it, stand for it, and defend it against all enemies.

6. The elder must be an ensample to the flock. He must be above reproach in his manner of life, in his dedication to Christ, and in his disposition toward all men.

The secondary duties of an elder are those duties which relate to the flock — that is, those duties and obligations which an elder must take for the welfare of the flock.

The secondary duties of elders are:

1. The elder must take heed to the flock. He must be concerned for the welfare of every member. He should have no

favorites, and he should show no partiality.

2. The elder must take the oversight of the flock willingly. He must desire the work because of his sincere interest in the souls of men. He must be an overseer of souls.

3. The elder must feed the flock. He must instruct the flock in the sound doctrine. He must be a teacher of that which is good. This responsibility requires diligent and continuous preparation.

4. The elder must rule well the flock. He must rule the flock, the church, as a father would rule his family — not in a permissive way and yet not as lording over God's heritage.

GREAT NEED OF THE CHURCH

There is no greater need in the church today than the need for qualified and consecrated elders to rule and oversee the congregations. Each congregation should be willing to submit to the leadership of its elders. The church is not a democracy; rather, it is God's heritage and is to be supervised by qualified men. No church can reach its spiritual zenith without qualified men to serve as elders or overseers.

QUESTIONS

What qualifications must an elder have that other Christian men may not necessarily have?

Discuss the wisdom of having a congregation governed or directed by a plurality of well qualified men rather than a government by one person.

Must an elder be characterized by every qualification—whether negative or positive—in a reasonable degree?

Is there a danger in an eldership's regarding themselves somewhat as a Board of Directors? Discuss.

Should elders regard themselves as leaders, protectors, or both?

16

As in Bible times
DEACONS
SERVE THE CHURCH

By Ben S. Flatt

Deacons are an important part of the working program of the New Testament Church. A proper understanding of their responsibilities is vital to the success of church growth. Although the Bible has relatively little to say about deacons, sufficient information is given and adequate guidelines are defined to produce the logical conclusions concerning the authority of deacons, their qualifications, the process of selection, their assigned duties, and the performance of those duties. The application of these principles will help avoid both of two extremes, either making deacons the same as elders and overseers, or letting them be deacons in name only, accomplishing very little.

MEANING OF THE WORD

The term which is translated "deacon" is from an original word which means "servant." It is defined as "one who executes the commands of another . . . a servant, attendant, or minister" (Thayer). The original word, in both noun and verb forms, appears over 90 times; however, the specific rendering of "deacon" occurs only 5 times in our basic English texts (Philippians 1:1; 1 Timothy 3:8, 10, 12, 13). Elsewhere, the term is translated as minister, servant, ministering, ministration, to minister, serving, service, to do service, relief, administration, minister unto, minister to, administer, and

81

serve. In every place where the word is used, whatever the form, the idea of "service" is presented.

AUTHORITY FOR DEACONS

That God has authorized deacons in the church can be easily seen. The specific "office of a deacon" is identified (1 Tim. 3:10, 13). An outline of qualifications is given to instruct the church about the type of men needed (Acts 6:3; 1 Tim. 3:8-10). The early church was commanded by the twelve apostles to select and appoint men to serve in this capacity (Acts 6:2-3). And some, who were serving in the church at Philippi were included in the salutation of Paul's epistle to that church (Phil. 1:1).

THEIR QUALIFICATIONS

Although the qualifications of the deacons are not as strict as those of elders, they are, nevertheless, quite improtant. The word "likewise" (1 Tim. 3:8) indicates that it is just as necessary for deacons to possess the specified qualities for the office of service as for the elders to have the qualities of leadership. The required traits which are listed in two passages of Scripture (Acts 6:3; 1 Tim. 3:8-10, 12), deal with three concepts: character, ability, and relationships with others.

Four involve character traits:

Grave. There must be a high degree of maturity which produces balanced, serious thinking.

Not double-tongued. Integrity is a key. One must be honest with all people at all times, never being two-faced.

Not given to much wine. At a time when little water was used because of health reasons, wine was used for drinking purposes. Warning was issued about being given to wine in excess or for other purposes. A deacon, like every Christian, should avoid the evils of strong drink.

Not greedy of filthy lucre. Men should not be lovers of money or covetous of it.

Three emphasize ability:

Holding the mystery of the faith in pure conscience.

It was necessary to have a clear understanding of the Word of God to stand for truth and to labor within its boundaries.

Full of the Holy Spirit. Because the Holy Spirit dwells in us through faith (Galatians 3:14) and that faith comes through the word (Romans 10:17), the man would need to be guided by the word given by inspiration.

Full of wisdom. Men charged with being deacons should be able to use common sense and good judgment in carrying out their assigned tasks.

Three are concerned with relationships to others:

Husband of one wife. To be a deacon a man must have one, and only one wife.

Ruling house well. The control of one's family is an indicator of ability to function in other areas.

Of good report or blameless. One's reputation can help or hinder, depending on what is thought about that person by the community and the church.

SELECTION OF DEACONS

Very little detailed teaching is given to govern the selection of deacons. The brethren were told to ". . . look ye out . . . men . . . whom we (apostles) may appoint . . ." (Acts 6:3). Whatever approach is used, leaders of the church should involve the membership in suggestions and approval of men to serve as deacons. The context of Acts 6 reveals that the needs and circumstances of a given situation will determine when deacons are appointed and how many are required.

ASSIGNED DUTIES OF DEACONS

All the work of the church, including that of deacons, is overseen by the elders (Acts 20:28; Hebrews 13:7, 17). The deacons have authority only as they are assigned to be "over" some specific "business" (Acts 6:3). Each deacon should be delegated responsibilities which are clearly understood by the deacon, the elders, and the congregation. Deacons may assist the elders by performing assignments in all scriptural works, particularly material, physical, benevolent, and mission areas.

83

PERFORMANCE OF DUTIES

Many congregations suffer because deacons, as well as others, will not perform. Important programs of work accomplish little or nothing if left on paper or in the memory of a conversation. Until a task is assigned, a deacon can not function; however, when the request is given, he needs to move on to see that the job is done. Working within the guidelines of the desires of the elders, a deacon must be willing to make decisions and put forth immediate efforts to begin and complete his assignment.

OBSERVATIONS

The work of the deacon is important. He is not an elder, may never be qualified as an elder, and need not necessarily use his office as a stepping stone to be an elder. He can serve as a deacon, recognizing the value of that service. Deacons need to function regularly and be appreciated for their work's sake. When deacons have used the office well, they "purchase to themselves a good degree, and great boldness in the faith . . ." (1 Tim. 3:13).

Good deacons are a blessing. When they were appointed and did their work in the setting of Acts 6, the complaining stopped, the needs were met, the Word increased, the disciples multiplied, and the deacons grew in faith and service (Acts 6:7-8). Just as the church today needs good elders to lead, it also needs competent, willing deacons to serve.

QUESTIONS

What two extremes involving deacons exist today?

Does the meaning of the word "deacon" suggest the type of duty he has?

What biblical authority do we have for deacons?

Discuss the different types of qualifications required of men who can serve as deacons.

What is the scriptural relationship between elders and deacons?

What assigned duties can deacons perform?

17

The role of
PREACHERS
IN THE LORD'S CHURCH

By A. Kay Gardner

T he church of Christ seeks to restore the New Testament church. It is committed to following the biblical pattern in all things: doctrine, worship, work, organization, zeal and life. Its faithful preachers fill the God-ordained role of public proclaimers of the gospel. They heed the principles stated here.

PREACH THE GOSPEL

"Preach the word" (2 Timothy 4:2). The gospel *must* be preached! It is God's power to save sinners and the world's hope. It is spiritual light that scatters darkness; divine power that breaks down bulwarks of sin. Since Christ built his church there has been perpetual need for men, faithful and able, to declare the whole counsel of God (Acts 20:27). This urgent need exists now; it always will.

Early Christians, evangelists and inspired apostles set the example. They were absorbed with an overwhelming passion to carry the message of a glorified Lord to their perishing fellow-men. With a crucified and risen Savior as the heart of the message, they preached it with amazing conviction and strong affection for the cross (1 Corinthians 2:2).

The church goes the way the pulpit goes. Soft, compromising preaching produces weak, wavering congregations. Every generation needs to hear the "Old Jerusalem" gospel. When blood-atonement is eliminated the pulpit is powerless; the pew is impoverished. The pulpit will be despised in an age when gospel truth is no longer honored.

PASTORS ARE SHEPHERDS — EVANGELISTS ARE PREACHERS

According to the Bible, pastors (elders) are to pastor (shepherd) the flock (Acts 20:28). Preachers (evangelists) are to preach (2 Tim. 4:1-4). Preachers who preach and pastors who pastor is the right way; it is God's divine plan. Here denominations have stumbled. When the evangelist is doing the pastoring, God's way is being ignored or rejected. Elders are to discharge their duty as caretakers of souls and should not appoint the preacher as their deputy to care for sick straying sheep. Shepherds do not nurse ill lambs by proxy.

Preachers are to labor in the word, preaching, teaching, exhorting (Colossians 1:24-29; 2 Tim. 4:1-5). Many preachers have played "pastor" so long it will take a while for them to become evangelists again.

Elevating the "Reverend Pastor" to a level above the "average" member in the Lord's body is a result of superficial thinking. Men who preach may be placed on a lofty pedestal by those whose minds are clouded, and conclusions are conditioned by a denominational thought-pattern. In God's sight the greatest person is the most faithful servant; not one who has assumed an elevated position. Seemingly it is a basic paradox of Christianity that the way *up* is *down* (Matthew 20:25-28). One does not earn a high place before God by appropriating an impressive religious title.

RELIGIOUS TITLES NOT SCRIPTURAL

Distinctive dress and high-sounding titles feed clerical vanity that mocks the spirit of Christianity. Scribes and Pharisees delighted in pompous designations. These reflect an arrogant attitude displeasing to the Master. A full-grown "clergy-laity complex," entrenched in denominational thought and practice, is foreign to New Testament teaching.

The words of Jesus are authoritative and final. "Be not ye called Rabbi . . . call no man your father on the earth . . . neither be ye called masters" (Matt. 23:8-10). Here the Lord laid down the principle that condemns the wearing of ALL religious titles whether they be Reverend, Rabbi, Master, Father, Pope, Cardinal, Archbishop, Pastor, etc.

PREACH THE WORD

Assuming religious titles corrupt the religion that is pure and undefiled even as false teachers are a disgrace to Christ and a hindrance to his church (Acts 20:29-30). Their "mouths must be stopped" (Titus 1:11). Paul warns against teaching traditions of men and vain philosophy (Colossians 2:8). When the whole counsel of God is preached, believed and obeyed, all spiritual needs are satisfied (James 1:21; 2 Tim. 3:16-17). All that men need to believe, be, know, do or teach to please God is written in the Bible. God provides the effective tool; his eternal word. It is mighty, living, powerful and will accomplish its purpose (Eph. 6:17; Heb. 4:12; Isaiah 55:11). When hearers obey God's word a glorious three-fold result follows: (1) aliens are converted to Christ, (2) the wayward are restored, (3) the saved stay saved if they continue firm and stedfast unto the end (1 Cor. 15:58). In this way the church is strengthened and its influence for good is extended.

Preachers carry a heavy burden in a sin-sick world. They lead the fight against sin by calling Christians to take up the whole armor of God; fight the devil; withstand his wiles and quench his fiery darts (Eph. 6:10-18). In the Lord's church, conscientious preachers refuse to join the search for something new and different, nor do they make a blundering reach for "relevancy." They are not ashamed of centuries old fundamentalism. Knowing that the doctrine of redemption in Christ will always be relevant, they preach *The Old Jerusalem Gospel* and exhort sinners to obey it; to become servants of God; saved, with sins forgiven and souls set free (Rom. 6:17-18). They do not neglect duty while sinners perish in darkness. Their preaching promotes unity, truth and righteousness while opposing division, error and sin (Proverbs 14:34; John 8:32; 1 Cor. 1:10-13). They warn of the fatal danger in being ashamed of Christ and his words for by them we will be judged (Mark 8:38; John 12:48). They teach that we are saved by grace through faith; not by grace alone nor faith alone but by God's grace and man's obedient faith (Eph. 2:8-10; Rom. 1:5; Gal. 5:6).

They do not try to galvanize sin into respectability, nor do they "soft-pedal" sin by shading terminology. They call transgression of God's law *sin*, not "deviant behavior" (1 John 3:4; James 4:17). They are careful to distinguish between matters of *faith* and matters of *opinion*, then deal with each for what it is.

PREACH THE GOSPEL — HOW?

Faithful evangelists preach the gospel in this manner: *Fully* — "From Jerusalem and round about . . . I have *fully* preached the gospel of Christ" (Rom. 15:19). A man who will not preach the gospel fully should not preach at all.

Forcefully — Paul "*powerfully* confuted the Jews, and that publicly, showing by the scriptures that Jesus was the Christ" (Acts 18:28). "I am set for the defense of the gospel" (Philippians 1:16). Paul's preaching was powerful; it demanded a decision. Most of his sermons caused a revival or a riot. Need for strong preaching is constant.

Simply — "I fear lest . . . your minds should be corrupted from the *simplicity* and the *purity* that is toward Christ" (2 Cor. 11:3). The average word in the Bible contains fewer than five letters. Inspired preachers had no mania for big words.

Urgently — "Necessity is laid upon me: for woe is unto me, if I preach not the gospel" (1 Cor. 9:16).

Boldly — When the council in Jerusalem beheld the *boldness* of Peter and John they marvelled (Acts 4:13, 29, 31). Paul urged brethren at Ephesus to pray that he might "make known with *boldness* the . . . gospel, . . . and that I may speak *boldly,* as I ought to speak" (Eph. 6:19, 20). God's preachers do not fear lest they offend brother Social Drinker or sister Dancer. That would be weak and cowardly.

In Love — Christ placed evangelists, teachers and others in the church to minister unto the building up of the body of Christ by "speaking the truth *in love* . . ." (Eph. 4:11-15). "Let all that ye do be done *in love*" (1 Cor. 16:13).

In the church of Christ evangelists "hold the pattern of sound words . . ." (2 Tim. 1:13). They strive to please God, not men; they preach Christ, not themselves. They are not in the entertainment business; rather, they are fishers of men in the soul-winning business. Faithfully and courageously, worthy preachers expose and oppose error; they rebuke sinners and condemn sin (John 8:44; Acts 8:20-23; 13:9-11). By doing their work well they glorify God.

QUESTIONS

Explain why the pulpit is left "powerless" when blood-atonement is not preached (Romans 5:8-11).

Why is it wrong in the sight of God for men to wear religious titles? (Matthew 23:8-10)

Point out as clearly as you can the particular work in the church that God has assigned: (a) to gospel preachers (b) to elders.

Whose mouths must be stopped? (Titus 1:11) Why?

In this chapter, six characteristics of sound gospel preaching are listed, with scripture references that support them. Does the preacher where you worship so preach the gospel?

Are sinners made saints by faith alone, or by grace alone, or by grace *and* obedient faith? Prove your answer by scripture.

18

She wears only
BIBLICAL NAMES

By B. J. Barr

A s one looks about in the religious world, there are hundreds of names that supposedly represent the church for which Christ died. But a quick glance into the word of God clearly shows most of these names are unbiblical and unfounded. Since these names cannot be found within the context of our religious standard — the Bible, it is unwise and disrespectful to adopt them as followers of Christ.

WHY ARE MAN-MADE NAMES WRONG?

Simply, they are condemned in the New Testament. Paul, in his letter to the Corinthian church, wrote these words, ". . . that ye all speak the same thing, and that there be no divisions among you; but that ye be perfected together in the same mind and in the same judgment" (1 Corinthians 1:10). In the next few verses, Paul further discusses what he meant. "Now this I mean, that each one of you saith, I am of Paul; and I of Apollos; and I of Cephas; and I of Christ. Is Christ divided? Was Paul crucified for you? Or were ye baptized in the name of Paul?" (1 Cor. 1:12-13). To give honor to a person such as "Luther" over the name of Christ is to divert honor belonging only to Christ. To exalt an ordinance such as "baptism" is to lift it higher than the name which is above every name — Christ. To designate a manner of church government as "Episcopal" or Presbyterian" is to add what God never intended.

91

Paul warned the early church against man-made titles; we of the churches of Christ today accept his plea. There is something in a name. We must live by it and uphold it.

BIBLICAL NAMES FOR THE CHURCH

In the Bible, there are no exclusive names for the church. God refers to his church as:

"the church of God" (1 Cor. 1:2)
"church of the firstborn" (Hebrews 12:23)
"churches of Christ" (Romans 16:16)
"Body of Christ (Colossians 1:24)
"Bride of Christ" (Revelation 21:2)
"House of God" (1 Timothy 3:15)

Notice that these references *are not* denominational names. They do not refer to different churches, only to God's one true church. In each name we can see God and His Son's name being glorified. God has chosen these names for His church.

DOES NAME MAKE SCRIPTURAL CHURCH?

This question is a reasonable one because today there are many churches that wear the name, church of Christ. However, when we check further, we will find many practices not found in our New Testament pattern. The name is only a step in the right direction. Just being called the church of Christ, church of God, or church of the firstborn does not make it such. If the organization is not according to the scriptures, in work, worship and purpose then it is not Christ's church. Many churches have the right name but have corrupted the scriptural plan of worship by adding things God did not authorize. Any activity which cannot prove its right to be by the Scriptures, stands condemned (1 Thessalonians 5:21). Christ is the builder. He is the head over all things to the church, which is his body. (See Eph. 5:23-24; Col. 1:18).

THE CHRISTIAN NAME

The churches of Christ carry Christ's name on their buildings to show whom we represent. Yet, on a daily basis when we live and work in our various communities, we are not known as or called "church of Christ," but simply Christians. God refers to his people as Christians, saints, children, disciples, priests, and brethren. The name marks us as being owned by Christ (Acts 11:26). Every Christian is a saint because his sins are forgiven (Rom. 1:7). He is a child of God because he has been born again (1 Peter 1:22-23); a disciple because he is a learner of Christ (John 15:8). He is a priest because he is empowered to worship and serve God directly through Christ (1 Pet. 2:5). Christians are all brethren, because they are all children of the same heavenly father (Gal. 6:1).

Those who love and respect God's will appreciate the names given by him. We must use these names rather than names that indicate division and that disrespect God's authority. If you refer to your denomination to express your faith or religious conviction, there is too much in your name. Why not be a Christian only?

WHAT IS IN A NAME?

One may ask, what's in a name? There are many who feel that there is nothing in a name. I disagree, based on Acts 4:12. There is a name that is above all others, and that name is Christ. No other name has the power or authority of Christ's. If God saw fit to use this name, who are we to change it?

The story is told of a man arrested for making whiskey or home-brew. He came before the judge, who was a church going man. He decided to have some fun with the accused. The judge asked him, "What is your name?" The man replied, "My name is Joshua." "Are you the Joshua who made the sun stand still?", the judge asked. "No sir," the man replied. "I am the Joshua that made the moonshine."

The story is simple. There is something in a name. In order to please God, we must do all in word and in deed. We know that this is true when it comes to everyday things like the naming of our children. Have you ever heard of a mother naming her daughter, Jezebel; or her son, Judas? No parent would permanently scar a child with a name that is noted for being wicked or evil. There is something in a name!

93

WHY ONLY GOD-GIVEN NAME?

God has given Jesus as our means of salvation. His name is the only one by which man can be saved (Acts 4:11-12). To this name, "every knee must bow" (Philippians 2:9, 11). The common saying that one name is as good as another may be true in non-religious matters, but biblically, no name is as good as Christ's (Eph. 1:20-21). The church is the bride of Christ. A bride should wear the groom's name (2 Cor. 11:2). We who have been obedient to the will of Christ, are in the family of God. Should not the family wear his name? (1 Tim. 3:15; Eph. 3:14-15).

Marshall Keeble, a well known black evangelist, commenting on the importance of a name, related this illustration that a check is no good without a name. He told of a preacher who was conducting a meeting in a certain city. There was one lady who attended every night and heard him assert that there was nothing in a name. He said that they were to work out their salvation, and the name had nothing to do with it. He made this point over and over. One night this lady told him that she would like to make a contribution to his ministry. The next day he went by her house to pick up the money. She gave him a check and he went directly to the bank to cash it. The cashier returned the check to him saying that there was no name signed to it. "She must have forgotten to sign it," the preacher said, so he returned to the lady's house to get her to sign the check. To his surprise, she informed him that she had not forgotten to sign it but was only doing as he had preached and did not put her name on the check. The lady made her point, and taught him never to preach that again.

CONCLUSION

From the Scriptures and practical illustrations, we can see why the church must wear a Bible name. Our feelings may guide us contrary to God's word. But religiously, we are not governed by our feelings. What we believe must be based on facts (Rom. 10:17). Just any way or name is not God's way (Prov. 14:12). Let us do things that are according to God's plan. Only in his word can we find the right path (Psalm 119).

The church of our Lord should not wear names like Lutheran, Baptist, Methodist, Mormon, Catholic, Jehovah's Witnesses, etc., unless they can be found in his Book. We must practice the things Christ and the apostles left for us to do. Christ desires that we unite (John 17:20-23), but we cannot unite with error. We must come together under Christ's name. It is an honor to wear his name. We must please him if we expect him to receive us when he comes back for his church (John 14:2-3).

QUESTIONS

Discuss the lessons of 1 Corinthians 1:10-13 and the use of denominational religious names.

What name does God give to his church?

If a church wears a proper Bible name, does that mean God is totally pleased with them?

Is there any significance in the religious name we choose to wear?

In which name is salvation offered? (Acts 4:11-12).

19

The church has a divine mission
EVANGELIZING
THE WORLD FOR CHRIST

By Jerry Dyer

J esus came to a lost world to live a life that would set the perfect example for all people of all time (1 Peter 2:21-23). Because he lived such a life, he could be offered as a perfect sacrifice for the sins of the world (2 Corinthians 5:21). Having lived that life, set that example and given his life, he came back from the dead (Romans 1:4). A few days after his resurrection he went back to heaven to take his position at the right hand of God and become our mediator (1 Timothy 2:5). It was at this point in time when the purpose of his life (i.e., to seek and save the lost, Luke 19:10), was passed as a command to his disciples. That command is recorded in Matthew 28:18-20 and Mark 16:15-16.

Take time to read these passages and carefully observe the teaching of the Great Commission.

A. "Go Preach the Gospel" (Mark 16:15-16). "Go Teach" (Matt. 28:19). The word gospel means "good news." We have good news about his birth, life, example, death, resurrection, atonement and ascension to heaven. That is why Jesus came and that is why we must go preach and teach.

It is very important that we remember that this is a command and God expects us to obey his commands. Salvation will be our reward for obedience (Hebrews 5: 8-9). Eternal destruction will be our punishment if we fail to do his will (Matt. 7:21-23).

These passages use two different words, "preach" and "teach," that have the same ultimate purpose. Not everyone can preach nor should everyone preach (1 Cor. 12: 12-21). However, all Christians have the responsibility to teach the gospel.

B. "To Every Creature"; to "All the Nations." We go to all nations because all nations are lost without Jesus. Read and study the following scriptures:

1. *Second Thessalonians 1:7-9.* This passage says very clearly that there are two classes of people who will suffer "everlasting destruction from the presence of the Lord": (a) Those who do not "know God" and, (b) those who "do not obey the gospel." One will not be able to stand before God on the day of judgment and expect to be excused from eternal destruction because he did not know God and therefore did not obey the gospel.

2. *Romans 1:16.* shows that the only way God will save a sinner is through the gospel of Jesus. There is no other way. One dare not preach any other plan (Galatians 1:8-9).

3. *Ephesians 2:1, 3, 12* describes the condition of the man out of Christ. The Scripture says that people who are out of Christ are "dead," "separated," "excluded," "foreigners," "without hope," "without God." They are eternally and irretrievably lost without obedience to Christ. Could the Holy Spirit have made it any clearer?

4. *First Thessalonians 4:13* teaches that those who die "in Christ" have joy, pleasure, peace, etc. Those who die out of Christ *have no hope!*

5. *John 14:6* declares that Jesus is the *only* way to God. You can't go through any other prophet, savior, etc. There is none other.

6. In *Acts 17:30-31* Paul said that God would no longer overlook the ignorance of men today, whether it is "denominational darkness" or "idol worship." All the world will be judged by the same standard.

All the world is lost without Jesus. That is why he came and that is why we must go. There are some who say: "I'm sorry but I love people too much to condemn them." We would have to respond by saying: That is not Jesus' definition of love. Jesus said in John 14:15 that love demands obedience. To see that the Bible teaches that all people outside of Christ are lost and then fail to warn them, would be like the doctor who found that his patient was dying from a disease but refused to tell him because he did not want to be "judgmental and upset him." The "social gospel" that serves just the cultural needs of mankind will cause many people to be lost.

The simple truth is that *NO MAN CAN BE SAVED APART FROM CHRIST.* Those who extend *hope* to the non-Christian (be it those in the darkness of idol worship or in denominational error), do something the Bible never does and weaken the hands of disciples who are trying to get the gospel to all.

C. "Teach them to observe all things whatsoever I have commanded you." Paul teaches us this same truth in 2 Timothy 2:2: "And the things which thou hast heard from me among many witnesses, the same commit thou to faithful men who shall be able to teach others also." This is what is sometimes referred to as the second part of the Great Commission or "keeping the saved, saved." This passage presents four levels of teaching and learning. This passage shows the difference between a "terminal" and a "germinal" ministry.

1. *Things thou has heard* in the presence of many witnesses. God expects us to listen, learn and apply truth that we learn from listening to others. Of course, we are to search for ourselves as we listen (Acts 17:11).

2. *Commit to faithful men.* That which Timothy had been taught was not to stay with him. It must be shared with others. Paul says we need to do more than "keep the faith," we must share it with others. if we do not share it with others, our ministry is terminal, i.e., the truth has stopped with us.

3. *That they may be able to teach others also.* Here's where our ministry is tested. We must so teach and

motivate others that they will receive *and* send that message on to others.

POINT: God does not want us to allow new Christians to wither. We need to help them grow. We must teach them the whole truth (Acts 20:26-27). We must teach the truth in love (Eph. 4:15). We must teach the truth at the right time (1 Cor. 3:1-2; 1 Peter 2:2). We must teach others (2 Tim. 2:2).

D. "Lo, I am with you *always*, even unto the end of the world." Jesus promised that as we go, he will go with us. When we sit, we sit alone. There is no barrier high, wide or strong enough to keep the gospel out (Philippians 4:13). He will never fail nor forsake us as we go (Hebrews 13:5).

May God help us "go . . . make disciples of all the nations, baptizing them in the name of the Father, Son, and the Holy Spirit: teaching them to observe all things, whatsoever I (Jesus) have commanded you . . ." *This is the mission of the church.* Everything else we do as a child of God is sub-servient to that command.

QUESTIONS

Does the Great Commission apply to more than the eleven who received it? (Matt. 28:16-20).

Will all people of all nations be judged by the same standard?

Is it fair for God to judge all nations by the same standard?

Can a Christian be lost who does not seek souls?

Should all Christians be expected to be able to teach the plan of salvation to the lost?

Is there a "best" method to reach people who are lost?

Discuss a plan of action to reach the lost of your area.

20

The Church is
GOD'S BENEVOLENT HAND TO THE POOR

By Charles R. Williams

The church of the New Testament was built by Jesus Christ; for, in Matthew 16:18 Jesus said, ". . . and upon this rock I will build *my* church . . ." Not only is he its founder, but also its head. The apostle Paul stated this clearly when he wrote "and he put all things in subjection under his feet, and gave him to be the head over all things to the church" (Ephesians 1:22). As founder and head he is also our pattern for living as members of his church, "For hereunto were ye called: because Christ also suffered for you, leaving you an example, that ye should follow his steps" (1 Peter 2:21). Regarding our subject in this chapter we then ask, "What example did Jesus leave as to what kind of attitude we should have toward those who are in physical need?" We should also ask, "What commands or examples has he given to his church today in the New Testament concerning benevolence?"

JESUS WAS CONCERNED

In the writings of Matthew, Mark, Luke, and John which describe the life of Christ before he built his church, we discover him to be a person of great compassion. His greatest concern was of course with the sins and souls of the people, but while living among men he demonstrated his care and concern for the physical needs of the people as well. A good example of this was when his friend Lazarus died. When he went to the home of Mary and Martha and saw their sorrow and that of their friends the scriptures tell us, ". . . he groaned in the spirit, and was troubled . . . Jesus wept . . . he loved him" (John 11:33-36). There are many instances in Christ's life which demonstrate to us that to be like Jesus or to be Christ-like we will need to be concerned about the physical welfare of others.

JESUS HAD COMPASSION

Many came to Jesus for care. Jesus was moved with compassion because of their great needs: "But when he saw the multitudes, he was moved with compassion for them, because they were distressed . . ." (Matt. 9:36). He was concerned that people were hungry: "I have compassion on the multitude, because they continue with me now three days, and have nothing to eat" (Mark 8:2). Jesus then provided food for the people.

JESUS TAUGHT ABOUT CARING

Not only did Jesus show his compassion for others in need but he also taught great lessons on the subject. Perhaps the best known is the story of the good Samaritan (Luke 10:25-37). Jesus emphasized that the greatest commandment is to love God with all our heart, soul and strength, and the second greatest commanment is like it, to love our neighbor as we love ourselves. When a man in the crowd asked, "Who is my neighbor?" Jesus responded with the story of the Good Samaritan. The story is about a man who gave his time, energies, and money to help a stranger in need. The stranger had been beaten and robbed and was in need of medical attention, food, and a place to stay. He provided it all and as a result he received the praise of Jesus for his act of compassion. Jesus then told the man in the crowd, "Go, and do thou likewise."

Perhaps the most striking lesson that Jesus taught about our responsibility in helping others is found in the picture that he gives of the final judgment:

But when the Son of man shall come in his glory: and before him shall be gathered all the nations: and he shall separate them one from another, as the shepherd separateth the sheep from the goats; and he shall set the sheep on his right hand, but the goats on the left. Then shall the king say unto them on his right hand, come, ye blessed of my Father, inherit the kingdom prepared for you from the foundation of the world: for I was hungry, and ye gave me to eat; I was thirsty, and ye gave me drink; I was a stranger, and ye took me in; naked, and ye clothed me; I was sick, and ye visited me; I was in prison, and ye came unto me. Then shall the righteous answer him saying, Lord, when saw we thee hungry, and fed thee? or athirst, and gave thee drink? And when saw we thee a stranger, and took thee in? or naked, and clothed thee? And when saw we thee sick, or in prison, and came unto thee? And the King shall answer and say unto them, Verily I say unto you, Inasmuch as ye did it unto one of these my brethren, even these least, ye did it unto me.

Jesus continues to describe the scene by saying that those who did not render this service to others would go away into eternal punishment, but those who did render the service would go away into eternal life (Matt. 25:31-40, 46).

HELP THE STRANGER

We would note that in each of the above cases not only were friends or brethren to be helped, but the stranger as well. These are the exact instructions that are given to Christians in the New Testament church, "Let love of the brethren continue. Forget not to show love unto strangers . . ." (Hebrews 13:1, 2).

The apostle Paul wrote to several congregations and instructed them with these words: "So then, as we have opportunity, let us work that which is good toward all men, and especially toward them that are of the household of faith" (Galatians 6:10). The church's responsibility of helping the needy is not, therefore, limited to its own people.

WHAT METHODS ARE TO BE USED?

The Scriptures give us the command and responsibility of helping others but they do not tell us in any detail how to do it. Each autonomous congregation and individual has been left to decide upon their own, how the needs of the needy are to be met. The examples that we have are few. In Acts chapter six we find that some of the widows were being neglected. The apostles' answer to the problem was to appoint several men to oversee the work of seeing to it that their needs were met. This would be one of the responsibilities of deacons in the church today.

In 1 Corinthians 16:1-3, and 2 Corinthians chapters eight and nine we have the example of several men taking up a collection from several congregations to help the poor saints in Judea. James wrote that Christians are to care for orphans and widows: "Pure religion and undefiled before our God and Father is this, to visit the fatherless and widows in their affliction, and to keep oneself unspotted from the world" (James 1:27). James, however, does not tell us how the local congregation or the individual is to do this; therefore, it is left up to us to do it in the most expedient way.

A MEANS TO AN END

The most important care that the church and Christians render is the saving and teaching of souls. That is its main business. Even benevolence is a means to that end. But it is difficult for a hungry person to study or learn God's will. The church's responsibility is not to feed and clothe the world but to teach the gospel. Jesus' disciples are, however, to be a compassionate people, just as he was. As God says, ". . . we should remember the poor . . ." (Galatians 2:10).

IN SUMMARY

Christ is our example in attitude toward rendering service to others. He taught his disciples to love and have compassion for the unfortunate, and he practiced what he taught. If we are to walk in his footsteps and follow his example, we too must do the same.

The church is the body of Christ and he is its head. As members of his body Christians must reflect Christ in their lives, or as the apostle Paul says, ". . . so now also Christ shall be magnified in my body, whether by life, or by death. For me to live is Christ, and to die is gain"

(Philippians 1:20, 21); and, "...it is no longer I that live but Christ liveth in me ..." (Gal. 2:20).

In regard to methods of feeding the hungry, clothing the needy, taking care of orphans and widows, little information is given. We are simply told to do it. It must be left up to the decision of the elders of the local congregation just as God intended it. But whatever we do it must be in accordance with the purpose of the church; to reach souls, to teach the gospel, and help its members to grow and mature to be like Christ.

QUESTIONS

What was Christ's attitude toward those in need of food?

What great test will be applied on the day of judgment as to whether one is saved or lost?

What commands were given to the early church regarding the poor, the widows, the orphans, etc.?

What methods of caring may the church use today?

What is the main purpose of benevolence?

21

She teaches
THE NEW TESTAMENT PLAN OF SALVATION

By Joe R. Barnett

A cts, chapter 2, tells of three thousand people following God's plan of salvation on Pentecost. On this occasion Simon Peter climaxed his sermon about the resurrected Jesus, saying, "God hath made that same Jesus, whom ye have crucified, both Lord and Christ" (Acts 2:36).

The words struck hard, and his convicted hearers asked, "What shall we do?" Peter answered, "Repent, and be baptized every one of you in the name of Jesus Christ for the remission of sins, and ye shall receive the gift of the Holy Ghost" (Acts 2:38).

When the chapter ends, three thousand persons have been baptized. This account shows that salvation is not a strange experience which just "takes people over" without any will of their own. These people had strong feelings about their change, but the process was basically a decision-making one. Their personal decision was a matter of accepting evidence and obeying God's commands. They knew what they did was right because they did what God told them, not just because they "felt" they were right.

ADDED TO THE CHURCH

Churches of Christ do not speak of membership in terms of a formula which must be followed for approved acceptance into the church. The New Testament gives certain steps which are to be taken to become a Christian. When a person takes these steps and becomes a Christian he, in the same action, becomes a member of the church. No further steps are required to qualify for church membership.

On the first day of the church's existence, as noted above, those who repented and were baptized were saved. From that day forward all who were saved were added to the church (Acts 2:47). According to this verse it was God who did the adding. Therefore, in seeking to follow this pattern, we neither vote people into the church nor force them through a required series of studies. We have no right to demand anything beyond their obedient submission to the Savior.

SALVATION BY GRACE . . .

Because of our sins it is not possible for us to achieve salvation on our own. Salvation comes by the grace of God. The apostle Paul wrote, "For by grace are ye saved through faith; and that not of yourselves: it is the gift of God: Not of works, lest any man should boast" (Ephesians 2:8, 9).

. . . THROUGH FAITH

We are saved by grace . . . through faith. Grace is God's part. Faith is our part. It is very important to realize that the only kind of faith God recognizes is an active faith which involves obedience to his commands. We never earn salvation — it is God's gift. Yet, we cannot receive salvation without meeting the conditions upon which the gift is promised.

CONDITIONS OF SALVATION

Those conditions of salvation which are taught in the New Testament are:

1) One must hear the gospel, for "faith cometh by hearing, and hearing by the word of God" (Romans 10:17).

2) One must believe, for "without faith it is impossible to please him" (Hebrews 11:6).

3) One must repent of past sins, for God "commandeth all men everywhere to repent" (Acts 17:30).

4) One must confess Jesus as Lord, for he said, "Whosoever therefore shall confess me before men, him will I confess also before my Father which is in heaven" (Matthew 10:32).

5) And one must be baptized for the remission of sins, for Peter said, "Repent, and be baptized every one of you in the name of Jesus Christ for the remission of your sins . . ." (Acts 2:38).

A SINGLE PROCESS

Each of these steps can be isolated and discussed, but we should be aware that spiritual rebirth is a single process involving the complete response of the individual to God's love.

Yes, there is a call to believe. But "faith only" isn't sufficient. Those who follow God's plan are not simply asked to change the ideas they believe to be true. Their entire lives are are to affirm this change of conviction. *Belief* is an *inner* change, whereas *repentance* is an inner resolution which shows on the *outside* of one's life. *Confession* is a public commitment to that belief and determined change of lifestyle. And *baptism* is the decisive act in which the change is sealed and, by God's grace and the power of Christ's blood, one's sins are washed away (Acts 22:16).

EMPHASIS ON BAPTISM

Churches of Christ have a reputation for placing much emphasis on baptism. Such an emphasis is justified for there are more than one hundred passages in the New Testament which mention the word baptism in one of its forms.

The New Testament teaches baptism as an act which is essential to salvation (Mark 16:16; Acts 2:38; Acts 22:16) F.F. Bruce, the noted New Testament scholar, has observed that the idea of an unbaptized Christian is simply not entertained by the New Testament.

107

The New Testament sets forth the following purposes for baptism:

1) It is to enter the kingdom (John 3:5).
2) It is to contact Christ's blood (Romans 6:3,4).
3) It is to get into Christ (Galatians 3:27).
4) It is for salvation (Mark 16:16; 1 Peter 3:21).
5) It is for the remission of sins (Acts 2:38).
6) It is to wash away sins (Acts 22:16).
7) It is to get into the church (1 Corinthians 12:13; Ephesians 1:23).

SALVATION IS FOR ALL

Since Christ died for the sins of the whole world and the invitation to share in his saving grace is open to everyone (Acts 10:34, 35; Revelation 22:17), we do not believe anyone is predestined for salvation or condemnation. Some will choose to come to Christ in faith and obedience and be saved. Others will reject his plea and be condemned (Mark 16:16). These will not be lost because they were marked for condemnation, but because that is the path they chose.

Your decision about Christ is the greatest decision of your life. To reject him is spiritually and eternally fatal. We urge you to accept the salvation offered by Christ. Submit to him in obedient faith and become a member of his church.

QUESTIONS

What did the people on Pentecost do to receive remission of their sins?

Is it proper to "vote" people into the church?

Does salvation by grace exempt man from all responsibility?

What are the conditions of salvation taught in the New Testament?

Can you list three passages which show the importance of baptism?

Have you obeyed all of God's conditions for your salvation?

22

The Apostles' Pattern Is Followed In
THE PRACTICE OF BAPTISM

By Dub McClish

Perhaps there is no teaching of the New Testament over which more controversy has raged than the subject of baptism. This is not the case because the New Testament is ambiguous on the subject, nor because men are incapable of understanding its teaching. As we explore this subject it shall be our premise that God is the author of baptism through the teachings of the Bible. In the final analysis, it makes little difference what any man says on the subject, but it makes all of the difference what God says. If the teaching of the New Testament on the subject of baptism is unimportant, then how can anyone logically contend that the teaching of the New Testament on any subject is important? The Lord, through his word, must be allowed to tell us what both the action and purpose of baptism are.

THE "WHAT" OF BAPTISM

In the minds of most people, baptism is an act that may be administered in either of three ways: sprinkling water on the candidate, pouring water on the candidate or immersing the candidate in water. Some English dictionaries state that baptism is administered by either of these three actions.[1] However, it must be remembered that modern English dictionaries reflect the *current* usage of words, rather than their original meanings.

Consider the following evidence in the New Testament, apart from the original meaning of the word "baptism." The baptism of John, which involved the same action as the baptism commanded by Christ and preached by the apostles, required "much water" (John 3:23). A case of baptism is described in Acts 8:38-39: "And they both went down into the water, both Philip and the eunuch; and he baptized him. And when they came up out of the water . . ." The apostle Paul twice uses the term

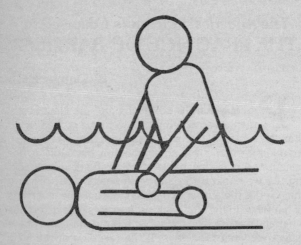

"burial" to describe what takes place when one is baptized (Romans 6:4; Colossians 2:12). This evidence obviously points to only one action — immersion.

A study of the Greek word for "baptism" yields the same conclusion. "Baptize" and its related forms was not an English word, originally. It was transferred into English directly from the New Testament Greek word, *baptidzo*. One may consult any standard lexicon of the Greek New Testament and learn that *baptidzo* means to dip, plunge, submerge or immerse when used literally.[2] When used figuratively (e.g., Mark 10:38), it means to overwhelm. If this Greek word were translated, rather than merely transliterated, the New Testament would read "immerse" everywhere it presently reads, "baptize."

For those who truly believe the Bible to be the inspired

word of God, the description of baptism in the New Testament is sufficient, regardless of what mere men may say on the subject. However, it is worthwhile to notice a sampling of what religious leaders have said on the subject. The reader is asked to please understand that these are not cited for the purpose of embarrassing anyone or to "prove" some right and others wrong. Our only purpose is to exalt the truth of God's word. Consider the following:

Martin Luther ("Father of the 16th century Reformation," founder of the Lutheran Church): "The term 'baptism' is a Greek word; it may be rendered into Latin by *mersio* — when we immerse anything in water, that it may be entirely covered with water."[3]

John Calvin (16th century reformer, a founder of the Presbyterian Church): "The word 'baptize' signifies to immerse and the rite of immersion was practiced by the ancient church."[4]

John Wesley (founder of the Methodist Church): "Buried with him — alluding to the ancient manner of baptizing by immersion."[5]

Catholic Dictionary: "In Apostolic Times the body of the baptized person was immersed, for St. Paul looks on the immersion as typifying the burial with Christ, and speaks of baptism as a bath."[6]

All of the above quotations have two things in common: (1) They are unanimous in their definition of baptism as immersion; (2) They all come from members of churches that have substituted sprinkling and/or pouring for immersion. Their scholarship and honor require them to refute their own practice, however. It cannot be rationally argued that New Testament baptism was and is anything less than immersion. To adopt any other view requires a denial of New Testament authority.

THE "WHY" OF BAPTISM

There are two basic schools of thought on the purpose of the baptism commanded by Jesus Christ: One says that baptism is an act of obedience of one who *has already been saved,* providing access to denominational

111

membership after salvation has been granted through faith alone. In this view, baptism is part of one's obedience to Christ because he is already a Christian. The other view contends that baptism is the final act of obedience one submits to *in order to be saved* or forgiven of his past sins. In this view a person is not saved until he is baptized, at which time he is also added to the church because he is saved. What does the Bible say?

Jesus told the apostles that as they preached the gospel, "He that believeth and is baptized shall be saved" (Mark 16:16). Note the order: (1) believe; (2) baptized; (3) saved. The order is *not* (1) believe; (2) saved; (3) baptized if one wished to join a church. In this verse baptism is made a condition of salvation, as plainly as is faith.

When the apostles began to fulfill the command to "go preach," they told people, "Repent ye, and be baptized everyone of you in the name of Jesus Christ unto the remission of your sins . . ." (Acts 2:38). What relation does repentance sustain to remission (forgiveness) of sins? (Notice that baptism is in the same relation to forgiveness of sins as repentance.) Those who argue that baptism *follows* forgiveness instead of preceding it, must also place repentance after forgiveness to be consistent. However, there is not a single instance of forgiveness granted apart from repentance in all of the Bible. "Remission of sins" is placed after baptism in this passage, even as "salvation" is in the previous passage. Saul of Tarsus was commanded to ". . . be baptized and wash away thy sins . . ." (Acts 22:16). This statement makes no sense at all if one's sins are forgiven before one is baptized.

The objection is sometimes raised that to insist that immersion in water is a scriptural condition of salvation equals a doctrine of "water salvation." If that is the case, then it is such scriptures as Mark 16:16; Acts 2:38; 22:16, etc., that should be blamed for the teaching, rather than those who believe it. However, such verses attribute no merit to water as a spiritual cleansing agent whatsoever. These verses do not say *what* the cleansing agent is. They only tell us *when* the cleansing occurs. It is plain from other scriptures that the blood of Christ is the agent of cleansing or forgiveness (1 Peter 1:18-19; Revelation 1:5, etc.). The old song is absolutely correct: "What can wash away my sin? Nothing but the blood of Jesus."

When does this washing occur or how does one gain access to the precious cleansing blood of Christ? Besides the references already cited, consider also Romans 6:3: "Or are ye ignorant that all we who were baptized into Christ Jesus were baptized into his death?" It was in the act of his death that Jesus' cleansing blood was offered for the sins of mankind (Hebrews 9:26-28). By what means is the sinner able to participate in the death of Christ, where he offered his precious blood? The inspired apostle answers conclusively: "we are baptized into his death" (Rom. 6:3). This is in perfect harmony with every other scripture on baptism. The purpose God has revealed in his word for baptism is not that of Christian obedience, done because one has already been saved. Rather, it, along with a confessed faith in Christ and repentance of sins, is the act in which one comes to participate in the death of Christ. It is therefore the act from which one comes forth to live a new life (Rom. 6:4). It is the act upon which one is added to the church of Christ, because he has been saved and the church is God's depository of saved people (Acts 2:41, 47; Ephesians 5:23). Only when one understands that salvation is not bestowed *until* one is scripturally baptized, can one appreciate the apostle Peter's pronouncement that baptism saves us (1 Peter 3:21).

SUMMARY

The Scriptures teach that the baptism, which Christ ordered to be preached to all men, is a burial in water. It brings one into salvation, or forgiveness of sins, through the blood of Christ. It is our earnest plea that all men return to what the Bible teaches on this subject, both in their teaching and practice.

William Allen Neilson (Ed.-in-Chief), et. al., *Webster's New International Dictionary of the English Language* (Springfield, Mass.: G. and C. Merriam Company, 1957). p. 216.

2 *The Analytical Greek Lexicon* (New York: Harper and Brothers, n. d.), p. 65; and Joseph Henry Thayer, *A Greek-English Lexicon of the New Testament* (New York: American Book Company, 1889), p. 94; and Walter Bauer, William F. Arndt and F. Wilbur Gingrich, *A Greek-English Lexicon of the New Testament and Other Early Christian Literature* (Chicago: University of Chicago Press, 1957), p. 131; etc.

3 T. W. Brents, *The Gospel Plan of Salvation* (Nashville, Tenn.: Gospel Advocate Company, 1957). p. 280.

4 *Ibid.,* pp. 280-281.

5 *Ibid.,* p. 334.

6 O. C. Lambert, *Roman Catholicism Against Itself* (Winfield, Ala.: O. C. Lambert, 1954), vol. I, p. 173.

QUESTIONS

Who alone has the right to determine both the action and purpose of baptism?

From what source alone can men learn God's will on the subject?

What does the Greek word for "baptism" literally mean? Where did God ever give any man the right to change this practice?

Is salvation or forgiveness of sins placed before or after baptism in such scriptures as Mark 16:16, Acts 2:38, Acts 22:16 and 1 Peter 3:21?

What is the perfect and only cleansing agent for our sins?

According to Romans 6:3, how does one become a participant in that cleansing agent, which Christ offered in his death?

23

As in Bible times
ADULTS ARE
THE SUBJECTS OF BAPTISM

By Bobby Duncan

P eople are lost and stand in need of salvation because of the guilt of their own sins — not the sins of their ancestors. The doctrine that babies inherit the guilt of Adam's transgression is not true. If it were, then Jesus would have been born guilty of sin.

BABIES ARE INNOCENT

Concerning little children, Jesus said, "of such is the kingdom of heaven" (Matthew 19:14). He never would have said that if little children are hereditarily totally depraved; he might have said instead: "of such is the kingdom of the devil."

In speaking of his deceased baby, David said, "I shall go to him, but he shall not return to me" (2 Samuel 12:23). David knew his baby was in a safe condition. It was guilty of no sin, for it had not transgressed God's law, and "sin is the transgression of the law" (1 John 3:4).

INFANT BAPTISM GREW OUT OF THE
FALSE DOCTRINE OF INHERITED GUILT

We emphasize the fact that there is no blessing little babies need which is conferred by means of baptism. Had it not been for the false doctrine of inherited guilt there likely never would have been the practice of baptizing infants. Notice the following statement from a nineteenth century author: "Infants are included in

115

Christ's act of redemption, and are entitled thereby to the benefits and blessings of his church."[1] Another writer wrote: "On the contrary, we have presumptive and positive arguments for the apostolic origin and character of infant baptism . . . in the universal virtue of Christ, as the Redeemer of all sexes, classes, and ages, and especially in the import of his own infancy, which has redeemed and sanctified the infantile age."[2]

In his *Treatise on Baptism*, John Wesley wrote: "If infants are guilty of original sin, then they are proper subjects of baptism; seeing, in the ordinary way, they cannot be saved, unless this be washed away by baptism" (*Doctrinal Tracts*, p. 252).

If babies were in need of redemption, and if baptizing them were the means of securing it for them, then we would not oppose infant baptism. But we have already seen that babies are not lost, and do not need redeeming. No verse in the Bible hints that they should be baptized.

FOUR PREREQUISITES TO BAPTISM

In the New Testament, four things characterized those who were baptized: (1) they had been taught the gospel of Jesus Christ, (2) they believed that Jesus Christ is the Son of God, (3) they had repented of their sins, and (4) they had confessed their faith in Jesus Christ. While each of these might not be specifically mentioned in the record of each case, each is clearly implied.

In the Great Commission, Jesus commanded: "Go ye therefore, and teach all nations, baptizing them in the name of the Father, and of the Son, and of the Holy Ghost" (Matthew 28:19). This verse clearly shows that those who are to be baptized are those who have first been taught.

Mark 16:15, 16 contains these words of Jesus: "Go ye into all the world, and preach the gospel to every creature. He that believeth and is baptized shall be saved; but he that believeth not shall be damned." This makes it abundantly clear that belief of the gospel must precede baptism.

116

Peter was inspired of the Holy Spirit to command: "Repent, and be baptized every one of you in the name of Jesus Christ for the remission of sins . . ." (Acts 2:38). The apostle was addressing a great multitude who had just been taught the truth concerning Jesus Christ, and who believed what they had heard. But they must also repent before they could properly be baptized. On this occasion those that "gladly received his word were baptized . . ." (verse 41).

Confessing Jesus as the Christ is an absolute necessity. Jesus himself said, "Whosoever therefore shall confess me before men, him will I confess also before my Father which is in heaven. But whosoever shall deny me before men, him will I also deny before my Father which is in heaven" (Matthew 10:32, 33). Romans 10:9 shows that the confession must be made before one can be saved: "That if thou shalt confess with thy mouth the Lord Jesus . . . thou shalt be saved." The next verse shows that this confession is made on the way to being saved: ". . . and with the mouth confession is made unto salvation."

Acts, chapter 8, contains an example of conversion in which each of these four prerequisites to baptism is clearly seen. Notice verses 35-39: "Then Philip opened his mouth, and began at the same scripture, and preached unto him Jesus. And as they went on their way, they came unto a certain water: and the eunuch said, See, here is water; what doth hinder me to be baptized? And Philip said, If thou believest with all thine heart, thou mayest. And he answered and said, I believe that Jesus Christ is the Son of God. And he commanded the chariot to stand still: and they went down both into the water, both Philip and the eunuch; and he baptized him. And when they were come up out of the water, the Spirit of the Lord caught away Philip, that the eunuch saw him no more: and he went on his way rejoicing."

Infants cannot be taught the gospel, nor can they believe it. They have no sins of which to repent, and are totally incapable of repenting. They cannot confess with the mouth, the Lord Jesus. This being true, infants can-

117

not be baptized in harmony with the teaching of the New Testament.

WHAT ABOUT "HOUSEHOLD" BAPTISMS?

In a strained effort to justify infant baptism, some have cited cases of "household" baptism such as Lydia's household (Acts 16:15), the jailer's household (Acts 16:31-33), and the household of Stephanas (1 Corinthians 1:16) — as proof that infants were baptized. But there is nothing in any of these instances to indicate infants were baptized. There is no proof there were any infants in any of these households; and even if there were, there is nothing that suggests they were baptized. With the New Testament teaching on baptism for a background, one would necessarily conclude that no infants were baptized.

THE EARLIEST MENTION OF INFANT BAPTISM

Those who favor infant baptism seek to authenticate its antiquity by citing the writings of Tertullian, who mentioned the practice around A.D. 200.[3] But notice the following from one of the most candid writers the Methodist Episcopal Church has produced: "Tertullian is the first writer in the Church who makes any express mention of the custom of infant baptism. Before his time, A.D. 200, there is not an allusion to the custom from which its existence may be fairly inferred. It is frequently argued, that the practice of infant baptism must have been an apostolic institution, because it prevailed, and became universal, without the least opposition from any source whatever. But, however strange it may seem, the fact is, that the first Father, or writer, by whom the practice is noticed, condemns it as having no foundation either in reason or revelation."[4]

CONCLUSION

The fact cannot be overemphasized that infants are safe; they are not lost. The New Testament writers said nothing about infant baptism. The only way one can practice baptizing infants is to depart from the teaching of Christ. If all people would return to the teaching of the New Testament for every religious practice, infant baptism would be abolished altogether. Churches of Christ seek to follow the New Testament in all matters of faith and practice.

---

[1] McClintock, John and James Strong, *Cyclopedia of Biblical, Theological, and Ecclesiastical Literature* (1895; rpt. Grand Rapids: Baker Book House, 1968), Vol. I, p. 648.

[2] Schaff, Philip, *History of the Christian Church* (Grand Rapids: Wm. B. Eerdmans Pub. Co., 1910), Vol. I, p. 470.

[3] McClintock and Strong, ibid., Vol. I, p. 648.

[4] Bledsoe, Albert T., *Southern Review* (St. Louis, 1874), Vol. XIV, p. 339.

QUESTIONS

Are babies born with the guilt of sin upon them?

To what did Jesus compare the kingdom of heaven in Matthew 19:14? Why?

What reason did John Wesley give for thinking infants should be baptized?

What four things characterized subjects for baptism in the New Testament?

Do the "household" baptisms in the New Testament prove infants were baptized? Why?

The first writer to mention infant baptism wrote around what date? Did he favor it, or did he oppose it?

What would happen to the practice of baptizing infants if all people should begin following only the New Testament?

24

God Assigned a Special
ROLE FOR WOMEN IN THE CHURCH

By James O. Baird

There is a great deal of confusion today as to woman's role both in the home and in the church. This uncertainty provides a good opportunity to study afresh what the Bible teaches on the subject. As the church is the pillar and ground of the truth (1 Tim. 3:15), it is most important that the church reflect Biblical truth about woman's role.

HOW JESUS DEALT WITH WOMEN

A good place to begin a study of woman's role in the church is with the earthly ministry of Jesus. We understand, of course, the church did not begin while Jesus was on earth (Matthew 16:18), but after he ascended into Heaven (Mark 9:1; Acts 1:8; Acts 2:1-4). Nevertheless, we can learn something about women's role in the church by studying how Jesus considered them during his earthly ministry.

We know that none of the apostles were women (Matt. 10:2-4). However, some of Jesus' closest disciples were women. Luke 8:2-3 mentions Mary Magdalene, Joanna, Susanna, and "many others" who helped provide financial support for Jesus and the apostles as they went about preaching. Later, when the apostles fled the crucifixion scene in fear, certain faithful and sorrowing women remained to watch his death on the cross (Matt. 27:55-56).

121

From these and other references in the Gospels, we learn that Jesus in no way dealt with women as being inferior to men as far as being his disciples was concerned. In selecting men rather than women to be his apostles, he did make some distinction in the *roles* men and women should fill. These two basic principles, i.e., (1) equality of worth in Christ's sight, and (2) difference in role assignments for men and women, were clearly taught in the early church, and should, of course, be reflected in the church today.

WOMAN'S ROLE IN THE CHURCH

When the church began on the Day of Pentecost, women, as well as men, came into it in great numbers (Acts 5:14). There were no distinctions made in conditions of membership between the sexes. Furthermore, the importance of women to the whole church is reflected by the concern which the early church had for widows who needed care and help (Acts 6:1-6).

The good works of women are frequently mentioned in Scripture. Dorcas is cited as an example of faithful, loving service (Acts 9:36-39). Lydia is revealed as being a woman of great hospitality, "constraining" Paul and his company to abide in her house (Acts 16:11-15). Phoebe is described as a "servant of the church that is in Cenchreae" (Romans 16:10). The many good works of women in the church is further reflected as Paul describes the qualifications for women who were to devote full time to Christian work and to be supported by the church. In 1 Timothy 5:9-10 these qualifications included widowhood, being sixty or more years of age, having no kin of their own to support them, and being "well reported of for good works." These good works were then stated as (1) bringing up children, (2) showing hospitality to strangers, (3) washing the saints' feet, (4) relieving the afflicted, and (5) diligently following every good work.

Woman's role in the private teaching of God's Word is also referenced in Scripture. In Acts 18:26 Priscilla, with her husband, Aquila, privately taught a good, but misinformed preacher (Apollos) "the way of God more accurately." Titus 2:4 commands older women to train younger women in Christian living.

A key verse in understanding the importance of women in the eyes of God is Galatians 3:28, "There can be
neither Jew nor Greek, there can be neither bond nor
free, there can be no male and female, for ye all are one
man in Christ Jesus." In the world of Jesus' day, there
were sharp distinctions among people by which they
looked upon each other as inferior or superior and, because of these differences, separated themselves from
each other. These differences included religious background (Jew and Greek), special status (slave or slave
owner), or sex (male and female). Paul wrote that none
of these distinctions was valid as far as worth is concerned. He did not mean, certainly, that when one became a Christian he or she ceased to be a man or a
woman, a slave or a free man, a Jew or a Gentile. None
of these, however, should cause separation, because all
are of equal preciousness in Christ Jesus.

DIFFERING ROLES FOR MEN AND WOMEN

Although the church is to hold unswervingly to the
view that women and men are equally valuable in the
eyes of God, it must also reflect the New Testament
teaching that men and women are to fill different roles in
the church.

For instance, in the Lord's plan for church government each congregation is to be led by elders and deacons (Philippians 1:1). In listing the qualifications for
elders (1 Tim. 3:1-7; Titus 1:5-9) and for deacons (1 Tim.
3:12) being the "husband of one wife" is mentioned. This
obviously excludes women form these roles; only men
are to be elders and deacons.

Although women can teach privately, as we learned
from the example of Priscilla, women are forbidden to
teach men publicly (1 Tim. 2:12). The common practice
today of women being accepted as preachers is not a
practice approved in the New Testament and should not
be practiced in the church (1 Cor. 14:34).

The great emphasis today on the rights of women
should not cause Christians to question the Lord's forbidding women to assume certain roles in the church.

123

Even if no reasons for this action were given we should accept by faith what God has revealed. Some reasons, however, were given. Consider the following:

1. Woman's role in the church reflects the original act of creation in which man was first created (1 Tim. 2:13).

2. Woman's role in the church reflects that it was the woman who was first deceived by Satan and fell into sin (1 Tim. 2:13).

3. Woman's role in the church is closely connected to her unique role in the home. Woman alone can give birth to children (1 Tim. 2:15). The man must care for and provide for his wife and love her as Christ loved the church (Ephesians 5:25). The woman's willing submission to her husband is most likely to call forth the best of his care (Eph. 5:22, 33). In order for there to be the greatest amount of happiness in the home, God has established different roles for men and women in the home. This difference is likewise to be reflected in the church.

SUMMARY AND CONCLUSION

In summary, we have found: (1) The church should teach what the Bible states about the role of women, regardless of what others are teaching and practicing. (2) Christ accepted women as his followers on the same basis as men, although he appointed no women apostles. (3) Women were among the earliest members of the church and an important part of its life. They were outstanding in their abilities to extend hospitality, to help provide for the needy and to express serving love which is to characterize the church as the family of God. (4) In God's sight men and women are to accept each other as being of equal value because God respects both equally. (5) God has ordained there are certain roles in the church which a woman cannot fill, and has given reasons why he made this distinction.

The church must uphold what God has set forth in this and all other matters.

QUESTIONS

How do we know that women were among the followers of Jesus while he was on the earth? Give the Scripture.

How do we know none of the apostles were women? Give the Scripture.

What is a Scripture which teaches women were members of the church in Jerusalem?

What woman is mentioned in Acts 9 as an example of one helping the needy?

What woman is mentioned in Acts 16 as being one who provided outstanding hospitality?

How do we know women are not to be elders and deacons? Give the Scripture.

Are the reasons the Bible gives for not permitting women to teach publicly, reasons which are based on passing social customs or more permanent reasons? Look up the verses which deal with this subject and discuss your conclusions.

25

She upholds God's Standards for
GODLY LIVING

Dan Jenkins

After the Hebrews crossed the Red Sea God set before them the high calling He had in view for His people. "Ye shall be holy, for I am holy . . ." (Leviticus 11:44). In a world that was given over to the ungodly living that often characterized pagan nations, a holy God called upon His people to set new standards of righteousness — holiness as He is holy!

Should it be any surprise to us that the same language is used in reference to His church in the new covenant! God is unchanging and He asks the church, His people today, to partake of His nature (2 Peter 1:4), to follow His teachings on holiness. "But as He which hath called you is holy, so be ye holy in all manner of conversation: because it is written, be ye holy; for I am holy" (1 Pet. 1:15-16).

WRONG STANDARD OF HOLINESS

One's daily life demands that he seek some standard for righteousness, but what is that standard? Men often use the wrong standard for righteousness.

It would have been so easy for the nation of Israel to have sought to be like the nations about them. However, the Lord reminded them that they had been called out of Egypt (Lev. 11:45), and that they were not to determine righteousness simply by being like those nations. "After the doings of the land of Egypt, wherein ye dwelt, shall ye not do, and after the doings of the land of Canaan whither I bring you shall ye not do, neither shall ye walk in their ordinances" (Lev. 18:3). As the history of man has been a history of men not abiding by God's teachings, it is folly to think that righteous standards are to be found in following what others are doing. God's instructions, "Thou shalt not follow a multitude to do evil" (Exodus 23:2), should remind us that the standard of righteousness is not to be set by doing what most people are doing. Jesus himself shows that most people will not live by God's teachings (Matthew 7:13-14).

Some set as a standard of righteousness the standard taught them by their parents. If parents were sinless then they could serve as the standard, but this simply is not the case (Romans 3:23). Jesus envisioned that following him would sometimes mean turning from parents (Matt. 10:37). Parental teaching, as important as it is, cannot be the standard.

Some have thought that learned men should be the standard. However, Paul states the impossibility of men knowing the things of God apart from God. "What man knoweth the things of a man save the spirit of man which is in him, even so the things of God knoweth no man, but the Spirit of God" (1 Corinthians 2:12). No man knows the things of God! *Man cannot determine righteousness!*

THE ONE STANDARD OF HOLINESS

There is only one standard and that is God! God created man in His image (Genesis 1:27) and when man fell, God brought about Christianity and designed it so that we would be conformed to His image. As we behold the glory of the Lord we ". . . are changed into the same image (2 Cor. 3:18). God wants us to be like Him! We are to partake of His nature! *He is the standard of holiness!*

WHAT HOLINESS ISN'T

Galatians 5:19-21 lists many of the ungodly practices that have destroyed men of long ago and are yet prevalent in our day. To show how serious these practices are, the list ends with these words, "They which do such things shall not inherit the kingdom of God" (Gal. 5:21).

Christ's church must abhor these, for to be found guilty of them will bar the doors of heaven. These are the words of a holy God telling us exactly what He wants us to avoid.

There are sexual sins listed — adultery, fornication, uncleanness, lasciviousness. Adultery is unlawful sex between two people, with at least one of these being married. Fornication is immorality of every sort. It is the Bible word to describe any sort of sexual sin. Uncleanness literally means impurity and refers to those thoughts and actions that lead to immorality. Lasciviousness means absence of restraint, indecency, and includes unchaste behavior of dress, speech and action. How unfortunate that men have left God's wonderful design of sex and have perverted it and set up their own standards in this area.

There are the sins of idolatry and witchcraft. Idolatry can be either the outward worship and service of an image made with hands (see Psalm 115:3-7 for discussion of the folly of such worship) or the covetous service of any material thing (Colossians 3:5). Witchcraft refers to sorcery, superstition, the occult and horoscopes. To follow such is to deny that God controls this world, that He determines what happens in our lives (Daniel 4:17).

There are sins of attitudes — hatred, variance, emulations, wrath. Hatred is the opposite of love and refers to bitterness of spirit and hostility toward others. Variance is the strife that results from hate. Emulations means jealousy and the uncontrolled desire to have what others have. Wrath is violent anger. Jealousy smolders in the heart, wrath is the same attitude outwardly shown.

There are sins of false teaching and division — strife, seditions, heresies. Strife often brings about factions, the taking of sides and divisions into parties. Seditions literally means "standing apart" and refers to the divisions into selfish groups. Heresy is the teaching of one's opinions that give rise to division.

There are the sins of drunkenness and revellings. Drunkenness is the indulgence in strong drink to which

128

so many are addicted. Revellings are the wild drinking parties that are found in every society.

There are other lists in the Bible (Rom. 1:26-32; Col. 3:5-10), but this list should help us to see that God ex-expects His people to be holy, to have as their standard of righteousness His holy nature.

AN EXAMPLE OF HOLINESS

In this same section of Galatians the Holy Spirit has another list that shows us much of what is involved in holiness. "But the fruit of the Spirit is love, joy, peace, longsuffering, gentleness, goodness, faith, meekness, temperance" (Gal. 5:21-22). These are attributes of our God that He expects us to have. Take each of these words, read the Old Testament and you'll find they de-scribe our God. Take each of these words, read the New Testament and see each of them displayed in the life of Jesus. God's standard for holiness has been lived on this earth, we can see it without fault in our Savior. As he was tempted in every way we are (Hebrews 4:15), it makes no difference when we live or where we live — we have the example of holiness we need! Peter describes this perfect life in these words, ". . . Christ also suffered for us, leaving us an example that ye should follow his steps; who did no sin, neither was guile found in his mouth; who when he was reviled, reviled not again; when he suffered he threatened not . . ." (1 Peter 2:21-23). Christ our example — this is God's visible standard of holiness! *We are to be like him!*

THE CHURCH AND HOLINESS

Many today have lost sight of God's holiness and the result is a world of sin. Some who claim to be religious may condone sin but the true church cannot be of this nature. She serves the Lord, she seeks his way and lives by his teachings of morality. When she ceases to do this he rejects her (Revelation 2:5) and she is as worthless salt, useless in his hands (Matt. 5:13). In an age when society is seeking new lifestyles, when it is seeking a new morality, the church of Christ upholds His standard of holy living.

QUESTIONS

To what two groups has God said, "Be ye holy, for I am holy"?

What are some wrong standards of holiness? Why are they wrong?

What is the one standard of holiness?

Discuss sexual impurity and examples in our own society.

Give illustrations of idolatry in our own day. Of witchcraft.

Define some sins of attitudes.

What is the fruit of the Spirit? Give examples from the life of Jesus.

What happens when a church ceases to live and teach God's standard of holiness?

26

She honors and upholds
GOD'S TEACHING ON MARRIAGE AND DIVORCE

By Wayne Jackson

Marriage is a covenant between a man and a woman wherein they agree to become joined to one another for the purpose of establishing a permanent home. Marriage was instituted by God with the creation of Adam and Eve. The first couple, being made male and female, were designed for marriage (Genesis 1:27), and so, it was the purpose of God that man and woman should have the privilege of becoming "one flesh" in the divinely organized arrangement of wedlock (Gen. 2:24).

The preservation of the marriage relationship is vitally important to the well-being of society as a whole. First, within the family unit there is provided a sphere of stability wherein one has the right to a family name, security of property, and an intimate atmosphere of love and trust. Second, marriage contributes to community solidarity. No society could long exist without marriage. In fact, "There are no societies in which marriage does not exist."[1]

Marriage, in harmony with God's original plan, is certainly an honorable state: "Let marriage be had in honor among all, and let the bed be undefiled . . ." (Hebrews 13:4). And while there may be times of extreme stress or difficulty when it might be in one's best interest not to marry (cf. 1 Corinthians 7:26, 28, 32, 35, 40), the general principle would be, "It is not good that man [or woman]

131

should be alone" (Gen. 2:18). The Bible makes it clear that "forbidding to marry" is contrary to the will of God (1 Timothy 4:1-3).

Holy matrimony, as designed by God, certainly has many benefits. First, as just indicated, it provides for intimate personal companionship (Gen. 2:18). Mankind, created in the image of the triune Godhead (Gen. 1:27), is *social* in disposition. Second, marriage is the legitimate avenue by which children are to be brought into the world (Gen. 1:28; 4:1; 1 Tim. 5:14). Jehovah never intended that children be the product of animalistic breeding experiments! Third, matrimony affords man and woman a moral and responsible means of satisfying the God-given sexual appetites of their bodies. The sexual "bed" is undefiled *within* valid marriage (Heb. 13:4).

God's divine ideal for the marital union is that it should last as long as both parties are alive. Death of one of the marriage partners, of course, terminates this relationship (Romans 7:2; 1 Cor. 7:39) and there is no "marriage" beyond the resurrection of the dead (Matthew 22:30).

Divorce — Since God is the author of marriage, it is His prerogative, *and His alone,* to determine when a marriage can be dissolved while both partners are still living. What, therefore, is the divine will concerning divorce? Ideally, God "hates" divorce (cf. Malachi 2:16), for even when a valid divorce is allowed by the Lord, there has been a violation of the marriage covenant by at least one of the parties. No divorce can involve *two* innocent persons; one of them may be, but at least one will be guilty.

Under the Old Testament system, if a man's wife "found no favor in his eyes" because he found some unseemly thing in her, he could write her a "bill of divorcement" and "send her out of his house" (that is, divorce her) (Deuteronomy 24:1). Yet, this was not consistent with Heaven's original ideal. God, through Moses, only *tolerated* it due to the "hardness of heart" characteristic of the Israelite people (Matt. 19:8). Jesus Christ, however, in discussing this very matter, declared that "from the beginning it hath not been so" (Matt. 19:8). The grammar of this verbally inspired passage implies that God's original marriage plan, as instituted in Eden, *had ideally never changed,* though a relaxation of it had been allowed under the Mosaic economy.[2] Then, in anticipation of his New Covenant law, Jesus proceeded to *restore* marriage to its original intent. Accordingly, the Lord said: "And I say unto you, Whosoever shall put away his wife, except for fornication, and shall marry another, committeth adultery" (Matt. 19:9). Several things may be said of this remarkable verse.

First, the passage is obviously of *universal* application, that is, the whole human family lies under obligation to it. The term "whosoever" is equal to "every one" (cf. Matt. 5:22, 31, 32). God expects, therefore, every human being who is capable of entering the marriage union, to be responsible to His martial code.

Second, Christ taught that no one can "put away" [the word means "divorce"] his [or her] companion unless the divorce is on the basis of fornication. The term "fornication" is general in meaning; it denotes "every kind of unlawful sexual intercourse."[3] The Lord thus allows divorce, and subsequent remarriage, only on the grounds of fornication. From the positive angle, this means the *innocent* partner,[4] in a marriage that hs been violated by fornication (extra-marital sexual conduct), has the right of divorce, and, if desirable, remarriage. From the negative side, the passage teaches that one who divorces for some reason other than fornication is *not* at liberty to remarry.

Matthew 19:9 affirms that one who divorces a companion, unless the divorce be for fornication, "committeth adultery." In the Bible, *adultery* "denotes any voluntary cohabitation of a married person with any other than his lawful spouse."[5] The tense of this verb, as used here in the Greek New Testament, suggests the idea of continued action. In other words, the person who enters this illicit union "keeps on committing adultery" each time he is sexually intimate with the new partner. By the formation of a new "marriage," the individual "enters the realm of adultery,"[6] or, as Prof. William F. Beck rendered it in his translation, he is "living in adultery."[7] The reason why this new union is called "adultery" is

133

quite obvious; though the divorced person has joined himself to a new mate [according to human legal requirements], according to the law of God, he *is still married to his original wife.* The new union is thus not approved by God.

In Matthew 5:32 Christ taught that "*every one that putteth away his wife, saving for the cause of fornication, maketh her an adulteress . . .*" She is not an adulteress simply because she has been put away, of course. But this divorced woman will likely marry again, and in so doing, she will be entering an adulterous union.

Some have attempted to establish that there is another reason for divorce, namely if a Christian, who is married to an unbeliever, is deserted by that infidel mate, the Christian is free to form a new marriage. It is claimed that proof for this view is to be found in 1 Corinthians 7: 15, where, in the case of an unbeliever leaving the Christian, the Christian "is not under bondage." Some contend that the Chrsitian is thus released from the "bondage" of marriage and so may remarry. However, this is not the case. The term "bondage" literally means "enslavement" (see Titus 2:3 where the same Greek word is translated "enslaved"), and *the marriage relationship has never been viewed as an enslavement!* The apostle is simply saying that if the unbeliever threatens to depart if the Christian does not forsake Christ, then the Christian may "let him depart." One is not obligated to be enslaved to that unbelieving spirit of rebellion. But, as one scholar notes, "Nothing is said about a second marriage for the believer; it is vain to put words in Paul's mouth when he is silent."[8]

The New Testament teaching regarding divorce and remarriage is very strict, especially in view of modern society's loose and compromising views of morality. And there is no question but that many people have, through ignorance, involved themselves in some heart-breaking, though immoral, relationships. But this important truth must be observed; while we should be compassionate towards the weak and sinful by attempting to help them, *we cannot lower the standards of the Holy Scriptures to a degenerate society!* Rather, we must encourage and challenge noble people to rise to the elevating authority of God's inspired Truth. Christianity requires great sacrifices; it has even cost many their very lives. But regardless of the costs, let us be brave enough to seek the Truth, the whole Truth, and nothing but the Truth. Churches of Christ urge their fellow-citizens to respect and extol the virtues of the home as ordained by Almighty God.

[1] Ashley Montague, *The Cultured Man*, New York: Permabooks, 1959, p. 240.

[2] M. R. Vincent, *Word Studies in the New Testament*, Wilmington, DE: Associated Publishers & Authors, 1972, p. 65.

[3] William Arndt & F.W. Gingrich, *A Greek-English Lexicon of the New Testament*, Chicago: University of Chicago Press, 1967, p. 699.

[4] By "innocent" we mean one who has not only been sexually faithful to his [or her] spouse, but also who has not, by means of designing schemes, *driven that partner to fornication.*

[5] J. Theodore Mueller, "Adultery," *Baker's Dictionary of Theology*, Grand Rapids: Baper Book House, 1960, p. 27.

[6] *Dictionary of New Testament Theology*, Grand Rapids: Zondervan, 1976, II, p. 583.

[7] William F. Beck, *THE NEW TESTAMENT in the Language of Today*, St. Louis: Concordia, 1963, p. 37.

[8] Lewis Johnson Jr., "1 Corinthians," *Wycliff Bible Commentary*, London: Oliphants, 1963, p. 1240.

QUESTIONS

Who is the original author of marriage?

What is the significance of two becoming one flesh?

Name and discuss some benefits of marriage.

Under what circumstances does God allow divorce and remarriage?

Why did Moses allow the Hebrews to divorce for many causes?

Upon what did Jesus base his teaching on divorce?

To be pleasing to God, those unlawfully divorced should . . .?

How can we strengthen our marriages against the ravages of divorce?

27

The Scriptures Are
HER DISCIPLINE

By B. C. Carr

I n every successful organization there must be discipline. Where there is no discipline, confusion reigns. God is not the author of confusion (1 Corinthians 14:33). He has prescribed in his word the standard to be used for correcting those who err. Because of abuses and misunderstanding upon this subject, many have rejected the idea of discipline altogether. We need to turn to the word of God and be instructed on this very important subject.

A GOD OF DISCIPLINE

In spite of the fact that God is a God of love (1 John 4:8), he is also a God of severity. "Behold therefore the goodness and severity of God: on them that fell, severity; but toward thee, goodness, if thou continue in his goodness: otherwise thou also shalt be cut off" (Romans 11: 22).

When Adam and Eve sinned in the garden of Eden they were driven from the garden (Genesis 3). They had disobeyed God and were punished. When Cain killed his brother Abel he was punished (Gen. 4:9-13). Because of the wickedness of those who lived in the days of Noah, God sent the flood to destroy them (Gen. 6:13). At the giving of the law on Mt. Sinai, God commanded that His people, "remember the sabbath day to keep it holy" (Exodus 20:8). While in the wilderness; a man decided to gather sticks upon the sabbath day. God instructed that he be stoned to death (Numbers 15:32-36). A whole generation of Israelites died in the wilderness because of their murmuring against God (Num. 14:26-35). Paul reveals that twenty-three thousand fell in one day because of fornication (1 Cor. 10:8). Along with the other things listed in this context, Paul states that they were written for our admonition (1 Cor. 10:11). Surely we recognize that God is also a God of severity toward those who do evil.

DISCIPLINE IN THE EARLY CHURCH

The Lord intended that his church should exercise discipline. In Matthew 16:18, Jesus promised to build his church. Before it was established, he gave instructions about discipline. "Moreover if thy brother shall tresspass against thee, go and tell him his fault between thee and him alone: if he shall hear thee, thou has gained thy brother. But if he will not hear thee, then take with thee one or two more that in the mouth of two or three witnesses every word may be established. And if he shall neglect to hear them, tell it to the church: but if he neglect to hear the church, let him be unto thee as an heathen man and publican" (Matt. 18:15-17). It is recognized that the first steps toward reconciliation are to be taken by the individuals involved in the offence, however, it must also be noted that the church is to be involved in action if the matter is not settled otherwise.

The church was still young when the Lord acted to bring swift punishment upon Ananias and Sapphira, his wife (Acts 5:1-10). These, who were members of the early church, had lied about giving. God shows his displeasure by bringing death upon them immediately. The result was that great fear came upon all the church and as many as heard these things (Acts 5:11). This did not hinder the growth of the church, as some might think, but believers were the more added to the Lord (Acts 5:14).

When Paul wrote to the church at Corinth, he rebuked them for their toleration of sin. There was a man among them guilty of fornication. They had not done anything to correct this matter. Paul, the inspired apostle, gave this instruction: "In the name of the Lord Jesus Christ, when ye are gathered together, and my spirit, with the power of our Lord Jesus Christ, to deliver such an one unto Satan for the destruction of the flesh, that the spirit may be saved in the day of the Lord Jesus" (1 Cor. 5:4-5). Please note this was to be action by the church. The church of the New Testament had an obligation to exercise discipline. This was to be done in the name (by authority) of the Lord Jesus Christ.

TERMS USED TO DESCRIBE DISCIPLINE

The Scriptures use different terms to describe discipline. We should be careful to use only Bible terms. Often we hear of someone being, "churched" or "turned out of the church." This is not biblical language.

The Scriptures speak of "withdrawing yourselves" (2 Thessalonians 3:6). In the same context we are told to, "have no fellowship" with the works of darkness (Eph. 5:11). In writing to those at Rome, Paul instructed the saints to "mark and avoid" some (Romans 16:17). To the Corinthians, Paul commanded to "deliver to Satan" the fornicator (1 Cor. 5:4-5). Later in the same chapter he instructs brethren not to "company with" nor "eat with" certain sinful brethren (1 Cor. 5:9-11).

WHO IS TO BE DISCIPLINED?

From the passages of Scripture above it is easy to see that those who are to be dealt with so severely are children of God who have sinned. They are bringing reproach upon the name of God and the church purchased with his blood. The list of sins varies with each passage cited, but all have sinned. There should be no partiality in the discharge of this sacred duty. It should include *"every"* brother who walks disorderly (2 Thess. 3:6). It is to be limited to those *"among you"* (2 Thess. 3:11). We are not obligated to take action toward all who are in the world (1 Cor. 5:9-13).

THE PURPOSE OF SUCH DISCIPLINE

Discipline should never be taken for vengeance sake (Romans 12:19). It should not be done in spite or out of

138

hatred. We are still to admonish the erring as a brother (2 Thess. 3:15). It is to make the brother ashamed (2 Thess. 3:14). Our aim should be to destroy sin, but to save the sinner (1 Cor. 5:5). Those punished are to learn from the experience that they might not sin (1 Tim. 1:20). They should have a greater respect for God and his church.

When the church acts in unity in this respect, its purity is preserved. Only a pure church will be presented to God (Eph. 5:27). When sin goes without rebuke, its influence is like leaven and will corrupt others (1 Cor. 5:6-7). Evil communications (companions) corrupt good manners (1 Cor. 15:33). God will not bless us if we fail in this duty (Joshua 7).

QUESTIONS

Can we afford to ignore the teaching of the Scriptures on this subject?

Why do you think so little discipline is practiced today?

Can the preacher or only a few members carry out God's plan of discipline?

List some sins mentioned that demand a withdrawal of fellowship.

What are the proper motives for exercising discipline?

If the parents who fail to discipline their child, sin against the child, what of elders who fail those in their care?

28

Rather than on the Sabbath
SHE WORSHIPS ON THE LORD'S DAY

By Roy H. Lanier, Jr.

T he Church of the Lord Jesus meets on the first day of the week for regular worship. At that time, she eats the Lord's Supper in memory of the death and resurrection of Jesus, she has a time for exhorting and teaching God's word. She also worships in other ways when assembled, in the songs, prayers and contribution. The Lord's church meets on Sundays for some very special reasons.

WHY WORSHIP ON SUNDAY?

First, churches worship on Sundays because some special events happened on that day.

1. Jesus rose on the first day of the week (Mark 16:9). This verse states, "Now when he was risen early on the first day of the week . . ."

2. The Holy Spirit came upon the apostles that day. "And when the day of Pentecost was fully come, they were all together in one place . . . And they were all filled with the Holy Spirit and began to speak in other tongues, as the Spirit gave them utterance (Acts 2:1-4)." This day of "Pentecost" literally means "fifty days." It was a special feast of the Jewish Law which was to be observed fifty days after their Passover Feast. It is to be "on the morrow, after the sabbath" (Leviticus 23:11, 15). So, the day on which the apostles received the Holy Spirit and

140

began their work in preaching the gospel was on a Sunday.

3. The church of the Lord Jesus Christ began that day. When the apostles began to preach salvation in the name of Christ, men repented and were baptized into Christ (Acts 2:37-42). They were added together in fellowship and began to evangelize the entire world. From this moment on in the New Testament, one can see a change, for the Church of the Lord was now in existence.

4. The churches met on Sunday to remember, in a special meal of worship, the death and resurrection of Jesus (Acts 20:7).

5. These churches continued to meet throughout the years on Sundays, and were given additional instructions about other things. They were told to "lay by in store" on this first day (1 Cor. 16:1-2). They were also to use this time for "exhorting one another" (Hebrews 10:25).

Second, the churches of Christ worship on Sundays because of a very important principle. Jesus said when his disicples went into all the world, they were to teach the disciples "to observe all things, whatsoever I commanded you . . ." (Matt. 28:20). Now, when one sees the early churches observing the Lord's Supper on the first day of the week, it follows that the *apostles taught them to do so.* If the apostles thus taught them to eat the Lord's Supper on the first day of the week, it was done in order to follow the commandments of Jesus. So, the example of the churches in the New Testament is very important, as they were being taught personally by the apostles.

Third, the evidence of historians is overwhelming that the churches met on Sundays for worship in honor of Christ.

1. *Ignatius* of Antioch said, "Let every friend of Christ keep the Lord's Day as a festival, the resurrection day, the queen and chief of all days (of the week)."[1] Ignatius lived between 37 A.D. and 108 A.D. and is known as a reputable historian.

141

2. *Justin Martyr* lived between 100 and 165 A.D. He said, "And on the day called Sunday, all who live in the cities and the country gather together to one place . . . bread and wine and water are brought . . . there is a distribution to each, and a participation of that over which thanks have been given . . . But Sunday is the day on which we all hold our common assembly, because it is the first day on which God . . . made the world; and Jesus Christ our Saviour on the same day rose from the dead."[2] Justin shows the practices of the early congregations continued on into the Second Century.

These scholars, along with many others, can be quoted to show the practice of the early centuries. They do not give us sacred teaching; they only show how the early Christians worshipped.

THE OLD TESTAMENT SABBATH

It is true the Law of Moses taught the Jews to "remember the sabbath day, to keep it holy" (Exodus 20:8). This covenant was one given the Israelites only (Deuteronomy 5:1-3, 12-15). It was a sign between God and Israel, the children descended from Abraham (Ex 31:17). It was the seventh day, a day on which the Jews were to rest (Ex. 20:9-10). They did not know about nor observe the sabbath day until they were given the Law at Mount Sinai, when they left Egypt with Moses (Nehemiah 9:13-14). It was right for the Jews to observe the sabbath, but this law was not given to Christians. In fact, Christians are taught in specific terms not to follow the Law of Moses (Romans 7:1-6). That law was fulfilled and ceased at the cross (Ephesians 2:14-16; Colossians 2:14). If Christians follow Jesus, they will follow his new covenant (Hebrews 8:6-8). And, under this new covenant, Jesus led the early Christians to worship on Sundays.

WHAT DOES THE BIBLE TEACH?

It teaches a worship assembly on the first day of the week, Sunday. On that day Christians remember the sacrifice of Jesus, they exhort one another, they give of their means, they sing and pray.

If we intend to imitate them and restore the practices

of the early churches, we will meet on Sunday and worship the Lord also.

---

[1] *The Ante-Nicene Fathers*, Vol. I, page 63.

[2] *The Ante-Nicene Fathers*, Vol. I, page 186.

QUESTIONS

When did the New Testament churches assemble for the Lord's Supper?

When did Paul instruct churches to give?

Does this indicate a regular practice of churches in meeting?

What event does the Lord's Supper memorialize?

When was Jesus raised?

What was the day when churches assembled according to historians?

If we imitate the early churches and restore their practice, when would we assemble?

29

Churches of Christ seek to
RESTORE
THE ORIGINAL CHURCH

By John Waddey

C hurches of Christ throughout the world are pleading for the restoration of the original Christianity of the New Testament. Perhaps you ask, "just what do you mean by this?" The question deserves a clear answer.

Restore is defined "to bring back to or put back into a former or original state" (Webster). Applied to Christianity, it suggests that we are seeking to put back into its original state, the church of Christ. But that suggests that the church has suffered deterioration over the years. Any person who carefully reads his New Testament and then examines the Protestant/Catholic "versions" of Christianity will be struck by the differences in the original and the modern varieties. Every aspect of primitive Christianity has suffered from attempts of men to change it to their liking.

CHANGES

The *form of church government* has been changed from simple congregational government with local elders to a complex pyramid government over the universal church (Compare Ephesians 1:22; Philippians 1:1).

Names by which the church was known have been eclipsed by denominational names such as Anglican,

Methodist, Lutheran (cp. 1 Corinthians 1:1; Romans 16:16).

The *recipient of baptism* has been changed by many from believing adults to infants (cp. Mark 16:15-16).

The *form of baptism* has been altered by many from burial by immersion to pouring or sprinkling water upon the head (cp. Rom. 6:3-5).

The *creed* of the church has been displaced by human doctrines that overshadow the will of Jesus (John 12:48; 2 John 9-10).

The *form of worship* has suffered as additions and subtractions have been made (cp. Acts 2:42; Eph. 5:19).

The gospel *plan of salvation* has been obscured by schemes advocating salvation by good works or by faith alone (cp. Acts 2:37-40; James 2:24).

The *unity* of the one church has been shattered by denominationalism with its myriad of competing bodies (cf. John 17:20-23). These and other changes have robbed believers of a clear vision of what Christianity was originally like. The seriousness of the matter is seen when we recall that an all-wise, infallible God designed the church and that sinful, fallible men have presumed to change it. No one can ever hope to improve on God's work.

NOT A NEW DENOMINATION

To *restore* does not imply that we create a new denomination better than existing ones. Christ built his church (Matthew 16:18) and declared it to be "one body" (Eph. 1:22; 4:4). Denominational division is condemned in Scripture (1 Cor. 1:10; Rom. 16:17). Even a better denomination would still be unacceptable, for it is the work of men competing with the true church of God. It is not in man that walketh to direct his own steps or build his own church (Jeremiah 10:23).

NOT A REFORMATION

We do not propose to *reform* an existing denomination. Martin Luther and John Calvin set out to reform the corrupt, medieval Catholic church. They learned as did others that such institutions are *impervious* to reform. A reformation is an "amendment of what is defective, vicious, corrupt or depraved" (Webster). Had the reformers succeeded in correcting some or all the abuses of Catholicism, the finished product would still have been the Roman Catholic church, not the church of the Lord established in Jerusalem (Matt. 16:18).

Our goal is to go beyond all the sects and denominations which have evolved, to the original Christianity preached and practiced by the apostles of Christ. The church which Jesus established was exactly what God wanted it to be. Its faith, worship and practice perfectly met the needs of humanity. Every attempt by uninspired men to improve upon, or modernize Christianity has only succeeded in corrupting it. The collector of fine art objects does not settle for an imitation, no matter how fine. He diligently searches until he finds the original. So do we. Like the jewelry merchant, having found the pearl of great price, we are willing to invest all to possess it (Matt. 13:45-46). We would be simply Christians, nothing more. Since the words of Christ will judge us in the last day (John 12:48), those words must be heeded in this life.

STRIVE FOR THE IDEAL

In restoring the church of the New Testament, we would not seek to be like the church at Corinth, Jerusalem, or Laodicea. Every congregation then as now was made up of human materials. While the design and blueprint of Christianity was conceived in heaven, the disciples that constitute a congregation are always human, and prone to sin (Rom. 3:23). As a consequence, every congregation reflects that human weakness in imperfection. Some are good but others are average or poor. But the ideal is set forth *in the divine plan* and every Christian in every age should strive to measure up to it. If we dedicate ourselves to following the Bible in all matters of faith and practice, then we will be the same kind of Christians as were the apostles.

A UNIVERSAL APPEAL

The idea of restoring New Testament Christianity has

a universal appeal to all men. It looks to that one *universal church* founded by Jesus who is its savior (Matt. 16:18; Eph. 5:23).

A *universal book* (the Bible) is set forth as the only rule of faith and practice, the only authoritative and complete repository of all that is necessary to serving God and preparing for eternity (2 Timothy 3:16-17).

Its *confession of faith is universal*; that Jesus Christ is the Son of God (Matt. 16:16).

Universally accepted Biblical names are used: Christian, disciples, brethren, saints, church of Christ (Acts 11:26; Matt. 23:8; Rom. 16:16).

Its teaching on *baptism* and the *Lord's Supper* is *universally appealing* for they are observed precisely as Christ instructed (Mark 16:15-16; Colossians 2:12; Matt. 26:26-29).

It has a *universal aim* which is to exalt and spread the kingdom of God on earth as it is in heaven (Matt. 28: 18-20).

Could any honest soul object to such spiritual principles as:

Wearing the name of Christ to the exclusion of all human names . . . Faith in the living, reigning, Christ as the only creed of the church . . . The New Testament of Christ being the church's only book of discipline . . . The recognition of the complete authority of Christ over his church . . . Christ's one church being exalted above all manmade institutions . . . All the commands of Christ being obeyed by his people . . . The ideals of Christ exemplified in the lives of all who wear his name . . . Unity in Christ by faith, repentance and baptism into him?

This would supersede all denominationalism to the end that there should be one body with Christ as both head and foundation.

The concept of Restoration is *not new*. It is an ancient and constant need in religion. Students of church history find many voices who made this plea. It is not a *local movement*. Around the world independent groups have sprung up with the announced goal of restoring original

Christianity. This common commitment cannot but bring these disciples together in Christ if sincerely followed. It is *not a governmental or institutional movement*. Rather, God-fearing individuals are making their way out of the darkness of religious confusion into the pure light of God's eternal truth. It is our prayer that you too will commit yourself to be an undenominational, New Testament Christian, a member of the church one reads of in the Scriptures.

QUESTIONS

What is the difference in restoration and reformation in religion?

Why do we need restoration?

Discuss the church of the Bible that should be our pattern.

Where would we look for guidelines for restoring the church?

What is the difference between Christ's original church and a modern denomination?

30

She urges all men to
UNITY UPON THE LORD AND HIS NEW TESTAMENT

By Mack Wayne Craig

I n a world divided into religious bodies of every doctrine and practice, Churches of Christ plead for the unity of all believers in Jesus Christ on the basis of the Word of God. Although most of us are accustomed to religious division, stop and ask yourself: Is this really God's plan for His people? Did Jesus die to bring about such confusion as exists among those who claim to wear his name? Those of us who cannot find this condition in harmony with the Word of God are pleading that all men put aside denominational ties and stand together united in Christ on the truth presented in the Bible.

It is clear from studying Jesus' teaching that this was his purpose for his followers. During the final hours before his death, Jesus' prayer for the disciples and all believers makes his attitude clear: "Neither pray I for these alone, but for them also which shall believe on me through their word; That they all may be one; as thou, Father, art in me, and I in thee, that they also may be one in us: that the world may believe that thou hast sent me" (John 17:20-21). We note in this prayer two important truths: first, Jesus expects his followers to be one in the same sense that he and the Father are one. Can you imagine asking Jesus what to do to be saved and being told something different from what God would say? Yet this is the result of religious division, as different churches

149

teach doctrines which do not agree with those taught by others.

A second truth which must be noted from Jesus' prayer is his statement that believers in years to come would learn and follow him through the word or teaching of the apostles" (John 17:20). Many seem to have decided that

EPHESIANS
4:4-6

they have the right to believe and teach whatever pleases them, with little concern over whether it is the message of God through the apostles. Jesus here makes it clear that his disciples can only be made by accepting the teaching set forth by the apostles, and that these disciples must and will then be one because they believe and teach the same thing.

These truths are emphasized by the apostle Paul in correcting the sin of denominationalism which arose in the Corinthian church. The idea of religious denominationalism is to separate or divide into different groups, each with its own peculiar doctrines and practices, but all claiming to belong to Christ. It is based on the idea that men have the right to interpret truth for themselves, and to decide what doctrines they wish to hold. It grows out of the Roman Catholic position that the *church* is the final authority, with the right to decide on doctrine, rather than *Christ* as final authority, to whom the church bows in obedience. Listen to Paul's message: "Now I beseech you, brethren, by the name of our Lord Jesus Christ, that ye all speak the same thing, and that there be no division among you; but that ye be perfectly joined together in the same mind and in the same judgment" (1 Corinthians 1:10). Does this requirement for unity of doctrine made by Paul fit the practice of religious groups today?

Denominationalism developed out of the efforts of sincere people to reform the Roman Catholic Church. Men like Martin Luther, John Calvin, John Knox, John and Charles Wesley, and many others became convinced of the need for change in the religious practices of the church. Each began to teach and emphasize various areas in which he believed reform was needed. Unfortunately, the result was that those who followed them developed into new religious groups with creeds and doctrines which still did not go back to the teaching of the apostles who were guided by the Holy Spirit. This practice has continued so that hundreds of churches exist today, in spite of Jesus' prayer and Paul's instruction that we all be one.

The tragic result of this has been the conclusion by many that what is called Christianity must be false. If Jesus is the Way, why can his followers not walk together? Did you note in Jesus' prayer that this is the reason for which he requires that we be one? He said ". . . that the world may believe that thou hast sent me" (John 17:21). The divisions in Christianity cause young people in divided homes to lose interest in the call of Jesus; how much more are people from non-Christian backgrounds confused by the differences among those who call themselves Christian!

God's plan for our salvation included his provision of truth as the foundation for life. This truth has been given us in the Bible, which God has preserved for us through the centuries. It was his purpose from the beginning that disciples of Jesus should stand together on his Word. Note the following:

1. Jesus claimed all authority in sending the apostles to teach his word: "All power is given unto me in heaven and in earth. Go ye therefore, and teach all nations, baptizing them in the name of the Father, and of the Son, and

of the Holy Ghost: Teaching them to observe all things whatsoever I have commanded you" (Matthew 28:18-20). The apostles were not at liberty to teach or interpret as they pleased, but were bound by the message of Jesus.

2. The Holy Spirit was given to the apostles to make sure that they would teach only the will of God and Christ. On the night of his betrayal, Jesus promised to send the Holy Spirit to accomplish this purpose: "But the Comforter, which is the Holy Ghost, whom the Father will send in my name, he shall teach you all things, and bring all things to your remembrance, whatsoever I have said unto you" (John 14:26). After his resurrection Jesus commanded the apostles to wait in Jerusalem for the coming of the Holy Spirit: "But ye shall receive power, after that the Holy Ghost is come upon you: and ye shall be witnesses unto me both in Jerusalem, and in all Judea, and in Samaria, and unto the uttermost part of the earth" (Acts 1:8).

3. Since the apostles could not always be present to teach the truth revealed by the Holy Spirit, they wrote the message which would be needed through the centuries. In doing this, God guided them by the Holy Spirit so the message had to be accurate and true. Listen to Paul's statement of this truth: "How that by revelation he made known unto me the mystery; (as I wrote afore in few words, Whereby, when ye read, ye may understand my knowledge in the mystery of Christ) Which in other ages was not made known unto the sons of men, as it is now revealed unto his holy apostles and prophets by the Spirit" (Ephesians 3:3-5). We have the privilege of reading and studying the words of the apostles and others guided by the Holy Spirit. To write creeds or single out special ideas for emphasis is to ignore the revelation of God's truth which is the basis for following Jesus.

4. This message of truth set forth in the Bible will make us all that God wants us to be. Notice Paul's statement to young Timothy: "But continue thou in the things which thou hast learned and hast been assured of, knowing of whom thou hast learned them; And that from a

child thou hast known the holy scriptures, which are able to make thee wise unto salvation through faith which is in Christ Jesus. All scripture is given by inspiration of God, and is profitable for doctrine, for reproof, for correction, for instruction in righteousness: That the man of God may be perfect, throughly furnished unto all good works" (2 Timothy 3:14-17).

Those who misunderstand the plea of churches of Christ for unity on the Word of God sometimes reply: "You think that you're right, and everybody else is wrong." This is not our position. We are convinced that the *Bible* is true and right, and that any of us is right only to the extent that we accept and follow what it says. Why not turn away from all human doctrines and unite on the Word of God as the only rule of faith and action?

QUESTIONS

What two important truths about unity does Jesus' prayer teach?

What is the idea of religious denominationalism?

What does this idea grow out of?

How did denominationalism develop?

What has been the result of denominationalism?

How did Jesus' guarantee that the apostles would speak the truth?

How can we know that truth today?

31

She Proclaims for All Men
FELLOWSHIP IN CHRIST

By Jim Massey

C hrist's church is Christ's people, "called out" from other people who are not Christ-like. Jesus loved all men of all races and tasted death for "every man" (Hebrews 2:9). His death was God's means of overcoming the broken fellowship between God and man, caused by sin.

Because God and Christians have wonderful companionship when sins are forgiven in Christ, this fellowship provides the way for all races and segments of society to be one with each other. All colors, economic levels, and social distinctions become "one in Christ Jesus" (Galatians 3:28). Christ's church shows Christ's oneness to all men.

God's plan to forgive all men in Christ required selection of a special race, the Jews, the descendents of Abraham, to bring Christ into the world. These Jews missed the point of their special privilege and became proud racists in their vain superiority over other nations (the Gentiles). But godliness (God-like-ness) opposes national or personal self-elevation, because "God is no respecter of persons" (Acts 10:34).

No racial prejudice ever surpassed Jewish hatred for Gentiles. But Ephesians 2:14 shows that Jesus "is our peace, who made both one, and broke down the middle wall of partition." Verse 15 says that he abolished in his flesh the hatred, that he might create of Jew and Gentile "one new man, so making peace." Verse 16 explains how Jew and Gentile were both reconciled to God and to one another by the cross and in one body, the church.

The church of Jesus Christ, therefore, is God's eternal plan for human and divine togetherness for all men. The universal levelling produced by a common salvation in Jesus' death results in a universal fellowship of Christ-like love and concern. Early Christians "had all things common" (Acts 4:32) and functioned unselfishly for the good of each other as do parts of a human body (Romans 12:5).

Today's world is full of hatred between races, castes, religions, colors, economic levels, and proud individuals. All hatred comes from our separation from God, but love comes from God. "He that loveth not knoweth not God, for God is love" (1 John 4:8). God's love is the only source of genuine fellowship to heal our world's bigotry and hatred.

The good news (gospel) message that God so loved the whole sinful world that he gave his only-begotten Son to die for it (John 3:16) is the only basis for peace among men. No legislation by law-makers nor sincere efforts by social peacemakers can solve the real problem — man's sin and necessary separation from God's holiness.

God is holy and pure. He cannot stand sin. His presence before Moses made ordinary dirt "holy ground" (Exodus 3:5). His name is holy and reverend (Psalm 111: 9). Angels sing, "Thou alone art holy" (Revelation 15:4). Man must be holy because God is holy (1 Peter 1:16). Without holiness no man can have fellowship with God (Hebrews 12:14).

But man is not holy by nature, he is sinful. He is basically un-God-like, or ungodly. The thoughts of man's heart are only evil continually (Genesis 6:5). There is not a just man on the earth that doeth good and sinneth not (Ecclesiastes 7:20). There is none righteous, no not one (Romans 3:10). All men have sinned and come short of the glory of God (Romans 3:23). Man is fleshly, sold

155

under sin (Romans 7:14). In his flesh dwells no good thing (Romans 7:18).

Because God's nature is angered by sin, He must punish every sin. He has eyes too pure to look upon sin (Habbakuk 1:13). Evil is an abomination to God (Proverbs 15:8). His wrath is revealed against all ungodliness and unrighteousness (Romans 1:18). Every sin must receive a proper punishment (Hebrews 2:2). If God failed to punish a single sin, he would be imperfect in justice. He would be like an unfair judge, partial and corrupt. But because he is perfectly just, God must punish every sin.

This shows why Jesus had to die for sinners. The very nature of God cannot stand sin. But the very nature of man is to practice sin. Because God is perfectly just, he must punish man's sin. And a perfect standard of right and wrong doesn't remedy man's sin problem. Law only exposes man's guilt and his need to be forgiven of sin. By the basic nature of God and man, the only way man could be forgiven by God was for God to find a way to punish sin and yet to forgive man, the sinner. Jesus' death was the answer.

Christ suffered in the place of sinners. Because God must punish sin, man's sins were punished upon Jesus. His death was a substitute sacrifice for us. He has borne our griefs and carried our sorrows. He was stricken, afflicted, and smitten of God. He was wounded for our transgressions. He was bruised for our iniquites. He was chastened so that we could have peace with God. With his stripes we are healed. God has laid upon him the sins of us all. God's demand for sin's punishment was satisfied when he saw the travail of his soul (Isaiah 53:4-12). Christ suffered sin's penalty in man's place.

The word "atonement" means "at-one-ment." It is the price paid which enables peace to be restored between enemies. Him who knew no sin, God made to be sin on our behalf that we might be made righteous because of him (2 Corinthians 5:21). Jesus bore our sins in his body on the cross, and by his stripes we are healed (1 Peter 2:24). Christ suffered for sins, the just for the unjust, that he might bring us to God (1 Peter 3:18). All have sinned and come short of the glory of God, but forgiveness of sins freely justifies or makes man righteous in Christ (Romans 3:23, 24). This is possible because God has given Jesus as a sin-offering that satisfies God's anger against sin. God now can both punish sin and also forgive the sinner who trusts in Jesus (Romans 3:25,26).

A man from Ethiopia was riding in his chariot, reading the prophet Isaiah about God's suffering Lamb upon whom man's sins were laid (Acts 8:28). The preacher Philip began at this Scripture and preached unto him Jesus (verse 35). The Ethiopian then wanted to be baptized (verse 36). They stopped the chariot, went down into the water, and the man was baptized (verse 38). He then came up out of the water rejoicing because his sins had been forgiven in the death of Jesus (verse 39).

The Ethiopian African had been taught by Philip, a Jew — racism had been erased by the atonement message of Jesus. The death of Jesus erases hatred between God and man and between men and other men. Christians have all things common in Christ's one body, the church. Men of different races and status become new men in Christ, who then proclaim the saving message of the cross to a world of sinners of all races alienated from God and from one another.

QUESTIONS

What causes the separation of fellowship between God and man?

What was God's purpose for the Jews, and how did they corrupt this purpose?

What body is God's plan for human togetherness?

Where does hatred come from?

Where does love come from?

Name two characteristics of God which cause him to separate from man.

Explain the meaning of "atonement."

What was the Ethiopian reading, what did he hear preached, what did he do, and why did he rejoice?

Why would Philip, a Jew, associate with an Ethiopian?

What message will saved sinners give their lives to proclaim?

32

Men can forfeit their salvation by
TURNING AWAY FROM CHRIST

By George W. DeHoff

Man is created in the image of God. He became a sinner by going astray from him. Adam and Eve were created pure, holy and innocent. They were God's children by creation but being in the image of God, they had the power of choice. They chose to do wrong. The devil had told them "Ye shall not surely die" (Genesis 3:4) but God has said "The soul that sinneth, it shall die" (Ezekiel 18:20). Adam and Eve were separated from God because of their sin. Man is a free moral agent before and after conversion — he is capable of choosing to follow Christ and thus become a Christian. In the same way, he is capable of choosing to reject our Blessed Lord by refusing to be faithful to him.

God loves his children and wants them to be saved. Throughout the Bible — more than 2,000 times God has warned his children against unfaithfulness, falling away, drifting away and sometimes outright rejection of their Heavenly Father. If it were impossible for him to fall away, then all of these warnings would be meaningless. They are given because God loves us and wants us to go to heaven.

Biblical examples of those who became children of God and then turned back and were lost are abundant. "God spared not the angels that sinned but cast them down to hell" (2 Peter 2:4). Christians are told "Make

158

your calling and election sure" (2 Peter 1:10). Paul said, "Let him that thinketh he standeth take heed lest he fall" (1 Corinthians 10:12). The beloved apostle Paul buffeted his body to bring it into subjection lest that after he had preached to others he himself should be a castaway (1 Corinthians 9:27). Our Lord has told us, "If a man keep my sayings, he shall never see death" (John 8:51). If we live after the flesh, we shall die but if we mortify the deeds of the flesh, we shall live (Romans 8:13).

Every Christian has an obligation to abide in, remain in and continue in the teaching of Christ (1 John 2:24) in order that he may serve God now and go to heaven at the end of the journey. It is this faithfulness which God's people seek to encourage.

GOD'S EXAMPLE — ISRAEL

The Israelites were God's children during the Old Testament period. "Ye are the children of the Lord your God" (Deuteronomy 14:1). They were an holy people unto the Lord. Notice from 1 Corinthians 10:1-10 the many things God said about them: (1) They were baptized into Moses. (2) They ate spiritual food. (3) They drank spiritual drink. (4) They were overthrown in the wilderness. (5) They lusted after evil things. (6) They were idolaters. (7) They committed fornication. (8) They fell — 23,000 in one day. (9) They tempted Christ. (10) They murmured. Some were even killed in the very act of fornication (Numbers 25:8). God said that those who are guilty of these works of the flesh cannot be saved (Galatians 5:19-21).

It is often said that if one is once a child of God, he is always a child of God. It is possible for a child to be disinherited. God said he would disinherit his disobedient children. "I will smite them with pestilence, and disinherit them" (Numbers 14:12). God is longsuffering and gives his children opportunity to repent but he will by no means clear the guilty (Numbers 14:18).

What happened to Israel is an example for us today. We are God's children. He has reserved for us a home in heaven but he will disinherit us if we prove unfaithful. If we forget God we will be cast into hell. "My people have

159

forgotten me days without number" (Jeremiah 2:32). "The wicked shall be turned into hell, and all the nations that forget God" (Psalm 9:7).

THE BOOK OF LIFE

When we become Christians, God writes our names in the Lamb's Book of Life. "Whose names are in the book of life" (Philippians 3:13). Our names may be written in prominent places but none can compare with having them written in heaven. But God will blot out of that book those who will not do right. "Whosoever hath sinned against me, him will I blot out of my book" (Exodus 32:33). Those whose names are not written in the book of life will be lost. "And whosoever was not found in the book of life was cast into the lake of fire" (Revelation 20:15). How important it is that we have our names written in this book by becoming Christians and, then, how very important that we live in such a way that God will not blot our names out!

ETERNAL LIFE

God teaches through His Bible that Christians have eternal life. This everlasting life is in Christ (John 6:40). The Bible is written to cause us to believe and thus have "life through his name" (John 20:31). Those who will not come to Christ will not have eternal life (John 5:40).

Christians receive eternal life in the world to come. While here we are "In hope of eternal life" (Titus 1:2). Eternal life is promised to Christians (1 John 2:25). We receive this life after the good fight of faith has ended (1 Timothy 6:12). Jesus said this reward is in the world to come (Mark 10:29-30). Our resurrection from the dead is "unto the resurrection of life" (John 5:28-29). After the judgment day, the righteous go away into life eternal (Matthew 25:46).

How wonderful to know that while we live here we are sowing the seed of the kingdom day by day and that at the end of the journey, we receive life everlasting (Galatians 6:8).

Here on earth all things are fragile — we break them, lose them or they wear out. But at the end of the journey, when the battles have all been fought and the final victory is worn, we receive a crown of life that fadeth not away.

KEEP THE FAITH

It is possible for children of God to believe the truth, become Christians and later (1) Depart from the faith, (2) Heed seducing spirits, (3) Take up with doctrines of devils, (4) Speak lies in hypocrisy and (5) Have their consciences seared (1 Timothy 4:1-2). It is said concerning some that they have damnation because they have cast off their first faith (1 Timothy 5:12) and of others that their faith was overthrown (2 Timothy 2:18). Some made shipwreck of faith (1 Timothy 1:19) and others believed for awhile and then fell away (Luke 8:13).

The Lord cast his own servant into outer darkness (Matthew 25:14) and took away from the vine those who would not bear fruit (John 15). Notice these were in the vine — in Christ who is the vine — and were later taken away by the Lord himself. They were cast into the fire.

God's grace never fails but it is possible for us to fall from grace (Galatians 5:4). If we could be saved in that condition, we would be saved without the grace of God!

If a brother sins, he does not need to be baptized again — he is already God's child. He needs to repent and pray (Acts 8:22). By walking in the light as given in God's Word, we have fellowship with other Christians and the blood of Christ cleanses us from all sin (1 John 1:11). This daily cleansing comes to those who faithfully serve the Lord. Those who will not serve him, who reject his faith and turn from his grace, will be finally lost.

Our great task is to remain faithful to our Blessed Lord and to teach others to love and serve him.

QUESTIONS

Who was the first to teach man that he could not lose his salvation? (Genesis 3:4).

Discuss our freedom to make choices and the possibility of turning away from Christ.

Name some Bible examples of children of God who fell away and were punished.

161

Would a loving God actually disinherit a rebellious child? (See Numbers 14:12).

What would be the consequence if a Christian's name was blotted out of God's book of life? (Exodus 32:33).

If God's grace never fails, how could a Christian ever be lost?

33

She proclaims the truth about
THE HOLY SPIRIT IN
THE LIFE OF THE CHRISTIAN

By John Waddey

F ew topics have received such attention in our generation as that of the Holy Spirit and the Christian. Much of the teaching heard lays heavy stress upon a direct operation of the Spirit on the heart of alien sinners to bring them to salvation, and supernatural enlightenment and guidance for Christians. We will examine these points in light of God's Word and see what is actually promised.

The Holy Spirit is a divine person, a member of the holy godhead. It is erroneous to think of him as merely a power, influence or feeling. Masculine pronouns are applied to the Spirit (John 14:26). Attributes of personhood are given him. He speaks (Revelation 2:29); he leads (Romans 8:14); he forbids (Acts 16:6). The Holy Spirit plays a vital role in our salvation. We are baptized into the name of the Father, the Son and the Holy Spirit (Matt. 28:19). He is the seal of our salvation and the "earnest of our inheritance" (Ephesians 1:13-14).

TO WHOM IS THE HOLY SPIRIT GIVEN?

Contrary to popular opinion, God's Spirit is not given to alien sinners to convert them. "Because ye are sons, God sent forth the Spirit of his Son into our hearts" (Galatians 4:6).

The Spirit through the inspired Scripture works on the

163

minds and hearts of sinners, convicting them (John 16:8; 1 Peter 1:23). When the sinner believes the gospel message, repents and is baptized, he receives remission of sins and the gift of the Holy Spirit (Acts 2:38). Thus the Spirit comes, not to make us sons, but because we have become Sons of God. God's Spirit is only given to those who in faith obey Christ. "We . . . receive the promise of the Spirit through faith" (Gal. 3:14). Jesus said "He that believeth on me . . . from within him shall flow rivers of living water. But this spake he of the Spirit, which they that believed on him were to receive . . ." (John 7:38-39). Peter tells us of "the Holy Spirit whom God hath given to them that obey him" (Acts 5:32). Jesus said, "how much more shall your heavenly Father give the Holy Spirit to them that ask him?" (Luke 11:13). The context makes clear that he gives this gift to his children!

We should be reminded that Scripture speaks of a baptism of the Holy Spirit which only the apostles and Cornelius received (Acts 1:5; Acts 11:15-17) and the miraculous gifts of the Spirit given by the hands of the apostles (Acts 8:12-18). (Only the apostles could pass the gifts along to others, the recipients could not.) There also is a general gift or indwelling of the Spirit which all receive at baptism. This is non-miraculous (Acts 2:38). Holy Spirit baptism was promised to the apostles, but never commanded of disciples. Only two cases of it are recorded at the first reception of Jews and Gentiles into Christ's kingdom. Both cases involved open displays of supernatural power (see Acts 2:1-13 and 10:44-48). Today there is but one baptism (Eph. 4:5). This baptism of the Great Commission is in water (Acts 8:37-38).

OBLIGATIONS IMPOSED

It is a remarkable privilege to receive God's Spirit in our lives. Such carries with it heavy responsibilities. "Know ye not that your body is a temple of the Holy Spirit which is in you, which ye have from God? and ye are not your own; . . . glorify God in your body" (1 Cor. 6:19-20). "If any man destroyeth the temple of God, him shall God destroy; for the temple of God is holy, and such are you" (1 Cor. 3:17). Thus any habit or practice that would defile our body and soul must be cast aside, be it fornication, drug abuse, indulgence in intoxicating beverages, gluttony, tobacco or any like thing.

We must "walk by the Spirit, and . . . not fulfill the lust of the flesh" (Gal. 5:16). By that, Paul means to order our lives by the Spirit's instructions found in the Scripture. "For the *law of the Spirit* of life in Christ Jesus, (makes) me free from the law of sin and death" (Rom. 8:2). "For as many as are led by the Spirit of God, these are sons of God" (Rom. 8:14). The Holy Spirit has given us the Bible to guide our path (2 Peter 1:20-21).

Christians must put away all things in their lives that would grieve the Holy Spirit (Eph. 4:25). In Ephesians 4:17-5:14 the apostle catalogs that ugly list of sins we must put away if we would please our heavenly guest. At the same time we must fill the vacuum in our lives by bringing forth the fruit of the Spirit: "love, joy, peace, longsuffering, kindness, goodness, faithfulness, meekness, self-control . . ." (Gal. 5:22-23).

BLESSINGS THE SPIRIT IMPARTS

Although no miraculous power or leading is promised to us today, the blessings bestowed by the indwelling Spirit are manifold. When at our baptism we receive the gift of the Spirit (Acts 2:38) it is likened to God's *seal* or stamp of approval or ownership (2 Cor. 1:22). His presence in our life is the *earnest* or assurance of our ultimate reward in heaven (Eph. 1:13-14). Our possession of the Spirit is an *assurance* of our sonship: "hereby we know that we abide in him and he in us, because he hath given us of his Spirit" (1 John 4:14). "The *love of God* hath been shed abroad in our hearts through the Holy Spirit which was given unto us" (Rom. 5:5). We "*abound in hope,* in the power of the Holy Spirit" (Rom. 15:13). Christians are "*strengthened* with power through his Spirit in the inward man" (Eph. 3:16). "And in like manner the Spirit *helpeth our infirmity*" (Rom. 8:26a). When we do not know how to pray as we ought, "the Spirit himself *maketh intercession* for us . . . according to the will of God" (Rom. 8:26-27). Paul urges us to pray "at all seasons in the Spirit" (Eph. 6:18). By the Spirit (we) "put to death the deeds of the body" (Rom. 8:13); thus we find help to overcome those powerful habits of sin which have attached themselves to us. When we walk in the fear of the Lord we enjoy "the comfort of the Holy Spirit" (Acts 9:31). The Holy Spirit leads the Christian in paths of righteousness. "For as many as are led by the Spirit of God, these are the sons of God" (Rom. 8:14).

Many claim the Spirit whispers words in their ear or overpowers their mind, but such is not Biblical. The Holy Spirit leads us through the instruction of the Scripture he caused to be written. Scripture came as "men spake from God, being moved by the Holy Spirit" (2 Pet. 1:21). In Ephesians 5:19 Paul instructs us to be filled with the Spirit and sing. In Colossians 3:16 he says "Let the words of Christ dwell in you richly" and sing. Thus with David we pray "Show me thy ways, O Jehovah; teach me thy paths, Guide me in thy truth and teach me . . ." (Psalm 25:5). Truly Scripture "is a lamp unto my feet, and light unto my path" (Ps. 119:105). It is the medium by which God's Spirit leads us. Led by the Spirit we enjoy "the communion of the Holy Spirit" (2 Cor. 13:14) and the . . . "fellowship of the Spirit" (Philippians 2:1). In a similar way "the Spirit himself beareth witness with our spirit, that we are children of God" (Rom. 8:16). In his word, the Spirit has told us the conditions of salvation; i.e., faith (Hebrews 11:6), repentance (Acts 17:30), immersion (Mark 16:16). When our spirit can truthfully say, I have met these terms" then the Spirit's Word says "he that believeth and is baptized shall be saved" (Mk. 16:16).

EVIDENCE OF THE INDWELLING SPIRIT

Those who have God's Spirit in their hearts will reflect it in their attitude and conduct. They will love the Bible which the Spirit caused to be written. "I have longed after thy precepts" (Ps. 119:40). "I love thy precepts" (Ps. 119:159). Sinners receive "not the love of the truth that they might be saved" (2 Thessalonians 2:10). Spirit filled men will confess that Jesus Christ is come in the flesh (1 John 4:2). They will be led by the Spirit's word (Rom. 8:14) and mind "the things of the Spirit" (Rom. 8:5). With the Spirit's help they will be mortifying the sinful desires and practices of the old life (Rom. 8:13). In their lives will be seen "the fruit of the Spirit . . . love, joy, peace, longsuffering, kindness, goodness, faithfulness, meekness, self-control . . ." (Gal. 5:22-23).

The Holy Spirit and Salvation

The implanted word of God which the Spirit inspired is able to save our souls (James 1:21). In every case of conversion recorded in the Acts of Apostles, souls were saved only after hearing the word of God taught and obeying the divine will (Compare Acts 2:1-47). The Lord today will open your heart even as he did Lydia's by the preaching of the gospel (Acts 16:11-15). He will remove your sins even as he did Saul of Tarsus' when you respond by being baptized (Acts 22:16).

Without God's Spirit, you cannot be saved (Rom. 8:9). It is impossible to receive the Spirit apart from Christian baptism (John 3:5). We urge you today to let Christ save you "through the washing of regeneration (baptism) and the renewing of the Holy Spirit" (Titus 3:5). In so doing you will find "righteousness, peace and joy in the Holy Spirit" (Rom. 14:17).

QUESTIONS

How do we conclude that the Holy Spirit is a person?

To whom is the Holy Spirit given?

In Scripture, who received the Baptism of the Holy Spirit?

Name three obligations of those who have the Spirit.

Discuss the blessings the Holy Spirit provides Christians today.

What is the evidence of the Spirit dwelling in one's life?

34

She believes the
MIRACLES OF BIBLE TIMES ARE NO LONGER AVAILABLE

By Claude A. Guild

The above title does not mean the church today denies the miracles of creation, the flood, the walls of Jericho story, the virgin birth of Christ or his resurrection. Miracles confirmed the sonship of Jesus. "These are written that ye may believe that Jesus is the Christ, the Son of God . . ." (John 20:31). To disbelieve these miracles and look for modern-day miracles outside the Book demonstrates our lack of faith in the Bible and the Son of God it reveals.

MIRACULOUS GIFTS

Like scaffolding, a temporary platform for workmen on a new building, miraculous gifts were temporary to enable the early church time to mature and grow. Instruction had to be given in the absence of a written, confirmed, complete and perfect revelation. These gifts were to last "till we all attain unto the unity of the faith, and of the knowledge of the Son of God, unto the full-grown man, unto the measure of the stature of the fulness of Christ . . ." (Ephesians 4:13).

These gifts came through the laying on of the apostles' hands. The apostles had to go to Samaria to lay hands on those Philip had converted and bestow gifts on them, because Philip could not do it (Acts 8:16). Paul laid his hands on twelve men at Ephesus and they spoke in tongues and prophesied (Acts 19:6). The seven deacons, including Philip, received the laying on of hands of the apostles (Acts 6:6). Paul laid his hands on Timothy to enable him to receive a special gift (2 Timothy 1:6). Finally, Paul longed to go to Rome, "that I may impart unto you some spiritual gift, to the end ye may be established" (Romans 1:11).

It is very, very important that we keep in mind the third-persons with reference to miraculous gifts. Only the apostles could give the nine miraculous gifts (1 Cor. 12:4-11). The ones upon whom they laid their hands could not impart the gifts to the third-person Christians. If they could, why didn't Philip bestow the gifts on the Christians in Samaria? Therefore, when the apostles died, their hands died with them and the ability to bestow gifts by "the laying on of hands" died also.

We must keep in mind that there are other measures of the Spirit. One, Christ possessed the Spirit "without measure" (John 3:34). Two, there was the baptismal measure of the Spirit for the apostles and the household of Cornelius (cf. Acts 2:1-4; Acts 10:44-45). Holy Spirit baptism was always spoken of in promise and not commanded (Matthew 3:11; Acts 1:4-5). There is the general measure of the Spirit. I like to call it the kinship measure of the Spirit. This measure is received by every child of God and makes us kin to God (cf. Rom. 8:9; 1 Cor. 6:19-20; 3:16-17; Acts 5:32; Eph. 1:13-14).

THE NINE GIFTS

The miraculous gifts are named in Paul's letter to the Corinthians. He states: "For to one is given through the Spirit the word of wisdom; and to another the word of knowledge according to the same Spirit; to another faith in the same Spirit; and to another, gifts of healings, in the one Spirit; and to another workings of miracles; and to another prophecy; and to another discerning of spirits; and to another divers kinds of tongues; and to another the interpretation of tongues . . . dividing to each one severally even as he will" (1 Cor. 12:8-11). These gifts relate specifically to the infant church when it did not have the completed revelation of God as we have today. There was a special need then that does not exist now.

169

The gifts were to confirm the word (Hebrews 2:1-4). They helped the church grow and keep out false teachers (Eph. 4:11-15).

The word preached by the apostles was oral. They didn't have a New Testament like we have today. It was being written. Therefore, they had these gifts and could bestow them on others to confirm the spoken word. "How shall we escape, if we neglect so great a salvation? which having at the first been spoken through the Lord, was confirmed unto us by them that heard him; God also bearing witness with them both by signs and wonders, and by manifold powers and by gifts of the Holy Spirit, according to his own will" (Heb. 2:3-4). When my wife and I married in Altus, Oklahoma, forty-two years ago, our marriage license was signed and sealed by the county clerk of Jackson County representing the State of Oklahoma. I do not have to go back to Altus once a week, or once a year to see if it is still confirmed. Since Paul said it "was confirmed," and it is in the past tense, we learn two important lessons: First, the signs, wonders and gifts of the Spirit were manifested through the miraculous gifts. Secondly, for us to look for confirming signs today, exemplifies our lack of faith in the miracles of the apostles and the genuineness of the word of God.

THAT WHICH IS PERFECT

After discussing the nine miraculous gifts in the 12th chapter of First Corinthians, Paul wanted to point up a "More excellent way" (1 Cor. 12:31), hence he points to the way of love in the 13th chapter. He puts a deadline and dateline on the miraculous gifts by saying, "Love never faileth: but whether there be prophecies, they shall be done away; whether there be tongues, they shall cease; whether there be knowledge, it shall be done away. For we know in part, and we prophesy in part; but when that which is perfect is come, that which is in part shall be done away" (1 Cor. 13:8-9).

This passage is like the man on the Jericho Road. "He fell among robbers who both stripped him and beat him, and departed, leaving him half dead" (Luke 10:30). The Pentecostal people have misused and abused this passage with a desire to perpetuate their glossolalia or tongue speaking positions. The three chapters (12-13-14) viewed in the context will not allow the miraculous gifts to be permanent; but spiritual gifts, the more excellent way, are to remain (13:13). But what does the phrase "When that which is perfect . . .," mean? It does not mean that evidence of salvation was the baptism of the Holy Spirit and evidence of the baptism of the Holy Spirit was the ability to speak in tongues. Wayne A. Robinson, Vice President of the Oral Roberts Evangelistic Association, gave up his association with Oral Roberts because of the abuse of these gifts. Referring to the questions "Are all apostles? are all prophets? are all teachers? are all workers of miracles? have all gifts of healing? do all speak in tongues? do all interpret? . . ." (1 Cor. 12:29-30), Robinson said, "How about answering the same question that Paul posed to the Corinthians: 'Have all gifts of healing? do all speak with tongues?' Internally, I admitted that the implied answer to each question was 'no.' . . . The New Testament clearly teaches that all Christians have the Holy Spirit, and the overriding evidence of this presence is never tongues."[1]

This passage does not refer to the second coming of Christ. The grammar alone will not allow it. Gary Workman states, "Paul uses a neuter article and substantive (an adjective used as a noun). It could therefore be translated, 'the perfect thing.' Jesus, however, is spoken of not as a thing but as a person. Thus, he is consistently referred to in masculine terms. Jesus would therefore be a 'he who, not a 'that which.' "[2]

When the scriptures were completed; the oral message spoken and the gifts to confirm that message were recorded, we received that "perfect law, the law of liberty" (James 1:25). It is therefore the New Testament that circumscribes his church today. H. Leo Boles said, "We have a perfect record of these gifts which were bestowed to help confirm the preaching of the word; there was no need for a continuation of them after his full gospel had been revealed and confirmed and a record made to preserve it."[3]

Frank Pack states it very well: "It is incorrect to simply

assume that because a spiritual gift is listed in the New Testament period, it must exist today . . . The form of the questions in 1 Corinthians 12:29-30 ('do all speak with tongues?') points out the self-evident fact that not every Christian was meant to possess every gift, since all Christians were not apostles, nor all prophets, neither did all speak with tongues, nor work miracles of various kinds."[4]

Finally, with reference to 1 Corinthians 13:9, "For we know in part, and we prophesy in part;" we have always had perfect knowledge in quality but not in quantity. Likewise, we have always had perfect prophecy in quality but not in quantity. But when Jesus' revelation came, miraculous gifts ceased and we have today perfect knowledge and prophecy in quality and quantity.

[1] Robinson, Wayne A., *I Once Spoke in Tongues*, (Tyndale House, Wheaton, Ill., 1973) pp. 55, 141.

[2] Workman, Gary, *Spiritual Sword*, (Getwell Rd. Church, Memphis, Tenn., April, 1981) p. 13.

[3] Boles, H. Leo, *The Holy Spirit, His Personality, Nature, Work*, (Gospel Advocate Company, Nashville, Tenn., 1971), p. 175.

[4] Pack, Frank, *Tongues and the Holy Spirit*, (Biblical Research Press, Abilene, Texas, 1972), pp. 106-107.

QUESTIONS

In what sense are the miracles of the Apostolic Age like scaffolding?

How did we receive miraculous gifts?

Why were miracles given?

Did all first century Christians have miraculous gifts?

At what point in history did the miracles cease?

If divine miracles ceased to be given at the end of the first century, how do we account for the claims of modern day miracle workers?

35

She proclaims
SALVATION TO WHOSOEVER WILL ACCEPT

By Clarence DeLoach, Jr.

To whom is the call of the gospel to be issued? Is it a call arbitrarily offered to some but withheld from others? Are some predestined to be saved and others to be lost? Has individual destiny been irrevocably fixed before birth?

A very large segment of the religious world has been conditioned by the complex theological system advanced by John Calvin. Calvin's teaching, generally designated "Calvinism," is summed up by five basic ideas, one related to or growing out of another. Those five cardinal doctrines are (1) the unconditional election and reprobation of particular men, (2) a limited atonement, (3) total depravity, i.e., man's inability to respond to God without divine intervention, (4) irresistible grace, and (5) the perseverance of the particular elect.

The basic error within these basic tenents of Calvinism is the denial of man's volition. Man was created as a being with the prerogative of choice. Adam and Eve were given the freedom of choice. God ordered them not to eat of the tree of knowledge of good and evil. The consequences of their choice were made clear. The first couple understood the directives and God urged them to make the right choice. However, God did not force the right decision, because the greatest good is chosen good. Sadly, Adam and Eve "transgressed the law" and

173

sinned against God. (See Genesis 2:15-3:19; 1 John 3:4.)

JESUS AND THE HUMAN WILL

Jesus makes it clear that the will of man is involved in serving him. Of some he said, "Ye will not come to me, that ye might have life" (John 5:40). Note the implications of this passage in relation to salvation. It is personal — "*ye* will not come to me"! It involves the will — "ye *will* not come"! One may accept or reject — "Ye will *not* come"! Man is active rather than passive in conversion — "Ye will not *come* to me"!

Jesus' great invitation was *universal* in scope. Matthew records him saying, "Come unto me, all ye that labor and are heavy laden, and I will give you rest" (Matt. 11:28). The very fact of invitation implies the choice of acceptance or rejection.

Concerning the exercise of the will, Jesus said, "If *any* man (note any man, not just those predestined) willeth to do his will, he shall know of the teaching, whether it is of God, or whether I speak from myself" (John 7:17). Thus, *doing* and *knowing* the teaching of Christ is a matter of the human will.

GRACE AND THE HUMAN WILL

In writing to Titus, Paul affirmed that ". . . the grace of God that bringeth salvation hath appeared to *all men,* teaching us that, denying ungodliness and worldly lusts, we should live soberly, righteously, and godly in this present world" (Tit. 2:11-12). Please observe from this passage (1) that God's grace has appeared to *all* men, (2) that it brings salvation and (3) it teaches. If God's grace has been made available to all men — why aren't all men saved? The answer, by implication is simple! All men have not exercised their wills to embrace the teaching of grace, and respond favorably to it.

SALVATION INVOLVES THE TOTAL MAN

By creative design, God made man an intellectual, emotional and volitional creature. With the *intellect* man is capable of receiving and understanding factual information. With his *emotions,* he is capable of being stirred

174

and touched by what he receives. The volition or will of man enables him to *act* upon what he understands. The gospel message reaches the intellect, stirs the emotions and activates the will.

On the day of Pentecost we see an example of the intellect, emotions and will being reached. The apostle Peter presented *evidence* from the Old Testament Scriptures, from his miracles, and the resurrection which proved Jesus to be the son of God. He reached their minds by evidence and reasoning. Their hearts were stirred upon learning the truth about Christ. Upon inquiring, they were told what to do (Acts 2:38). Their wills were activated as they "gladly received the word and were baptized" (Acts 2:41).

GOD WANTS ALL TO BE SAVED

God is not aloof to man's salvation! God longs to save! He wants all men to come to the knowledge of truth (1 Timothy 2:4). "For God so loved the world, (not just a predestined few) that he gave his only begotten Son, that *whosoever* believeth in him should not perish but have everlasting life" (John 3:16).

Of God's longing to save, the apostle Peter said, "The Lord is not slack concerning his promise, as some men count slackness; but is long-suffering to usward, not willing that any should perish, but that all should come to repentance" (2 Peter. 3:9). The Hebrew writer said of Jesus, "That he by the grace of God should taste death *for every man*" (Heb. 2:9).

God seeks men through the gospel. The Thessalonians were "called by the gospel" (2 Thess. 2:14). Those who are called are "chosen of God, a royal priesthood, a holy nation and a peculiar people" (1 Pet. 2:9). The *called* are those who "hear, believe and are baptized" (Acts 18:8). They have exercised their volition and freedom of choice!

WHOSOEVER WILL

Interestingly, the Bible ends with an invitation. Jesus said, "The Spirit (the Holy Spirit) and the bride (the church) say, come, and let him that heareth say, come.

175

And let him that is athirst come. And *whosoever will* let him take the water of life freely" [Parenthesis and emphsis mine—C.D.] (Revelation 22:17).

It is the work of the bride, the church, to issue that invitation to all men until Jesus comes. Calvinism in general, and predestination of individuals in particular would nullify that invitation.

God is moving toward you with a message of love, salvation and hope. Will you exercise your prerogative to hear, believe and obey it?

QUESTIONS

From what human theological system does the doctrine of limited salvation spring?

What is meant by freedom of choice in religion?

How do such verses as Matthew 11:28 relate to the subject of limited atonement?

If God wants all to be saved (2 Peter 3:9) and has all power (Matthew 28:18), why are not all men saved?

How does God call men to salvation today (2 Thessalonians 2:14)?

36

She sets forth the Bible teaching on
THE NATURE OF MAN

By Robert R. Taylor, Jr.

Both Testaments raise the fundamental query, "What is man?" The Sweet Singer of Ancient Israel does in Psalm 8:4; the writer of Hebrews does so in Hebrews 2:6. Misconceptions abound in our world relative to the basic nature of man. Godless evolutionists view man as an evolved creature who in no sense has been created by a Divine Maker. Materialists view man as wholly mortal. There is nothing that survives him at death. Like Rover, the dog, he is dead all over at death. This view denies man a spirit or an entity that outlives his fleshly tabernacle of clay. The Calvinistic view of man denies his free moral agency. This widely entrenched system of religious thought has man, the helpless puppet, dangling on the strings of Jehovah's arbitrary decisions made for him before the foundation of the world. Hedonism (the pleasure principle) views men and women as playboys and playgirls. This was the old Epicurean concept that Paul met among Athenian philosophers in classical Athens in Acts 17. They pursue the principle of "Let us eat, drink and be merry today for tomorrow we die." No one needs to argue that this is the dominant life style of the masses in our day. This is why fornication adultery, incest, rape, perversions, etc., are widespread in our day and increasing annually. Then there is the Biblical view that will be set out briefly in this chapter.

MAN IS CREATED IN GOD'S IMAGE

Man is here as a result of a Creator's hand. The "Big

Bang" theory had nothing to do with his origin. Godless evolution, that totally lacks sense and sanity to sustain it, had nothing to do with man's origin. Man did not will himself into being. This the Psalmist makes crystal clear in Psalm 100:3. Jehovah willed man into existence. The Bible says, "Let us make man in our image, after our likeness . . . So God created man in his own image, in the image of God created he him; male and female created he them" (Genesis 1:26-27). Genesis 2:7 details the making of man from dust and how God breathed into his nostrils the breath of life and man became a living soul. Genesis 2:21-23 depicts so beautifully and majestically the marvelous making of glorious woman. Solomon affirmed that God made man upright (Ecclesiastes 7:29). The Psalmist declared that "it is he that made us, and not we ourselves" (Ps. 100:3). David declared himself to be fearfully and wonderfully made" (Ps.˙ 139:14). Jesus said God made male and female and they both have existed from the *beginning* of the creation (Matt. 19:4-5; Mark 10:6). Paul, on Mars' Hill, affirmed man to be God's created offspring (Acts 17:28-29). Man is here because God made or created him. He is not the product of aimless evolution that did not even have him in mind when the senseless process somehow started in the dim past. Man is not from *slime;* he is from the *Sublime.*

MAN IS A FALLEN CREATURE

There are 1,189 chapters in the Bible. Only two of them, Genesis 1 and 2, portray man as a creature of sinless perfection. From Genesis 3, the time when man first sinned, to the end of Revelation 22 man is viewed as one who has sinned and thus has come short of Jehovah's glory. Sin is lawlessness or transgression (1 John 3:4). Sin is a failure to do right (James 4:17). Sin is unrighteousness (1 John 5:17). Sin is an act or thought, word or deed which is contrary to God's will (Proverbs 24:9; Ephesians 4:29; James 2:9). The Bible teaches surely and certainly that man has fallen; yet George Gaylord Simpson says in *The Meaning of Evolution* that man has risen; that he has not fallen. The Bible exhibits the folly of this silly, Simpson sentiment. Isaiah 59:1-2; Romans 3:9, 23 and 1 John 1:8-10 are classic verses in the Bible which set forth man as a fallen creature — as a sinner.

MAN IS A POTENTIAL CHILD OF GOD

This is due to God's love which provides man a remedy and points him merically to a Savior (1 John 4:9; John 3:16-17; 1 Timothy 2:3-4; 2 Peter 3:9). By gospel obedience (hearing, faith, repentance, confession and baptism) man becomes a Christian. By a faithful life of work, worship, watching and waiting man prepares himself for the heavenly habitations in yonder's world. "Behold, what manner of love the Father hath bestowed upon us, that we should be called the sons of God: therefore the world knoweth us not, because it knew him not. Beloved, now are we the sons of God, and it doth not yet appear what we shall be: but we know that, when he shall appear, we shall be like him; for we shall see him as he is" (1 John 3:1-2).

MAN IS A DUAL OR TRIUNE BEING

Obviously, man is more than bone, muscle, blood and tissue. If man is nothing more than a creature of evolution and if the only difference between man and a mouse lies in the arrangements of molecules, then man is no better than a cockroach, a sheep, a pig or a horse. Jesus stressed that man is more valuable than a sheep, the sparrows or the fowls of the air. Yet this is just not true if humans and animals are all evolved creatures.

There are passages which set forth man as a dual being — possessive of body and spirit. In Ecclesiastes 12:7 Solomon speaks of the body which goes to dust from whence it came but the spirit goes to God its giver. James 2:26 speaks of the death of the body at the time the spirit vacates the tabernacle of clay. Jesus warns us not to fear killers of the body but fear him who is able to destroy both body and soul in hell (Matt. 10:28). These passages treat man as a dual being.

When a distinction is made between soul and spirit, as is sometimes the case in Holy Writ, then man is depicted as a triune being. Paul wrote the Thessalonians of this triune nature. Note his apostolic affirmation, "And the very God of peace sanctify you wholly; and I pray God your whole spirit and soul and body be preserved blameless unto the coming of our Lord Jesus Christ" (1 Thess. 5:23). The writer of Hebrews 4:12 speaks of the "dividing asunder of soul and spirit." Soul is used in a number of ways. (1) It may refer to the whole person as in the case of the three thousand souls added to the church in Acts 2:41 or the total number of people aboard ship on Paul's trip to Rome in Acts 27:37. (2) It may refer simply to physical life which man enjoys in common with lower forms of life. Psalm 78:50 employs this particular use of the word soul. (3) Soul may be used to refer to the intellectual nature of man. Paul's natural man in 1 Corinthians 2:14 is quite literally the "soulish man" (Guy N. Woods). (4) Soul is used as a synonym of that unique unity that bound early disciples together. They were of one heart and one soul (Acts 4:32). (5) The soul is used synonymously with the spirit to refer to man's immortal nature that survives the body and earthly life. When body, soul and spirit are all used, we are speaking of the fleshly tabernacle of clay, the earthly life that inhabits it and that immortal part which is made in God's image, in Deity's likeness.

SOME ERRORS REFUTED

The very fact that man has body, soul and spirit refutes materialism (imbibed and defended by ancient Sadducees, by modern atheists and by many so-called religionists) in telling fashion. In Luke 20 Jesus proved to the skeptical Sadducees that even though Abraham, Isaac and Jacob had long been dead physically when God spoke to Moses at the burning bush, that in a far higher sense the trio of patriarchs all lived as far as God was concerned.

The very fact that man is dual or triune in being refutes soul sleeping. Man does not cease to be at death. It is the body that sleeps in Mother Earth as Daniel 12:2 makes crystal clear. The spirit or soul is very much conscious. Abraham, Lazarus and the rich man of Luke 16:19-31 were all conscious in their widely separated compartments of Hades. The rich man knew he was in anguish and pain. Lazarus knew he was comforted in Abraham's bosom. Jesus promised the dying thief that his spirit and the penitent thief's spirit would be together that very day in Hadean Paradise (Luke 23:43). Jesus commended his spirit into the Father's hands (Luke 23:46). Joseph and Nicodemus took care of his bodily burial (John 19:38ff). The souls (not bodies) that John saw under the altar were very much conscious (Rev. 6:9-11). Man is conscious from death to judgment even though he possesses no body.

This is the Biblical doctrine of man's nature. He is body, soul and spirit. When soul and spirit are used interchangeably, then he is body and spirit or body and soul.

QUESTIONS

List and discuss the misconceptions relative to man's nature.

Contrast evolution's picture of man and the Biblical view of man.

Discuss the real origin of man.

How do evolution and the Scriptures differ drastically relative to man's fall?

What is man potentially?

Discuss man as a dual creature.

Discuss man's triune nature.

Refute some popular errors about man's nature.

Why is a correct understanding of man's nature so basic to understanding the Bible?

37

She teaches the Biblical
DOCTRINE OF THE GODHEAD

By Ray Hawk

C hurches of Christ have the responsibility of teaching only truth. If we waver or faint in this divine obligation, we lose what God has promised to those who obey His will (Matthew 7:21). It is therefore the loving duty and privilege of the church that she teach the Biblical doctrine of the Godhead.

DEFINING THE GODHEAD

The word "Godhead" is used three times in the English Bible (Acts 17:29; Romans 1:20; Colossians 2:9). According to Greek dictionaries and lexicons, each of these places has a different word, but they are each related to the other, meaning divinity or having the quality of deity. When the word "Godhead" is used, we think of the Father, the Son and the Holy Spirit being the sum total of Deity. We must not think of the Godhead in human terminology. God is not three men. Jesus the Word occupied a human body and came in the flesh to dwell among men (John 1:14). Of the Godhead, he is the only one spoken of as man (1 Timothy 2:5). He emptied himself of the nature or form of God and became a man (Philippians 2:6-7). He alone died and shed his precious blood for man (Acts 20:28). He was the person of the Godhead that was born of flesh, died, was buried and rose again (Phil. 2:8-11). He was man but also God. "And without controversy great is the mystery of godliness: God was manifest in the flesh, justified in the Spirit, seen of angels, preached unto the Gentiles, believed on in the world, received up into glory" (1 Tim. 3:16).

THREE PERSONS BUT ONE GOD

Many people today, as well as in the past, have failed to understand God. Some of this is due to the impossibility of a *finite* mind to understand an *infinite* being. There is nothing we can do about that. However, the rest of our inability to understand is a failure to study the revelation God has given of himself. We can understand that (Ephesians 3:4).

The Bible teaches the concept of one Deity. "One God" (Eph. 4:6). "But to us there is one God" (1 Cor. 8:6). "And the Lord shall be king over all the earth: in that day shall there be one Lord, and his name one" (Zechariah 14:9). There are no other gods. "I am the Lord: that is my name: and my glory will I not give to another (god), neither my praise to graven images" (Isaiah 42:8).

We recognize there are three personalities that are Deity. There is one Deity but three persons. We know one is referred to as the Father, another as the Son and a third as the Holy Spirit (Matthew 28:19). Are these three persons really one person? How can there be just one Deity but three persons sharing the Godhead?

First, we must recognize that the word "God" may also be translated "deity." The Father, Son and Holy Spirit share that one quality, nature or form called God. The Jews had a problem understanding this. When Jesus said, "I and my Father are one," "the Jews took up stones again to stone him" (John 10:30-31). The first time they tried to stone him was when he said, "Verily, verily, I say unto you, Before Abraham was, I am" (John 8:58). Jesus claimed for himself Deity. The Jews wanted to stone him for it. "Jesus answered them, Many good works have I showed you from my Father; for which of those works do ye stone me? The Jews answered him, saying, For a good work we stone thee not; but for blasphemy; and because that thou, being a man, makest thyself God" (John 10:32-33). They could not understand that Deity may be composed of two personalities with one taking upon himself humanity while the other personality was in heaven.

THE FATHER *AND* THE SON

The scriptures are very plain in showing the Father and the Son as two personalities. Even when Jesus said, "I and my Father are one" (John 10:30), we see two persons. I = Jesus, and My Father = Jehovah. Jesus did not say he and the Father were one person. That would make Jesus his own father and the Father his own son!

The very language of the New Testament points to two persons. God the Father is not human but divine. Jesus is divine but became human by entering a human body. "Wherefore when he cometh into the world, he saith, Sacrifice and offering thou wouldest not, but a body hast thou prepared me" (Hebrews 10:5).

The gospel of John is a good book describing the three personalities that make up the one Godhead or Deity.

1. John 3:16: We have a giver and the one who is the Gift. The giver is not the gift; therefore, we have two persons.

2. John 3:13: John shows us that Jesus ascended up to heaven after he came from heaven. The Father was in heaven and the Son was on earth. Two persons.

3. John 6:44-45: One cannot come to Jesus (one person) unless the Father (another person) draws him. If Jesus is the Father, when one comes to the Father, he has already come to the Son!

4. "Then said Jesus unto them, Yet a little while am I with you, and then I go unto him that sent me" (John 7: 33). If Jesus is his own Father, who was he going to go to? Who sent him? How could he go to him if he is that person?

5. "And yet if I judge, my judgment is true: for I am not alone, but I and the Father that sent me" (John 8:16). If Jesus is the Father, he would be alone for that would only be one person present. If the Father is another person, Jesus would not be alone.

6. "It is also written in your law, that the testimony of

184

two men is true. I am one that bear witness of myself, and the Father that sent me beareth witness of me" (John 8:17-18). Jesus said, "I am one" and the Father is the other witness. One plus one equals two persons. That fulfilled the law. One person playing two roles would not!

7. One should look at the following passages and see that they also speak of the Father *and* the Son. That's two persons. John 8:28, 42; 10:36; 12:27-30, 44, 49; 14:10, 15-17, 23-24, 26, 28.

8. In John 16:7-13 we see the Father (one person), Jesus (a second person) and the Holy Spirit (a third person). Three personalities, but one Godhead or Deity.

DID JESUS HAVE TWO SPIRITS?

Some have attempted to teach that Jesus the man had a human spirit, received at conception like other human beings, and the Jehovah or Father Spirit after he was born. When the human spirit is speaking to the Father, it is speaking to the Divine Spirit within the body of Jesus, according to them. Among the numerous reasons why this theory is false is the fact that Jesus said he would return to the Father from "whence he came." If the human spirit first existed at conception, how could it return to a place it had never been *unless* the Spirit of Jesus existed before conception as passages like Philippians 2:6-8 indicate? When Jesus on the cross said, "Father, into thy hands I commend my spirit" (Luke 23:46) we have a human spirit being given to a Divine Spirit as *both* reside in the body of Jesus! The passage should say, "I commend my spirit: and having said this, he gave up the ghosts"! Since death is the spirit leaving the body, and since this theory says Jesus' body contained two spirits, we find Jehovah and Jesus died! Who can believe that?

CONCLUSION

The Bible clearly illustrates that God manifests himself in three persons: the Father, the Son, and the Holy Spirit. Each is a person. The Father is not the Son. The Son is not the Holy Spirit. The Holy Spirit is not the Father, but each is Deity or God. Each shares in the one form, nature or quality of the Godhead.

QUESTIONS

Are there three gods taught by the Bible?

If the scriptures say someone sent another, would you say they are the same personality or would you believe there are two personalities involved?

Did Jehovah, the Father, shed his blood upon the cross or was it Jesus?

Who is the Comforter mentioned in John 14:26; 16:13?

If Jesus had a human spirit, existing at conception, how could it return to heaven since it did not come from heaven?

When Jesus died on the cross, how many spirits (ghosts) did he commend to the Father: one or two?

Do the Scriptures teach in any verse that Jesus is his own Father and the Father is his own Son?

38

She teaches the
FUTURE PUNISHMENT OF THE WICKED

By Albert Gardner

The account of the rich man and Lazarus reveals the two possible destinies of people after death. "And it came to pass, that the beggar died, and was carried by the angels into Abraham's bosom: the rich man also died, and was buried; and in hell he lifted up his eyes, being in torments, and seeth Abraham afar off, and Lazarus in his bosom. And he cried and said, Father Abraham, have mercy on me, and send Lazarus, that he may dip the tip of his finger in water, and cool my tongue; for I am tormented in this flame. But Abraham said, Son, remember that thou in thy lifetime receivedst thy good things, and likewise Lazarus evil things: but now he is comforted, and thou are tormented. And beside all this, between us and you there is a great gulf fixed: so they which would pass from hence to you cannot; neither can they pass to us, that would come from thence" (Luke 16:22-26).

Some have tried to dismiss the teaching given here by saying it is just a parable. This may be a parable but if it is, it is not called that by Luke. If it is a parable it is the only time Jesus named a person in a parable. However, it teaches the same thing whether it is a parable or not, for a parable is something that either did happen or could happen. A parable may illustrate and make the truth easy to understand, but it does not weaken the teaching.

187

HADES AND SHEOL

Hades is the place of departed spirits without regard to whether they are righteous or wicked. The Old Testament word translated *Sheol* has the same meaning as the New Testament word *Hades*. The rich man and Lazarus both went to hades but they were not together for they were separated by a great gulf.

Lazarus went to Abraham's bosom, a place of happiness. This is where Jesus went when he died. He told the thief, "Today shalt thou be with me in paradise" (Luke 23:43). He did not go to the place of torment and flames where the rich man was suffering. Peter quoted from David and said that someone's soul would go to hell (hades, ASV), and his body would not see corruption. He explains that David's body did see corruption and that David was referring to Christ. "He foreseeing this spake of the resurrection of the Christ, that neither was he left unto Hades, nor did his flesh see corruption" (Acts 2:31 ASV).

The rich man went to a place of torment, suffering, and flames. This is the place where sinful angels are kept till the judgment. They were "cast down to hell" (2 Peter 2:4). The Greek word "tartarus," translated hell in this verse, is used nowhere else in the New Testament.

UNIVERSALISM, PURGATORY, AND ANNIHILATION

There are three popular doctrines which relate to the problem of the suffering of the wicked. First, the Universalists teach that all will eventually be saved and that there is no eternal punishment. The rich man shows this doctrine to be false. Jesus taught there are two roads leading through life and one of them is the broad way "that leadeth to destruction, and many there be which go in thereat" (Matthew 7:13). In the resurrection, some will be saved and some will be lost (John 5:29).

Second, the Catholic doctrine of purgatory involves the souls of people suffering for their sins. When they are purged or cleansed, they will be permitted to go to heaven. The rich man wanted Lazarus to leave his place and come to comfort him, but he was told there was a great gulf separating them. There could be no change. There would be no passing from one state to another. There is no purgatory. There can be no purifying of the wicked after their death. If one in his lifetime turns his back on the only sacrifice which can take away sins, the only thing which remains is "a certain fearful looking for of judgment and fiery indignation, which shall devour the adversaries" (Hebrews 10:27).

Third, the Jehovah's Witnesses teach the annihilation of the wicked. When discussing the Greek word "gehenna" which is translated hell, they say "it signifies annihilation, not eternal torment."[1] They further state, "The Bible shows that it is only the incurably wicked that God will punish everlastingly — not with eternal torture, but by mercifully putting them out of existence forever."[2] Again, "Adam, therefore, went completely out of existence."[3] They say also, "As to 'eternal torment,' there is no such place."[4]

If one goes out of existence, obviously there would be no punishment, for there would be nothing to punish. But is there anything beyond the grave? Does one continue to exist after death?

When Jesus was transfigured, the apostles saw him talking with Moses and Elijah (Matt. 17:3). Moses had been dead about fifteen hundred years and Elijah had been gone for about a thousand years. Yet they still existed and were still Moses and Elijah. They were conscious. Moses did not go out of existence at death.

The rich man in Luke 16 did not cease to exist at death but was conscious, had a memory of his life and brothers, was in torment and talked about his present state after his death. Jehovah's Witness teaching about the dead going out of existence at death is a false doctrine.

In Luke 12:5 Jesus warned, "Fear him, which after he hath killed hath power to cast into hell." Hell is not death but *after* death one can be cast into hell. If hell is nothing more than death or extinction, why fear God more than man? Men can kill other men but there is something worse than death which we are to fear. Jesus said one

189

could "be cast into everlasting fire" (Matt. 18:8). It is a fire "that never shall be quenched" (Mark 9:43).

ETERNAL PUNISHMENT

The Bible is clear about the eternal nature of the punishment of the wicked. "And these shall go away into everlasting punishment: but the righteous into life eternal" (Matt. 25:46). It is easy to see that *Life* is the same in duration as is the *Punishment* of the wicked. If one is temporary, so is the other. If hell is temporary, heaven is also temporary.

The New Testament use of the words eternal and everlasting makes it clear what they mean. It is "everlasting punishment" (Matt. 25:46). The fire is "everlasting fire" (Matt. 25:41). There will be "eternal damnation" for some (Mark 3:29). Now consider how other verses use these words.

1. *God is everlasting.* "According to the commandment of the everlasting God" (Romans 16:26). Does everlasting mean unending or temporary? Will God cease to exist?

2. *The Holy Spirit is eternal.* "Who through the eternal Spirit offered himself without spot to God" (Heb. 9:14). Is the Holy Spirit temporary? When the world ends will he go out of existence?

3. *Redemption is eternal.* "Neither by the blood of goats and calves, but by his own blood he entered in once into the holy place, having obtained eternal redemption for us" (Heb. 9:12). Is it eternal redemption or will he have to be offered again? Is his work of redemption complete or was it for just a brief time?

4. *Salvation is eternal.* "He became the author of eternal salvation unto all them that obey him" (Heb. 5:9). Will obeying him still bring unending salvation?

5. *The kingdom is an everlasting kingdom.* The faithful will be in "the everlasting kingdom of our Lord and Savior Jesus Christ" (2 Peter 1:11).

If eternal punishment is temporary, does that mean God, the Holy Spirit, salvation, and the kingdom are temporary and will cease to exist? The same words in both Greek and English are used to describe the future punishment of the wicked that are used to describe God, the Spirit, salvation, and the kingdom. "Depart from me, ye cursed, into everlasting fire, prepared for the devil and his angels" (Matt. 25:41).

There will be eternal punishment for the wicked but we can avoid it if we will live soberly, righteously, and godly in this present world (Titus 2:11-12).

---

[1] *Good News To Make You Happy*, Watchtower Bible and Tract Society of Pennsylvania, Inc., p. 92.

[2] *Ibid.*, p. 97.

[3] *Children*, Watchtower Bible and Tract Society of Pennsylvania, Inc., p. 70.

[4] *Ibid.*, pp 71-72.

QUESTIONS

Describe the rich man and Lazarus after death.

What is the meaning of hades and sheol?

Does one go out of existence at death?

Name five persons or things which are eternal.

Explain Matthew 25:46.

39

She practices the
PRIESTHOOD
OF ALL BELIEVERS

By Hulen L. Jackson

I'm a priest. You're a priest. We're all priests in God's kingdom. Christ alone is the high priest. So the Bible teaches plainly. From the early apostacy of the New Testament church into the Greek and Roman Catholic churches came the separation of Christians into clergy and laity. The apostolic church did not believe nor practice such. From this departure came the teaching of Protestant bodies about "ordained preachers" who alone can serve the "sacraments" of the church to the laity, and the belief that the front of the church building where the communion table is kept becomes the "altar" where the ordained preacher or priest alone can serve communion. To go back to simple New Testament teaching and practice will eliminate all of this error.

WHAT IS A PRIEST?

The word translated "priest" in the New Testament means prince or servant but throughout the Bible a priest can not be separated from an altar or from the offering of sacrifices. A prophet served God for the people while a priest served the people in offering their gifts before God. The fathers did so in the Patriarchal age; the Levites did so in the Jewish age, and all Christians today as priests offer to God gifts and sacrifices. It can easily be proved from the New and the Old Testaments that God

192

has never allowed anyone to offer sacrifices save a priest in any age. Every Christian today, as a priest before God, brings his offerings and sacrifices before the Father.

OUR PRIESTHOOD TODAY AS THE CHURCH:

Even Jesus' high priesthood is not discussed in the New Testament until you come to the book of Hebrews and there the writer exalts him as our one and only and everlasting high priest in heaven serving us who are on earth. We will never have or need another. He has already given before God the one sacrifice for our sins once for all. But, our own priesthood is hardly mentioned even in Hebrews; you have to come to the writings of Peter and John to get such instructions. Hebrews 10:22 is oft considered a reference, based upon the Old Testament picture, to our priesthood today, serving in the True Tabernacle, the church. Study closely the following passages.

Hebrews 13:15-16

"Through him then let us offer up a sacrifice of praise to God continuously, that is, the fruit of lips which make confession to his name. But to do good and to communicate forget not: for with such sacrifices God is well pleased." This must be understood with the assumption that all Christians to whom he is writing are priests and therefore have the right to bring such sacrifices before God's altar in heaven. Whether the fruit here is singing or praying, I could not do so if I were not a priest. Vincent in his word studies of the New Testament explains that "offer up" in this passage actually means "bring up to the altar." A Christian does just that when he praises God either in song or in prayer.

1 Peter 2:5-9

Peter is writing to the dispersed elect-Christians in this letter and not just to apostles. In verse 5 Peter calls us "a holy priesthood" and also a "spiritual house," suggesting that Christians today are separated (holy) from the world and thus constitute not only a true temple but are the priests in that very temple of God. Then in verse 9 he adds the thought that we are also a "royal priesthood" exalting our spiritual state and relationship with God, calling us regal or kingly priests. And, as such in God's house today, we "bring up to the altar" which is in heaven, spiritual or living sacrifices. Only priests can do so. As a people for God's own possession, we all as priests approach the Father through our High Priest, Jesus the Christ (1 Timothy 2:5).

Revelation 1:6

John then adds in this verse the thought that Christ hath made us to be a "kingdom, to be priests unto his God and Father." Collectively we are his kingdom and individually we are priests in that kingdom. Yes, even John believed and taught that we are kingly or royal priests before God. Remember John wrote mainly to the seven churches of Asia — not to just a select clergy in those churches. In Revelation 5:10 John repeats virtually the same thought about us, saying that Jesus purchased out of every tribe and nation a people and made them into a kingdom of priests. That's who and what we are today.

Romans 12:1

"I beseech you therefore, brethren, by the mercies of God, to present your bodies a living sacrifice, holy, acceptable to God, which is your spiritual service." Note the words: *brethren, sacrifice, spiritual service*. Brethren (not just a select group called a clergy) were directed to offer or present sacrifices in spiritual service unto God. Recalling that only priests can offer sacrifices, this statement Paul makes implies necessarily that brethren are priests and thus can obey this command. Thank God daily that you are a priest and do not have to go through any man on earth to contact God or to offer your sacrifices, offerings and gifts unto the Father. What are some of these sacrifices we offer as Christians?

From Burton Coffman's fine commentary on 1 Peter (pages 96-98) may I list the following:

(a) Our faith is our sacrifice.
(b) The love of God is our sacrifice.
(c) Our repentance is our sacrifice.

194

(d) Our confession of faith in Christ is a sacrifice.
(e) Our baptism into Christ is our sacrifice.
(f) Our praise of God is our sacrifice.
(g) Our contributions are our sacrifices.
(h) Our songs are our sacrifice.
(i) Our prayers are our sacrifices.
(j) The whole life of honor and love on the part of devoted Christians is their sacrifice.

With such sacrifices God is well pleased and they are acceptable through Jesus Christ our Lord. I can offer up; you can offer up; we all can offer up spiritual sacrifices. Do so faithfully.

QUESTIONS

What is the origin of the clergy-laity classes found in most churches?

Who can serve as a priest in God's church today?

What are the duties of a Christian priest?

Who is the high-priest of the church?

According to Paul, through whom must we offer our worship? (1 Timothy 2:5).

Discuss the sacrifices Christians are to offer God.

40

Churches of Christ reject the
EMPTY FORMS OF RITUALISM

By Bill Nicks

There has always been a tendency on the part of men toward ritualism in their efforts to worship, whether worshippers of the true God or false gods. Ritualism has to do with ceremonies and forms: "In a derogatory sense, excessive devotion to prescribed ritual forms in worship" — Webster. It is the prescribing of certain "rites," such as the Liturgy, "the public rites and services of the Christian Church, specifically, as the Eucharistic rite, called the Liturgy in the Eastern, the Mass in the Western Church." These describe the deterioration of true worship into rites designed by uninspired men, and are a caricature of the true worship as prescribed by Christ.

The difference in true worship and false worship is clearly described in the Bible. Jesus said, "God is a spirit, and they who worship him must worship in spirit and in truth" (John 4:24). Ritualism is the opposite of worshipping in spirit and in truth. The Lord's supper was designed to remember Christ's death on the cross. His body that was given and his blood that was shed are signified in the first-day-of-the-week-partaking of the bread and fruit of the vine. These emblems represent his body and blood. Jesus said, "As oft as ye do this, do it in memory of me" (1 Corinthians 11:25).

There is a great difference in an emblem which the Lord has set for the purpose of impressing some truth upon worshippers, and in hollow rituals which men have

196

added. Even Old Testament worship had its emblematic observances, but not without meaning. For example, there was the instruction for the High Priest, with his holy garments, to first bathe himself, representing purification from sin, then to "kill the goat of the sin-offering, that is for the people, and bring his blood within the veil . . . and sprinkle it upon the mercy-seat." After this, he was to make an atonement for the holy place, and for the tent of meeting. This was a blood atonement for the sins of himself and "all the assembly of Israel" (Leviticus 16:4-19). After this, he was to "lay both hands upon the head of a live goat, and confess over him all the iniquities of the children of Israel, and all their transgressions, even all their sins; . . . and he shall send him away by the hand of a man that is in readiness into the wilderness: and the goat shall bear upon him all their iniquities unto a solitary land; and he shall let go the goat into the wilderness" (Lev. 16:20-22). Was this ritualism? No, because the Lord was impressing on Israel the heinousness of sin, and typifying the eventual plan of Jesus' coming into the world to shed his blood once for all, in contrast to the year by year shedding of the blood of bulls and goats (Hebrews 10:14). Even the laying on of the hands of the High priest held a significance:

> "The laying on of hands is not an act of blessing but is believed to be a real transference of guilt to the scapegoat. To drive out the goat meant to drive out sin itself . . . Alongside this, though more rare, is the laying on of hands as an act of blessing (Genesis 48:18; Isaiah 44:3). It is no doubt closely related to laying on of hands on the occasion of a man's installation in an office (Numbers 27:12ff). The laying on of hands, therefore, means if one compares the two very different acts of removal of sin and blessing . . . he passes on his special blessing or burdens to the scapegoat with the burden which he himself had carried."[1]

All Old Testament prophets condemned empty formality, but none went to the heart of the matter with more clarity and forcefulness than Micah:

> "Wherewith shall I come before the Lord, and bow myself before the high God? Shall I come before him with burnt offerings, with calves of a year old? Will the Lord

be pleased with thousands of rams, or with ten thousands of rivers of oil? Shall I give my firstborn for my transgression, the fruit of my body for the sin of my soul? He hath shewed thee, O man, what is good; and what doth the Lord require of thee, but to do justly, and to love mercy, and to walk humbly with thy God?" (Micah 6:6-8).

It is not true that the sacrificial system, which was appointed by the Lord for a purpose, was abandoned by the prophets. It continued until fulfilled by Christ, and even Christ died shortly after keeping the Passover. The condemnation which the prophets delivered was not for offering of sacrifices and keeping of the feasts, but for the failure of Israel to undergird their offerings with a sincere spiritual attitude and holy life. Many of them no doubt felt there was some magic ritual in the mere mechanical performance of empty ceremonies to change their lives from unholiness to purity. "For I desire mercy, and not sacrifice; and the knowledge of God more than burnt offerings" (Hosea 6:6).

NEW TESTAMENT

The same can be said of worship required under the New Testament. The problem is not with the institution of worship as required by the Lord. The problem is in the degeneration of true worship into ritualism. When our Lord was questioned, "Why eateth your Teacher with the publicans and sinners?", he heard it and said, "They that are whole have no need of a physician, but they that are sick. But go ye, and learn what this meaneth, 'I desire mercy, and not sacrifice: for I came not to call the righteous but sinners' " (Matthew 9:11-13).

There are at least two instances when true acts of worship prescribed by the Lord become ritualistic: (1) When such additions are made to the word of the Lord that the actions performed are not authorized by the Lord, and (2) When such acts that are prescribed by the Lord are done perfunctorily, hence done mechanically and without either interest or zeal.

As an example of ritualism in the Lord's supper, the additions to the simple memorial feast in what is called the Eucharist is a case in point. Priestly rites performed in the "mass" demand that Christ be crucified again and again, and that through the doctrine of "transubstantiation" the bread when consecrated by the priest becomes by a miracle the literal body of Christ, and the fruit of the vine becomes in the same way the literal blood of Jesus. Such was not intended by the Lord when he said, "This is my body, . . . this is my blood of the new covenant." This metaphorical expression obviously meant that the emblems represented his body and blood, and that Christians partook of the bread and fruit of the vine "in memory" of him (Matthew 26; Mark 14; Luke 22). Clearly, the New Testament teaches the priesthood of all believers (1 Peter 2:5, 9), but priestcraft actually interferes with the worshippers' communion with the Lord by its sacerdotal rites of human additions. These are innovations into true New Testament worship. Transubstantiation became a doctrine of Roman Catholicism in the Council of Trent (1560 A.D.).[2]

There is sufficient spirituality and inspiration available in the acts of worship in the New Testament, without additional doctrines which men have developed through councils and creeds. The wonderful Scriptures furnish us "completely unto every good work" (2 Timothy 3:16-17). Indeed, God's power has "granted unto us all things pertaining to life and godliness" (2 Peter 1:3). When we sing, we are to "sing with the spirit and with the understanding also," and when we pray, we are to "pray with the spirit and with the understanding also" (1 Cor. 14:15). God demands that the worshipper approach him with a sincere heart, offering up "a sacrifice of praise to God, that is the fruit of lips which make confession to his name" (Heb. 13:15). The Lord's supper, prayer, singing, teaching the word, and offering up our material gifts are all acts which are established by divine authority. The Lord's supper is a communion, or fellowship with the body and blood of Christ. It is also to be done in the assembly when saints are gathered together in his name in a spirit of togetherness (Acts 20:7). None of these are rites, but are to be observed with enthusiasm, zeal, and meaning. Devoid of the significance these have to build us up on our most holy faith, they will deteriorate and become meaningless rituals. With consecrated lives of holiness and devotion to God, they become instruments through which we are drawn closer to God in worship to Him through our Lord Jesus Christ.

QUESTIONS

What is meant by ritualism?

What is the difference in the ceremonies of Mosaic worship and the ritualism of Catholicism and Protestantism?

Give two instances when Christian worship can become ritualistic.

Discuss the difference in the New Testament doctrine of the Lord's Supper and the Catholic mass.

How can we avoid empty ritualism in our worship?

41

She teaches men to
GIVE TO GOD AND TO CAESAR

By Bill Burchett

Churches of Christ are careful to stress the Biblical concept of submission to duly constituted authority. Not only is the Christian to submit himself to God, he is to be subject to those agencies which God has authorized and ordained. Only in his submission to these is he showing true submission to God.

The Christian is a citizen of two kingdoms — one earthly and one heavenly. Some would argue that since our citizenship is in heaven (Philippians 3:20), we have no obligation to any earthly government. The apostle Paul, who penned the preceding passage, certainly did not limit his citizenship to heaven. He was a citizen of both Rome (Acts 22:26-29) and the kingdom of our Lord (Colossians 1:13), and obviously did not see an impossible conflict.

An attempt was made to ensnare Jesus on this same subject by the Pharisees (Matthew 22:15-22). Jesus, however, showed that instead of a conflict of duties, there was perfect harmony. He not only escaped the snare, but in his answer, he laid down a law for all time, "Render therefore unto Caesar the things that are Caesar's; and unto God the things that are God's." Christians, disciples of Jesus, those who are obedient to God, should take their stand for law, for loyalty, and for order.

201

GOVERNMENT ORDAINED OF GOD

Both the Old and New Testaments state vividly that earthly rulers have authority from God. "Blessed be the name of God for ever and ever; for wisdom and might are his. And he changeth the times and the seasons; he removeth kings, and setteth up kings" (Daniel 2:20-21). To Nebuchadnezzar the statement is made, ". . . for the God of heaven hath given thee a kingdom, power, and strength, and glory" (Dan. 2:37).

In the New Testament Jesus makes it clear to Pilate, "Thou couldest have no power at all against me, except it were given thee from above" (John 19:11). Paul, an apostle of God and a Roman citizen, writes to the Roman church, "Let every soul be subject unto the higher powers. For there is no power but of God: the powers that be are ordained of God. Whosoever therefore resisteth the power, resisteth the ordinance of God: and they that resist shall receive to themselves damnation" (Romans 13:1-2). In verse 4 of the same passage the apostle twice refers to civil power as "the minister of God," and repeats the thought again at verse 6.

Clearly civil government is ordained of God. Anarchy is not the Father's will for men.

SUBMISSION TO GOVERNMENT

Christians are to be obedient citizens. In fact, of all people, Christians ought to be among the very best citizens. The disciple's relationship to God is the decisive factor in all his other relationships. We are citizens of a heavenly kingdom, but while in the flesh we are citizens of nations as well. God has ordained civil government for these nations, and so we have a duty to Caesar as well as to God. In our relationship and duty to God, we find ourselves with various responsibilities, including submission to civil law.

Early Christians lived under a totalitarian form of government — the Roman dictators. Yet, God's word commanded and encouraged them to be obedient citizens. Paul wrote to the evangelist Titus concerning matters that should be preached to God's people. Among many other things he was to "put them in mind to be subject to principalities and powers, to obey magistrates, . . ." (Titus 3:1).

The apostle Peter likewise stresses the importance of submission. "Submit yourselves to every ordinance of man for the Lord's sake: whether it be to the king, as supreme; or unto governors, as unto them that are sent by him for the punishment of evildoers, and for the praise of them that do well. For so is the will of God . . ." (1 Pet. 2:13-15). In looking again at Romans 13:1-7, we see that Christians are to be in subjection to civil authorities. This is so not merely because of fear of the sword, but also for conscience's sake.

This submission or obedience to government, however, is not without qualification. It is qualified by our duty to God. If there arises a conflict between obedience to God and obedience to civil rulers, we must obey God rather than men (Acts 5:29).

OTHER RESPONSIBILITIES

Jesus, in responding to the Pharisees in Matthew 22:15-22, did not define the specific duties to either Caesar or God, but he left no doubt that we have a debt to both. When government is carrying out its God-ordained responsibilities (Rom. 13:3-4; 1 Pet. 2:14), and when we are receiving the protection of the government as well as the privileges provided, then we are certainly under obligation to support that government.

In addition to civil obedience and submission in general, there are some very specific duties and responsibilities pointed out in the Scriptures. The Christian is to make supplications, prayers, intercessions, and thanksgivings for government leaders (1 Timothy 2:1-4). Further, the Christian supports the government by paying his taxes (Matt. 22:21; Rom. 13:6). It is not ours to refrain from this duty because a government is not perfect, or because there is waste in government, or because we do not agree with all the programs of the government. Neither Jesus nor Paul qualified their tax remarks by such notions. On the other hand, Christians living in a democratic society should certainly participate in the betterment of government as they have opportunity.

Jesus teaches his followers to be attitude-conscious in all their dealings. It isn't surprising then to learn that his apostles encourage the development of a good attitude toward rulers. Christians are to respect and honor their governing authorities (Rom. 13:7; 1 Pet. 2:17).

Among the more controversial areas of responsibility is that of service to one's government. How is one to serve? Where is one to serve? What about the Christian and military service, police work, jury duty, etc.? Can he serve? Must he serve? While each individual should be fully persuaded in his own mind (Rom. 14:23), we do have examples of government service in God's word. The reader is encouraged to study carefully the cases of Erastus (Rom. 16:23), Cornelius (Acts 10 and 11), and the Philippian jailor (Acts 16).

PRIVILEGES AND RIGHTS

The Christian in a democratic society has the great privilege of helping in the formation of good government. He can vote on issues, help elect good officials, and assist in the influencing of proper legislation. To this writer, such should not only be seen as a privilege, but also as a duty.

Since the government is to punish the evil doer (Rom. 13:3-4), the citizen has the privilege of enjoying a sense of security brought about by law and order. While enjoying this privilege, the Christian will do those things which contribute to the preservation of law and order.

Another precious privilege is the right to due process. It is not wrong for the Christian citizen to respectfully demand his rights under the law (Acts 25:6-12).

And, certainly, the Christian can exercise his right to protection (Acts 23:12-35) as well as make his legal defense when accused (Acts 24:10).

IN SUMMARY

Our God does not authorize anarchy and chaos for the inhabitants of this world. It was no accident that Jesus came into the world at a time of strong government. In this world of Roman peace, Roman roads, and Roman law and order, Jesus established his church and sent his disciples into all the world with the gospel. His followers thus became citizens of two kingdoms. Nearly two thousand years have not diminished the truth which Jesus spoke, "Render therefore unto Caesar the things that are Caesar's; and unto God the things that are God's." An obvious separation of church and state, yet a solemn duty to both.

QUESTIONS

What is the importance of authority in our world?

What is the ultimate source of authority? Why?

Discuss the Christian's attitude toward all duly constituted authority.

Did Paul consider his Roman citizenship to be a matter of importance?

What was behind the Pharisees' question to Jesus about taxes?

How is civil government the minister of God?

List some Christian duties to government.

Can a Christian serve as a policeman or a soldier?

Does obedience to civil government have any limitations?

42

The church believes in
A VIRGIN BORN SAVIOR

By Rubel Shelly

C hurches of Christ believe, affirm, and defend the biblical doctrine of the virgin birth of Christ. It is a fundamental teaching of Scripture that the human race was (and is) incapable of saving itself (Ephesians 2:8-9), that the eternal Son of God came among us as a human being for our salvation (Philippians 2:5-11), and that the means of his coming among us was an *incarnation* (i.e., a "becoming-in-flesh") by means of his birth of the virgin Mary (1 Timothy 3:16).

THE DOCTRINE STATED

As one opens a New Testament, he or she cannot get past the first page without confronting the doctrine of the virgin birth. The writer Matthew says: "When his mother Mary had been betrothed to Joseph, before they came together she was *found with child of the Holy Spirit*" (Matthew 1:18). Joseph, perplexed over the fact that his wife-to-be was pregnant, was given this explanation by an angel in a dream: "Joseph, thou son of David, fear not to take unto thee Mary thy wife: for *that which is conceived in her is of the Holy Spirit*" (Matt. 1:20).

Another Gospel writer tells of Mary's pregnancy from her perspective. He tells how the angel Gabriel appeared to her to help prepare this young girl for the great event which would occur in her life. He told her, "And behold, thou shalt conceive in thy womb, and bring forth a son, and shalt call his name Jesus" (Luke 1:31). Startled at such a thing, for she was a virgin, the angel continued: "The Holy Spirit shall come upon thee, and the power of the Most High shall overshadow thee: wherefore also *the holy thing which is begotten shall be called the Son of God*" (Luke 1:35).

All four of the Gospels assume the doctrine of the virgin birth; two of them give details about it. And it is all the more amazing that one of these writers (i.e., Luke) is a physician whose training and experience would incline him to deny the possibility of such a birth. Careful historian that we know Luke to have been, he investigated thoroughly and affirmed without hesitation that Jesus of Nazareth was born of a virgin.

Some seven hundred or more years before the birth of Jesus, the Holy Spirit had moved the prophet Isaiah to foretell the miraculous birth of the Messiah. "Therefore the Lord himself shall give you a sign; *Behold a virgin shall conceive, and bear a son,* and shall call his name Immanuel" (Isaiah 7:14). Skeptics have tried to eliminate the phenomenon of predictive prophecy from the Bible, but this and many other divinely revealed predictions — all of which came to pass — make their efforts futile.

Isaiah predicted the virgin birth, New Testament writers recorded its occurrence, and it stands as a sign from God as to the identity of Jesus of Nazareth as the Son of God and Savior of the world.

THE IMPORTANCE OF THE VIRGIN BIRTH

By means of the virgin birth, *we are able to identify with certainty the Messiah* to whom the entire Old Testament had pointed. Throughout the Law, the Prophets, and the Psalms, the Spirit of God had been giving bits of information about this anticipated Redeemer which would enable people to recognize and believe on him when he appeared. He was to be a descendant of Abraham (Genesis 12:1-3), from the tribe of Judah (Gen. 49:10), and a member of David's family (2 Samuel 7:12-17). His coming was to be announced by a forerunner (Isa. 40:3; Malachi 4:5), and he was to be born in Bethlehem (Micah 5:2). Add to these prophecies and their fulfillments that of the virgin birth, and there is no doubt as to who the Messiah and Redeemer of mankind is.

By means of the incarnation, *we have a mediator* who is able to restore fallen men and women to the fellowship of a holy God. "For there is one God, one mediator also between God and men, himself man, Christ Jesus" (1 Tim. 2:5). His role as mediator depends on his having come in the flesh to share our humanity, but his coming in the flesh was by means of the virgin birth. Thus the virgin birth was an integral part of the redemptive program itself.

DANGERS OF DENYING THIS DOCTRINE

To deny the doctrine of the virgin birth is to deny the trustworthiness of the Bible. It has been demonstrated already that the Bible speaks clearly and forthrightly in claiming a miraculous, virgin birth for Jesus of Nazareth. If that claim is false, by what right do we accept as true any other doctrine about Christ?

A denial of the virgin birth most likely proceeds from a rejection of supernaturalism in general. In other words, one most likely rejects the particular miracle of the virgin birth because he has already rejected the possibility of *all* miracles. But if one rejects miracles in general and the virgin birth in particular, Christianity can never have any place in his life. Belief in Jesus requires belief in the supernatural events involved in his life (John 14:11). If he was not virgin born, bodily raised, and capable of performing signs in his Father's name, there is no good reason for us to regard his teaching as authoritative. Apart from the miracles in his life, he is just another moral philosopher or religious teacher.

Finally, to deny the virgin birth is to deny that we have a Savior. The virgin birth identifies Jesus as the promised Old Testament Redeemer and demonstrates his qualification to mediate between God and humanity. Without that identifying mark, we have no good reason to believe that he is the one whom heaven has provided to save mankind.

CONCLUSION

I appeal with you to believe on Jesus Christ as the Son

of God (John 8:24), to confess that faith from a penitent and sincere heart (Romans 10:10), and to identify yourself with his saving death, burial, and resurrection in the beautiful act of baptism (Rom. 6:3-4).

His incarnation by means of the virgin birth is in vain for you, unless you allow him to save you from your sin.

QUESTIONS

What is the meaning of the term "incarnation"?

Which Gospel writers devote the greatest amount of attention to the virgin birth?

Discuss Isaiah 7:14. Why have skeptics attacked this verse with such enthusiasm?

Why is the doctrine of the virgin birth so crucial?

What is at stake for the person who denies this doctrine of the Christian faith?

43

She preaches
THE DEITY OF JESUS

By Hugo McCord

The Bible church, being the "pillar and ground of the truth" (1 Timothy 3:15), is founded on him who is the truth, Jesus Christ (John 14:6). "Other foundation can no man lay than that which is laid, which is Jesus Christ" (1 Corinthians 3:11). "Upon this rock ['Thou art the Christ, the Son of the living God']," said Jesus, "I will build my church; and the gates of Hades shall not prevail against it" (Matthew 16:13-19). Peter, the apostle who made the good confession, "Thou art the Christ, the Son of the living God," if living today, would be embarrassed that some have said the rock on which the church was built was himself. Peter wrote that an Old Testament prediction, "Behold, I lay in Zion a chief corner stone, elect, precious" (Isaiah 28:16), was fulfilled, not in Simon Peter, but in Jesus Christ (1 Peter 2:6). The church today then that is truly Christ's church gives to him the preeminence in all things (Colossians 1:18). Only because he has all authority in heaven and on earth (Matthew 28:18) will he be able to save his church, his body, in heaven (Ephesians 5:23).

The non-human origin of Jesus is seen when we take a close look at the kind of person he was. With hardly an exception, both believers and unbelievers unite in joyful praise and in warm admiration for the person of Jesus.

A DESCRIPTION

Keeping youthful desires under control, Jesus as a lad

was turned toward religion. Though he knew he was the Son of God, he subjected himself as a youth to his earthly parents. Though he knew he would be a preacher, yet he learned hard physical work. Though not a husband, yet he respected wives and mothers. Though not a father, yet he loved little children. Though authoritative, yet he was meek and lowly. Though unschooled, yet he was the master teacher. Tired and hungry, yet consumed with soul-saving, he forgot his own needs. Obsessed by justice, he refused to embarrass a sinful penitent and instead rebuked her persecutors. Free from race prejudice, he was a friend of the hated Samaritans. Free from the love of money, owning not a pillow, he was content to be rich in good works. Free from worldly ambition, he rejected attempts to make him an earthly king. Free from selfishness, he worked early and late, going about doing good. Free from self-righteousness, he was a friend of sinners. Having respect for things sacred, he forcibly removed commercialism and thievery from the temple of God.

Jesus exposed the self-righteousness of a religious sect called the Pharisees. An acid tongue had he for duplicity, but toward penitence, he was gentle and easy to approach. Loving the unfortunate, even at the expense of his popularity, he helped those in need. Moved with compassion, multitudes of hungry people he fed. Grieved at death, and weeping, he comforted the broken-hearted.

Born in a stable to humble parents, never did he get above the common people. He washed feet, and plain men and women were comfortable in his presence. He had no quirks, no one-sided views on any subject. Devout exceedingly, yet he was no ascetic. His overall perspective was not of this world, yet he concentrated on his work in this world. He was a balanced, whole person. Perfectly he was able to combine piety and philanthropy.

Never hesitant, never making a mistake, he was in charge of every situation. Completely self-possessed, yet free of self-sufficiency, he obtained strength to help in time of need through private devotionals with his Father. Making the Father's will his will, unveeringly he denied himself to bless humanity. Loving his enemies, free from resentment, he excused his murderers and prayed for them. Loving his neighbor more than he loved himself, he won the benediction of his Father and the gratitude of sinners.

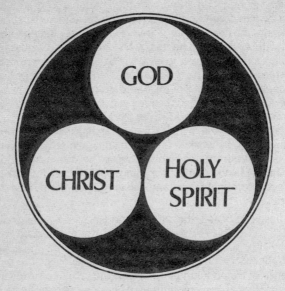

If Jesus had not claimed deity, his character would have claimed it for him. No mere human has approached the measure of the stature of the fulness of Christ Jesus. Eyewitnesses said they beheld his glory, the glory as of the only one of his nature, full of grace and truth. If he was not divine, his character remains forever unexplainable.

INSANITY OR DEPRAVITY OR DEITY

A contradiction ensues if one ascribes goodness to Jesus and yet withholds deity. A good man does not deceive. Jesus claimed deity and so convinced myriads that they committed their all to his leadership. If he is not divine, he is not a blessing. The world's greatest hoax he becomes, and the world's meanest man. Ingratiating himself, promising life abundant here and beyond the grave, yet unable to carry through, this man was a malevolent weakling. If he was sane, which is unquestioned, then if not God he was not good.

Inconsistent are the Unitarians, who admire Jesus as a man but refuse to recognize his deity. The Jehovah's Witnesses make Jesus more than a man, but withhold his equality with the Father (Philippians 2:6). The Scripture asserts that in him "dwells all the fulness of the Godhead bodily" (Col. 2:9). He lacks nothing, being the very image of the Father's substance (Hebrews 1:3). It is no wonder that Thomas exclaimed to Jesus, "My Lord and my God" (John 20:28).

JESUS UNINVENTABLE

The story of Jesus could not be fictional. If it were, then how the gospel writers came to conspire on that fiction, and where they obtained their idea about such a person, are both unexplainable. Their invention of such a person is unimaginable and becomes in itself a miracle.

---

* A large portion of this article is taken from Chapter VI of the author's book, *From Heaven or From Men?*, published by the Firm Foundation Publishing House, Austin, Texas.

QUESTIONS

Who is the foundation of the church?

What do we mean in saying Jesus is divine?

What is the definition of "deity"?

Discuss some of the evidences of Jesus' divinity.

Is it correct for us to call Jesus God?

What would be the consequences if Jesus were not divine?

44

She believes in
AN INSPIRED BIBLE

By Arlie Hoover

The question, "Why call ye me, Lord, Lord, and do not the things which I say?" is found in Luke 6:46. When Jesus asked this question he was criticizing those people, then and now, who try to make a false distinction between his *person* and his *word*. Some folks say, "I believe in Jesus so what does it really matter what I think about the Bible?"

But it does matter, say the Churches of Christ. It matters greatly what you believe about the Bible! Jesus himself will not let you make this false distinction between his person and his word. He often quoted the Scriptures as originating with God the Father (Matthew 19:4-5). When the Pharisees tried to replace God's commandment in the Law of Moses with their own tradition, he accused them of making void the word of God (Mark 7:13).

Jesus' strongest statement about the complete trustworthiness of the Bible is John 10:35. In a discussion over his divinity he cited Psalm 82:6 and then appended the fateful words, "The Scripture cannot be broken." Since Scripture cannot be broken, an appeal to Scripture is final; it can't be challenged or disproved or denied.

Christ's high view of the Bible comes out clearly in his constant references to the events in the Old Testament. He always treated them as true, actual, and historically reliable. He mentions, for example, the creation, the flood, the lives of Abraham, Isaac, Jacob, and David, the destruction of Sodom, the ordeal of Jonah, and many other episodes.

He never used these Old Testament stories as if they were myths or legends. On the contrary, their authenticity was essential to the point he was making. If Adam didn't really exist, then Christ's teaching on marriage falls to the ground (Matt. 19:4-6). If David didn't really eat the shewbread, then Jesus' defense of his own similar action is left limping (Matt. 12:1-4). If Jonah didn't really preach and Ninevah really repent, then Christ looks like a fool using this as an illustration of his own coming (Matt. 12:41). Those who have a low view of the Bible make our Lord look naive.

When we refer to the Bible as the inspired Word of God, therefore, it does not at all take away from Jesus' glory as the living, incarnate Word. In like manner, to call Jesus the Word of God does not at all turn the Bible into an inferior book. *Both* Jesus and the Bible are the Word of God! Jesus is the *personal* Word of God and the Bible is the *written* Word of God.

What do we mean when we say the Bible is the inspired Word of God? We mean simply that *God controlled the production of his word.* The job was not farmed out to subordinates. We mean that the writers of the Bible had special supernatural supervision when they penned the words of God. We mean that the Holy Spirit preserved them from all kinds of errors, errors of fact, errors of doctrine, and errors of judgment. We mean that the Holy Spirit even influenced their choice of language so that the words they used were the very words of God (1 Corinthians 2:13).

We take our stand, in sum, with all those conservative groups who affirm belief in *plenary verbal inspiration.*

Peter expressed it well: "No prophecy of Scripture is a matter of one's own interpretation, for no prophecy was ever made by an act of human will, but men moved by the Holy Spirit spoke from God" (2 Pet. 1:20-21 NIV). The literal meaning of the word "moved" in this passage is "carried along," as an ocean current might carry a ship through the water. Peter is saying that though humans were the necessary instruments of revelation, God himself is the ultimate source.

Paul told Timothy that "All Scripture is inspired by God" (2 Timothy 3:16). The phrase "inspired by God" translates a single Greek word, *theopneustos*, which literally means "breathed out by God." All Scripture is "God-breathed," exhaled by the Almighty! Few passages more clearly affirm the divine origin of the Bible.

One must not assume that our belief in plenary, verbal inspiration leads to a "dictation theory," whereby the Spirit of God used the Bible writers as one might use a tape recorder. Such a view would make the Bible writers into passive tools or robots. If the Scriptures were dictated in this way it would be difficult to explain passages like Luke 1:1-4 where Luke explains his dependence on sources. There is no contradiction between the personal research of the writer and the guidance of the Holy Spirit.

We actually know very little about the precise *method* of inspiration. How God did it is not explained in the Bible. The product, not the process, is what is important. However God did it, the result is His Word. What got written down was what He wanted written down.

The Bible, then, is our authority precisely because it is not the word of man but of God, the completely dependable Word of God, the Word of truth (John 17:17). Anyone who says "Jesus is Lord" and yet belittles the Word of God is inconsistent and hypocritical. We can demonstrate our submission to Christ's lordship only by our absolute, unconditional surrender to the teachings of His Word.

QUESTIONS

Study the context of John 10:35. Identify the precise issue in the argument between Jesus and the Jews. How did Jesus' use of Psalm 82:6 settle the issue?

Did Jesus accept the historical accuracy of the Old Testament? Illustrate your answer.

What is meant by "plenary, verbal inspiration"?

Discuss the meaning and the implications of *theopneustos* in 2 Timothy 3:16.

Criticize the "dictation theory" of inspiration. Is it required by the doctrine of plenary, verbal inspiration? Explain.

What are the dangers of a low view of the Bible?

45

She is saved by
THE BLOOD OF JESUS

By Basil Overton

T he apostle Peter wrote the following to Christians to encourage them as they were faced with persecution and suffering. "Forasmuch as ye know ye were not redeemed with corruptible things, as silver and gold, from your vain conversation received by tradition from your fathers; but with the precious blood of Christ, as a lamb without blemish and without spot" (1 Peter 1:18-19).

We think of silver and gold as being incorruptible, and we know blood is corruptible. But, Peter said silver and gold are corruptible, and he said the blood of Christ is incorruptible. Does this mean that the blood that was in the body of Jesus was not corruptible? If one had the literal blood of Jesus in a container, he would not be any better off as far as his being saved from his sins is concerned. How then is the blood of Christ incorruptible? How are we redeemed by it?

SIGNIFICANCE OF BLOOD IN THE BIBLE

Under the law of Moses, God forbade the eating of blood. He gave as the reason: "For the life of the flesh is in the blood: and I have given it to you upon the altar to make an atonement for your souls: for it is the blood that maketh an atonement for the soul" (Leviticus 17:11). "For it is the life of all flesh; the blood of it is for the life thereof; therefore I said unto the children of Israel, ye shall eat the blood of no manner of flesh: for the life of all flesh is the blood thereof: whosoever eateth it shall be cut off" (Lev. 17:14).

The Bible not only stresses that physical life is in blood, it also teaches that spiritual life is signified by blood. "When I say unto the wicked, Thou shalt surely die; and thou givest him not warning, nor speakest to warn the wicked from his wicked way, to save his life; the same wicked man shall die in his iniquity; but his blood will I require at thine hand" (Ezekiel 3:18). In telling Ezekiel this, God equated "his life" with "his blood" in referring to a wicked man. This means that if Ezekiel failed to warn a wicked man, God held Ezekiel responsible for the man's being lost or dying in his iniquity. Ezekiel was responsible for the man's spiritual life, and in the text the blood of the wicked man stood for his spiritual life.

When Judas took the thirty pieces of silver back to those who gave them to him for betraying Jesus, he said, "I have sinned in that I have betrayed the innocent blood" (Matthew 27:4). This means that Judas realized he had betrayed a man whose life was pure and sinless. "Innocent blood" means innocent life.

"When Pilate saw that he could prevail nothing, but rather a tumult was made, he took water and washed his hands before the multitude saying, 'I am innocent of the blood of this just person: see ye to it.' Then answered all the people, and said, His blood be on us and on our children" (Matt. 27:24-25). Pilate was trying to escape the responsibility of causing Jesus to lose his life, so he said he was innocent of the blood of Jesus. He was saying he was responsible for the taking of the life of Jesus. The crowd responded to Pilate and said they would take the responsibility for taking the life of Jesus, or they were willing to have his blood on them and their children.

Later the Jews did not like it because they sensed that the apostles intended to bring the blood of Jesus upon them (Acts 5:28). The apostles were also trying to bring the blood of Jesus upon those Jews, to have it applied to them in a spiritual sense so they could be saved from their sins.

219

WHY CAN JESUS' BLOOD SAVE ALL?

Just how precious is the blood of Christ? Why is it that his precious blood can save all sinners? As the song says, "There is power in the blood." How can there be so much power in the blood of Jesus? "In whom we have redemption through his blood, the forgiveness of sins, according to the riches of his grace" (Ephesians 1:7).

The reason the blood of Jesus is so powerful and can save all people from their sins is because his life was so much greater than ours. He did not sin! (1 Pet. 2:22-25). Even Judas acknowledged Jesus was guiltless. Judas did not say, "I have sinned, but Jesus did some things wrong too." Judas knew Jesus was sinless! Even Pilate, who desperately sought something wrong with Jesus, found no fault in him (Luke 23:14).

Paul declared that God has "set forth Jesus to be a propitiation through faith in his blood, to declare his righteousness for the remission of sins that are past through the forebearance of God; to declare, I say, at this time his righteousness: that he might be just and the justifier of him that believeth in Jesus" (Rom. 3:25-26).

Usually, in the letter Paul wrote to the church in Rome, God's righteousness refers to the standard of instruction to which we are to be slaves, and to which we are to submit (Rom. 6:16-18; 10:1-3). But in Romans 3:25-26 Paul stresses that he refers to the personal holiness and sinlessness of Jesus, or as he says "I say at this time his righteousness." This is the reason we can have faith in his blood. We can have faith in the blood of Jesus because his life was perfect. The only reason the death of Jesus is significant is because of the perfect life he lived. His blood stands for his life. This is the sense in which his blood is incorruptible.

OUR RELATIONSHIP TO THE BLOOD

We do not relate to the blood of Christ in some mystical manner. What the New Testament says about how we relate to his blood is very practical.

1. Some say it does not matter about the doctrine one believes as long as he accepts the blood of Jesus. How-

ever, the New Testament makes it clear we must accept the covenant of Christ in order to have the benefits of the blood of Christ. To accept the covenant, or testament of Christ, one must believe the doctrine in it.

When Jesus instituted the Lord's supper he said of the fruit of the vine, "For this is my blood of the New Testament which is shed for many for the remission of sins" (Matt. 26:28).

The blood of Jesus is not merely blood, but it is "the blood of the covenant" (Hebrews 10:29; 13:20). If what we believe and practice in religion is not in the covenant of Christ, or if it is not authorized by Christ in the New Testament, it is not under the blood of Christ and is therefore wrong.

2. Some have the notion that the Lord's supper is of relatively little importance compared to the blood of Christ. One man told me, "I will have you know I have been a Christian fifty years and I have never eaten the Lord's supper." One cannot have the benefits of the blood of Christ if he ignores or neglects the Lord's supper and does not eat at the Lord's table upon the first day of the week. The blood of Christ is symbolized on the Lord's table by the fruit of the vine. When we eat at the Lord's table we remember Jesus. He said concerning our eating at his table, "Do this in remembrance of me." Surely we remember his death, but his death means nothing without his perfect life, so we remember him; we remember his perfect life. When we neglect the Lord's supper we show how little we think of the blood of Jesus. When we show how little we think of the blood of Jesus, we show how little we think of his life, and how little we think of him.

3. Others think that it does not matter whether one is in the church or not as long as he believes in the blood of Christ. However, the church we read about in the Bible, the Lord's church, was purchased by his blood (Acts 20:28). One cannot be saved out of that which was purchased by the blood of Christ who gave himself for the church (Eph. 5:25). In the New Testament "the church" means "the saved." One can no more be saved out of

221

that church than he can be saved out of the saved. Instead of looking for a church that suits him, one should look in the New Testament and see what church the Lord wants him to be in. Redemption by the blood of Jesus is in Christ (Eph. 1:7). To be in Christ is the same as being in his body which is the church (Col. 1:2; 3:15; 1:18). Therefore, salvation by the blood of Jesus is in his church.

4. After showing from Acts 2:38 that baptism is for the remission of sins, a woman said to me, "Preacher, I do not see how baptism could be for remission of sins because the Bible says the blood of Christ was shed for the remission of sins." But on Pentecost, Peter told those who believed what he had said about Jesus, to repent and be baptized in the name of Jesus Christ for the remission of sins (Acts 2:38). So there has to be some sense in which Jesus shed his blood for the remission of sins, and also some sense in which baptism is for the remission of sins.

I explained it to the lady and her son and daughter-in-law as follows: The blood of Jesus was shed for the remission of sins in the sense that by Jesus giving his life for us, he made remission of sins available for all the lost. Why are not all the lost saved? Because not all the lost accept or acquire what Jesus made available by shedding his blood. One acquires what Jesus made available on Calvary's cross when he believes in him and trusts him by repenting of his sins, and confessing him as the Son of God, and by being baptized into him for the remission of his sins. Baptism is for the remission of sins in the sense that when one is baptized by the authority of Jesus, or in his name, he is baptized into Christ and into his death, and thus acquires what the Lord made available when he shed his blood (Rom. 6:3). Being baptized one gets into the spiritual relationship called in the New Testament "in Christ," or in the church, where the blood of Christ saves.

QUESTIONS

In Scripture the word "blood" often stands for _____ ?
Why is Jesus' blood so precious?

Discuss the relationship of Jesus' blood and the New Testament.

What is the purpose and value of the Lord's Supper?

What was the price paid for the church?

How does water baptism relate to Christ's blood?

46

The church contends that
GOD'S KINGDOM WAS ESTABLISHED ON PENTECOST, 33 A.D.

By M. H. Tucker

A long with redemption in Christ, the kingdom is the foremost theme in the Bible. These two are so interrelated that to misunderstand them is to misunderstand much of the Bible.

Many fanciful theories on the kingdom of God have been worked out by men which only obscure the real nature of the kingdom. One of the more prominent theories affirms that the kingdom has not been established, but will be set up when Christ returns. At that time, they say, Christ will rule on a literal throne in Jerusalem for one thousand years. Furthermore, this view states that the kingdom and the church are not the same institution; that the church was something added as an afterthought because the kingdom was rejected when Christ tried to establish it during his first advent. This theory is commonly known as premillennialism.

THE KINGDOM AND THE CHURCH

The kingdom and the church are the same institution. The two words express different aspects of that institution just as the words "body" (Ephesians 1:22-23) and "house" (1 Timothy 3:15) express different aspects of the church. The following considerations show that the kingdom and the church are the same.

(1) *Jesus used the words interchangeably.* In Matthew 16:18 he said, "I will build my church." In the same breath he said, "I will give unto thee the keys of the kingdom" (Matt. 16:19). If the two are not the same, Christ built one thing, but gave Peter the keys to another thing. If the kingdom has not been established, Peter and the other apostles have never used the keys, and one may wonder why they were given to them?

(2) *The Lord's supper was to be in the kingdom.* When Christ instituted the Lord's supper he said, "I appoint unto you a kingdom as my Father hath appointed unto me; that ye may eat and drink at my table in my kingdom" (Luke 22:29-30). However, the Lord's supper was observed in the church in Corinth (1 Corinthians 11:17-30), and in the church in Troas (Acts 20:7). Since the Lord's supper which was to be in the kingdom was observed in the church, the kingdom and the church must be the same.

(3) *The seed produces subjects of the kingdom and members of the church.* In the parable of the sower, Jesus called the word of God the "word of the kingdom" (Matt. 13:19). In Luke 8:11 the word of God is called the "seed". When the seed or the word of the kingdom was received into honest hearts it produced subjects of the kingdom. However, when the same seed was received by the Corinthians it produced members of the church. "Many of the Corinthians hearing believed and were baptized" (Acts 18:8). Later, when Paul wrote to these Christians he called them the "church of God which is at Corinth" (1 Cor. 1:2). God decreed that seed is to bring forth after its kind (Genesis 1:11). Since the word of God, the seed, produces subjects of the kingdom and members of the church, and since seed will produce the same product, it follows that to be a member of the church is to be a subject of the kingdom.

(4) *After Pentecost of 33 A.D., both the kingdom and the church are spoken of as a present reality.* Acts 2 is the pivotal point of Bible history. Recorded in this chapter are the events of the first Pentecost following the resurrection of Christ. Prior to this chapter the kingdom and the church are spoken of as future. Earlier Christ

said, "I will build my church" (Matt. 16:18). In the last verse of Acts 2 we learn that "the Lord added to the church daily such as should be saved" (verse 47).

In like manner, the kingdom was not a reality before Acts 2; it existed only in promise and prophecy. John preached, "the kingdom is at hand" (Matt. 3:1-2). Jesus preached, "The time is fulfilled, and the kingdom of God is at hand" (Mark 1:15). Furthermore, he said, "There be some of them that stand here, which shall not taste of death, till they have seen the kingdom of God come with power" (Mark 9:1). After Acts 2 the kingdom is said to be in existence. Members of the church at Colossae were in the kingdom. Paul said, "Who hath delivered us from the power of darkness, and hath translated us into the kingdom of his dear Son" (Col. 1:13). John said that he was in the kingdom (Revelation 1:9).

The above evidence clearly demonstrates that the church and the kingdom are the same. If one has been in existence since 33 A.D., the other has been in existence since then.

CHRIST IS NOW REIGNING

As previously stated, premillennialism teaches that the kingdom was offered to the Jews at his first advent but it was rejected. Therefore, the offer was withdrawn and the kingdom is held in abeyance until his second advent. At that time he will begin reigning on a literal throne in Jerusalem. That the above is false and that Christ is now reigning as King of Kings may be seen from the following considerations.

(1) *Christ cannot reign on earth.* An Old Testament prophecy states that no seed (descendant) of Coniah (Jeconiah) "shall prosper, sitting upon the throne of David, and ruling anymore in Judah" (Jeremiah 22:30). The genealogy of Christ in Matthew, chapter 1 lists Christ as a descendant of Jeconiah (Matt. 1:12). Since Christ is the seed of Coniah and since no seed of his can reign on David's throne on earth, it follows that Christ cannot reign on David's throne on earth. This does not forbid Christ from reigning on David's throne; it only forbids him from reigning on David's throne *on earth.*

In Luke 1:32-33 we learn that "the Lord God shall give unto him the throne of his father David . . ." Christ now reigns *from heaven*.

(2) Christ began reigning after his ascension. On Pentecost in 33 A.D. Peter affirms that the prophecy of David concerning one who would sit on his throne was fulfilled in Christ's resurrection. "Being therefore a prophet, and knowing that God had sworn with an oath to him, that of the fruit of his loins, according to the flesh, he would raise up Christ to sit on his throne; he seeing this before spoke of the resurrection of Christ . . ." (Acts 20:30-31).

(3) Christ will cease to reign when the end comes. Contrary to premillennialism, which affirms that Christ will *begin* to reign when he returns, the Bible teaches that he will *cease* to reign when he returns. "Then cometh the end, when he shall have delivered up the kingdom to God, even the Father; when he shall have put down all rule and all authority and power. For he must reign, till he hath put all things under his feet. The last enemy that shall be destroyed is death" (1 Cor. 15:24-26).

The kingdom of God is almost 2,000 years old. As king, Christ rules its subjects. The church of Christ is 2,000 years old; as head, Christ directs its members. Thanks be to God the kingdom shall stand forever (Daniel 2:44) and "the gates of Hades" will not prevail against the church (Matt. 16:18).

QUESTIONS

Describe the doctrine of premillennialism.

Discuss the idea that Acts 2 is the pivotal point of the Bible.

In addition to the word "church", what other terms describe the kingdom?

Give the date, geographicl location and the Bible chapter which tells of the beginning of the church.

Name two things that will take place when "the end comes."

47

She Affirms
SALVATION BY FAITH BUT NOT BY FAITH ONLY

By Batsell Barrett Baxter

Salvation is by God's grace. It is a gift from God, motivated by his love for us, and is provided through Jesus Christ. Grace means "unmerited favor." Salvation is an unearned, undeserved blessing, offered freely to all mankind, and made possible by the sacrificial death of Christ on the cross. In short, there was no way that man, the sinner, could earn or merit salvation, so God provided it for him as a gift. This is the Good News of the Gospel.

One of the clearest statements of this theme is from the pen of the apostle Paul in Ephesians 2:8-9, where he said, "For by grace have ye been saved through faith; and that not of yourselves, it is the gift of God; not of works, that no man should glory." This passage emphasizes that salvation is God's gift — a matter of grace. It would be impossible to overemphasize the fact that salvation is a gift from God — a matter of grace.

SALVATION BY FAITH

In Ephesians 2:8-9, mentioned above, there are several key words, two of which stand out. The first is *grace*, the unmerited favor of God which provides salvation as a gift for all men. The second key word is *faith*, which is man's response to God's free gift. Salvation is by grace — on God's side; and by faith — on man's side.

Now it becomes very important for us to understand what faith means. Exactly what is meant by faith? Many people define faith as a mental acceptance of certain facts. That is *historical faith* and we have historical faith about many things. We believe, for example, that certain cities exist and that certain people have lived though we have neither seen the cities nor known the people. That kind of faith, however, is not sufficient to save a man. The devils believe and shudder (James 2:19), but they will not be saved. *Saving faith* is something beyond the mental acceptance of the existence of God and of Christ. It is that, but it is more.

The theme of the book of Romans is "salvation by faith." When we study Romans we discover that faith meant, to the apostle Paul, a mental acceptance of the existence of God and Christ, plus an active commitment of his life. When a man has faith he not only believes, but also invests himself in Christ. The clearest way to convey Paul's meaning is to read a phrase from the opening sentence of Romans and another from the closing sentence. In the opening sentence we find the expression "unto obedience of faith" (Romans 1:5). Paul emphasized faith throughout the sixteen chapters which make up the book. *It is obedient faith — faith which includes within itself obedience to God's will.* When we come to the end of the book we find that Paul used the same expression, "Unto obedience of faith" (Romans 16:26). We are saved by grace, to which we must respond in obedient faith (Rom. 16:26). Grace is God's part and faith is our part. Faith, in order to be saving faith, includes within itself the obedience which God asks of us.

We are disturbed by those whose interpretation of faith leads them to preach, in many pulpits across the land and on many radio and television programs, that all one must do in order to be saved is to believe in one's heart. The emphasis often made is that whenever a person believes in the Lord and mentally commits himself to the Lord, he is immediately saved. Sometimes this is called "being born again," and is described as having happened while riding on an airplane, or on one's knees in prayer, or while facing some special trial of life. This interpretation of faith, commonly held by many people, is not the interpretation of faith reflected in the pages of the inspired Scriptures. Biblical faith is an obedient faith.

GRACE AND FAITH

What is the relation of grace and faith? "For God so loved the world, that he gave his only begotten Son, that whosoever believeth on him should not perish but have eternal life" (John 3:16). Both elements are in this passage — God's gift and man's response. Later in that same chapter there is this additional sentence, "He that believeth on the Son hath eternal life; but he that obeyeth not the Son shall not see life, but the wrath of God abideth on him" (John 3;36). In this sentence, believing is the positive side, while its opposite is disobedience, the negative side.

Salvation is God's gift; there can be no question about that. But, the gift must be appropriated by man's response in obedient faith. Grace makes salvation possible; obedient faith makes salvation actual. When man responds in Biblical faith to God's offer of salvation, he is neither earning nor deserving the gift, but only accepting it on the condition on which the Lord has promised to give it.

In this connection let us also read 2 Thessalonians 1:7-9: ". . . To you that are afflicted rest with us, at the revelation of the Lord Jesus from heaven with the angels of his power in flaming fire, rendering vengeance to them that know not God, and to them that obey not the gospel of our Lord Jesus: who shall suffer punishment, even eternal destruction from the face of the Lord and from the glory of his might." Notice that the vengeance of the Lord at the time of judgment will be rendered against: (1) Those that know not God, and (2) Those that obey not the gospel. These passages obviously indicate that obedience to the commands of God is imperative if one expects to be saved eternally.

Do not misunderstand this emphasis upon obedience. We do not *earn* salvation, but we must comply with the *conditions* laid down by the Lord in order to receive the free gift of eternal salvation. Christ said, "Even so ye also when ye shall have done all the things that are commanded you, say, We are unprofitable servants; we have done that which it was our duty to do" (Luke 17:10). Man cannot earn salvation through works of merit, but he must comply with the conditions that the Lord laid down in order to receive the gift of salvation.

NEW TESTAMENT EXAMPLES OF CONVERSION

In the book of Acts there are eight major conversions, given as models for all people of all time. In every case the gospel of Christ was preached, the people believed in their hearts, but they did not stop there. Their faith led them to make known their faith in some manner (confessing Christ as their Savior) and then they were baptized for the forgiveness of sins.

As an example, let's notice the beginning of the church on Pentecost, at which time 3,000 were saved. It all began with the preaching of a great sermon concerning Christ by the apostle Peter. Then we read, "Now when they heard this, they were pricked in their heart, and said unto Peter and the rest of the apostles, Brethren, what shall we do? And Peter said unto them, Repent ye, and be baptized every one of you in the name of Jesus Christ unto the remission of your sins; and ye shall receive the gift of the Holy Spirit . . . And with many other words he testified, and exhorted them, saying, Save yourselves from this crooked generation. They then that received his word were baptized: and there were added unto them in that day about 3,000 souls" (Acts 2:37-38; 40-41). Obedient faith is demonstrated very clearly in this example: They heard the gospel of Christ, they believed it, at which point they asked what they must then do. Peter told them to repent of their sins and to be baptized. When they had made their faith in Christ actual by obeying the conditions upon which salvation is given, the Scripture then tells us that they were added to the church or family of God. The same pattern is found in each of the other stories of conversion.

We are saved by grace — on God's side; we are saved

by faith — on man's side. But Biblical faith is more than mere belief. It is more than an intellectual commitment. It involves obedience: confession of Christ before men (Matthew 10:32-33), repentance for our sins (Luke 13:3), and baptism for the forgiveness of our sins (Acts 2:38).

QUESTIONS

In your own words, explain the meaning of "salvation by grace."

Since God loves all people, and since God's grace is extended to all people, does this mean that all will be saved?

Does "Biblical faith" include only the idea of believing that Jesus is the Son of God? Is salvation provided when one believes intellectually that Jesus is the Savior?

What are the "conditions of pardon" which the New Testament teaches?

Exactly, at what point does salvation come — When Christ died on the cross? When man believes that Jesus is his Savior? When man responds in obedient faith?

48

Christ's Church is
ESSENTIAL TO SALVATION

By Doyle Crawford

These words of Jesus, "I will build my church and the gates of Hades shall not prevail against it" (Matthew 16:18), reveal his determination to establish his church. Such determination shows he deemed the church important.

The word "Hades ("Hell" in the King James Version) in the Bible means, according to Webster, "The state or resting place of the dead."[1] Jesus died on the cross of Calvary (Luke 23:46) and entered the state of the dead. However, Peter affirmed in Acts 2:27ff that his soul was not left in that state. He was raised (Acts 2:32). Not even death itself could keep Jesus' soul nor prevent his building his church.

THE WORD "CHURCH"

A noted scholar of the language of the New Testament has remarked that the word "Church" (Greek — "ekklesia") meant: "(a) An assembly of Christians gathered for worship . . . (b) A company of Christians . . ."[2] in its Christian usage.

It is apparent that Christ built a company of Christians. Such would convey the idea of building of which Jesus spoke. It would be more natural to speak of building together people in a company than an assembly. Anywhere people follow the teaching of Jesus' New Covenant faithfully, they are recognized as the church of Christ.

233

PURCHASED BY BLOOD OF CHRIST

Paul, the apostle, conversed with the elders of the church from Ephesus and encouraged them in their responsibility to the church (Acts 20:17-28). He reminded them of the importance of this group and their duty. He declared the church to be that which Christ "purchased with his own blood" (Acts 20:28). To neglect their work in the Lord's church would have been to neglect that for which Christ died.

Jesus has not lessened the importance of this company for which his blood was shed. To neglect our duty to the church today is to abandon responsibility to the body for which Christ's blood was shed. I appeal to reason. Can one forsake such important duty and remain pleasing to God? Can one declare the church nonessential and refuse to be a part of it and yet obtain divine approval?

CHRIST, THE SAVIOR OF THE CHURCH

Ephesians 5:22-33 contains a beautiful analogy between the husband-wife relationship and the Christ-church relationship. Verse 23 states, "For the husband is the head of the wife, as Christ also is the head of the church, being himself the savior of the body." The apostle reasons that husbands and wives should imitate the relationship of Christ and the church.

Note that Christ is, "the savior of the body." The point was clear to first century Christians. They knew the church was the object of our Lord's continued grace. The apostle does not labor to prove the point. He uses what Christians already knew to be true to teach vital lessons on marriage.

Paul, the writer of Ephesians, knew of no other company or persons who had this special relationship with Jesus. Salvation was the blessing of the faithful in the church body. Can one leave the church and still enjoy salvation? How could that be when the church is that group of people being redeemed by Christ?

THE CHURCH IS GOD'S FAMILY

Paul wrote to Timothy that he might know, "How men

234

ought to behave themselves in the house of God, which is the church of the living God . . ." (1 Timothy 3:15). The word house is often used in the Scriptures to denote a household or family (cf. Acts 11:14; 2 Tim. 1:16). God's family is therefore also known as the church.

CHILDREN BY FAITH

Galatians 3:26 tells us that we become members of God's family by becoming his children through faith. The next verse tells us how that faith operates to make us family members. It says, "For as many of you as were baptized into Christ did put on Christ" (Gal. 3:27). When one by faith in Jesus is baptized into a proper relationship with him, one becomes a member of God's family, the church.

A TEST CASE

"And the Lord added to them day by day those who were saved" (Acts 2:47b). This was the account of many Christian converts after the Lord's ascension back into heaven. What was this group called that had converts being added to it day by day? Acts 4:23 refers to these people as a "company." These same people are called, "the church" (Acts 5:11; 8:2). How were these people added to the church? They received the word gladly and were baptized (Acts 2:41). Having obtained forgiveness, they were now sons of God, members of the family or church of God.

WHAT MEN SAY OR WHAT CHRIST SAYS

Man's response to the concept of the church varies. Some say it has no significance and no right to exist. Others say it is good but, other organizations are just as good. Some believe it is imperative to have a church yet, believe one is as good as another.

Jesus once came to his disciples and asked them, "Who do men say the Son of man is" (Matt. 16:13). After they had related the opinions that many held he asked, "But who say ye that I am" (verse 15). Peter replied that he was the Christ, the Son of the living God (verse 16). Jesus then commended him for believing the testimony of God rather than the opinions of men.

The facts about the church are much like the idea as to the person of Jesus. Men have many opinions. But, God has a revealed will about the church in the Scripture. What will you believe concerning the church? Will you believe men or God?

---

1 *Webster's New World Dictionary of the American Language*, College Edition, (Cleveland and New York: The World Publishing Company, 1960) p. 650.

2 Joseph Thayer, Greek-English Lexicon of the New Testament, (Grand Rapids: Baker Book House, 1977), p. 196.

QUESTIONS

The word "church" refers to both a _____ of Christians gathered for worship or a _____ of Christians.

According to Acts 20:28, what did Jesus purchase with his own blood?

Who is the head of the church (Ephesians 5:23)?

In the New Testament, when people were saved, they were added to a company known as the _____ .

Can one refuse participation in and duty to the church of our Lord and still be pleasing to God?

49

In her faith and practice
NO TRADITION OF MAN IS ACCEPTED AS BINDING

By J. A. McNutt

The original meaning of the word "tradition" has to do with delivering something into the hands of another. In a religious sense it would refer to the delivery of opinions, doctrines, practices, rites and customs from generation to generation by oral communication. The Jewish nation subscribes to an unwritten code of laws said to have been given to Moses, but handed down by word of mouth from one generation to another by the rabbis, but not recorded in the Old Testament. Among the Moslems it would cover the sayings and acts attributed to Mohammed, which were not recorded in the Koran. Other religious bodies today have a mass of traditional teachings and practices which they have added to their worship and ceremonies which are never once mentioned in the New Testament.

TRADITION MAY BE GOOD OR BAD

The nature of tradition is not determined by its oral or written form alone, but by its original source and content. Is it from God or men? Is it Biblically correct or does it contradict the word of God? Is it from heaven or from men? Paul praised the Corinthians for holding fast the ordinances (traditions) which he had delivered (1 Corinthians 11:2). He is here speaking of divinely inspired instruction, for he says, "For I have received of the Lord that which also I delivered unto you" (1 Cor. 11:23a).

237

Jesus condemned human tradition when it interfered with obedience to God, saying to the Jewish leaders, "Thus have ye made the commandment of God of none effect by your tradition" (Matthew 15:6b). Again, our Lord said to the Pharisees, "Full well ye reject the commandment of God, that ye may keep your own traditions" (Mark 7:9). Some religious bodies today reject the word of God and follow human traditions in their worship services.

REJECT HUMAN TRADITION

Being governed by a "Thus saith the Lord" and professing to "Speak where the Bible speaks and to be silent where it is silent," we cannot and will not accept the binding authority of human tradition. Paul told Titus to rebuke the church in Crete lest they should give heed to fables and the commandments of men, "That turn from the truth" (Titus 1:14-15). Again Paul wrote the church in Colossae saying, "Wherefore if ye be dead with Christ from the rudiments of the world, are ye subject unto ordinances (traditions), (Touch not; taste not; handle not; which all are to perish with the using;) after the commandments and doctrines of men?" (Col. 2:20-22). Have you observed certain so-called holy days from childhood? Were you baptized while still an infant? What about the rituals where you attend church? Are the traditional practices observed in churches today based on the word of God, or on human authority?

WHAT IS THE CHAFF TO THE WHEAT?

Jehovah inspired his prophet Jeremiah to issue some stern warnings to the false prophets, and to his people who were being deceived by them, in Jeremiah 23:28-29, "The prophet that hath a dream, let him tell a dream; but he that hath my word, let him speak my word faithfully. What is the chaff to the wheat? saith the Lord, Is not my word like a fire? saith the Lord; and like a hammer that breaketh the rock in pieces?" It is no time today for dreams and fables when souls are dying, and mankind is hungering for the bread of life. Chaff is dead and lifeless, while the word of God pulsates with energy and saving power (Romans 1:16). Chaff is worthless but the word of

God is living and powerful (Hebrews 4:12). A scientist can produce a grain of corn or wheat which seems to be identical with real grain, but he cannot inject the germ of life so that it will produce a living plant. Men can fabricate their dreams and proclaim their visions, but only faith in God and obedience to his gospel can save our souls (James 1:21; 1 Cor. 15:1-2).

THE PROBLEM OF ORAL TRADITION

We are aware that some claim that there is a body of inspired truth, spoken by Christ and endorsed by the apostles, which was never committed to writing. They tell us that these truths, although they were never committed to writing, have been handed down by word of mouth from the first century and are of equal authority with the written word in our New Testament. This theory of oral tradition poses a real problem when one considers how difficult it is for people to transmit a factual account around a room, much less an accurate message passed down through twenty centuries. How could such a message be reliable without each individual who passed it on being inspired? This would require continuing inspiration and special revelations. Of course we have had certain religious teachers who have claimed to be inspired, and claimed to be guided by the Holy Spirit. This, of course, conflicts with the Biblical claims of final and complete revelation (2 Peter 1:3). If we have all things that pertain to life and godliness as Peter affirms, and we do, what need would we have for present day revelation? Paul says, "That the man of God may be thoroughly furnished unto all good works" (2 Tim. 3:16). And Jude speaks of the faith, "Which was once delivered unto the saints" (Jude 3). This does not leave any valid reason for continuing revelation, but another perplexing question arises. If these teachers today are guided by the Holy Spirit why do they contradict and condemn one another?

WHY BE BOUND BY HUMAN AUTHORITY?

Man-made traditions set up barriers to fellowship and set aside the authority of the Bible. Human tradition introduces its own laws and restrictions. It binds that which God has loosed, and looses that which God has bound. It is just as evil to be a law maker in the church as it is to be a law breaker. It is difficult to say which is the worse, but God condemns them both. We read of the Jews, who condemned the man whom Jesus had healed, because he had violated their traditions relative to Sabbath keeping, by carring his bed (John 5:10). We are told that they persecuted Jesus and sought to kill him because he violated their tradition. Although Jesus kept the will of his Father he refused to be bound by their authority. In turn, Jesus charged the Pharisees with having transgressed the commandment of God, relative to caring for their parents, by using an excuse based on tradition (Matt. 15:3-6).

TRADITIONS CAN CORRUPT GOD'S WAY

Man-made tradition has often opened the flood gates to hundreds of innovations. These innovations have corrupted and changed the government of the church, and altered the doctrinal stance of the church as well. In an article in the *Gospel Advocate* of April 16, 1981, p. 243, Jim E. Waldron writes, "At this present stage in history, the 'Christianity' that most people see is covered with so much tapestry from the dark ages, so much hair-splitting from the various sects, so much infidelity from the modernistic theologians and so much Judaism from the Sabbatarians that the average man despairs to find the simple life of a disciple whose only desire is to serve the humble Man from Galilee. People are generally more upset by being shown that their traditions are wrong than they are when God and the Bible are attacked. Concerning Easter for example, one finds that to criticise the Easter festival is considered by many to be virtually blasphemous, when in reality the term 'Easter' comes from an ancient, mythological Anglo-Saxon goddess, 'Estre' (New Webster's Dictionary of the English Language, p. 273). The Easter celebration is based upon tradition and not Scripture." Similar statements could be truthfully made relative to the observance in the church of Lent, Christmas and certain other so-called holy days.

NOT A LAW MAKING BODY

It is not within the power or province of the church to

240

make laws or by-laws, to amend or change, to add too, or subtract from the revealed will of God. The church of our Lord is an absolute monarchy with Christ as King of kings, and Lord of lords. All power is vested in Christ the head of the church, and all authority is his both in heaven and on earth (Matt. 28:18-19). The church exists to proclaim the gospel and to execute the will of her Lord. The enactment of laws and decrees is not left to the discretion of the church. Professor John L. Girardeau, of Columbia Theological Seminary, in his book (*Instrumental Music In Public Worship*, p. 24) says, "The principle of the discretionary power of the church in regard to things not commanded by Christ in his word, was the chief fountain from which flowed the gradually increasing tide of corruptions that swept the Latin church into apostasy from the gospel of God's grace. And as surely as causes produce their appropriate effects, and history repeats itself in obedience to that law, any Protestant church which embodies that principle in its creed is destined, sooner or later, to experience a similar fate." Remember, it was our Lord who said, "In vain they do worship me, teaching for doctrines the commandments of men" (Matt. 15:9).

QUESTIONS

Give your definition of the word "tradition."

What tradition did Paul urge the Corinthians to "hold fast"?

Why did Jesus condemn the traditions of the Pharisees?

How reliable is oral tradition?

Give some examples of human tradition.

Is the church a law making body?

50

The church anxiously awaits
THE RETURN OF JESUS

By Guy V. Caskey

A mature Christian man said to me: "I wish Jesus would come down in our midst now and take us back to heaven with him." This frank, sincere statement arrested my attention. This was not a sudden, impulsive, irresponsible utterance of a man who despaired of life, who had grown weary of insoluble problems and so depressed with life's unfavorable circumstances it no longer held for him any attraction or meaning. It was, rather, an expression which disclosed his faith in the promise of the Lord to return, and revealed bright expectancy of his heart of a future life far better than this one on earth.

This statement of an unusual man prompted me to search the Scriptures for the promise that Jesus is coming again. I wanted to know the "how" and the "when" along with "what" would attend this most significant event. All of the answers to the questions people ask concerning this momentous occasion are not easily obtained. The reason for this, doubtless, is that God did not choose to divulge some things to us about the second coming of Christ. There are some matters, however, regarding this occurrence about which the Bible is very plain.

JESUS IS COMING BACK

The promise of his coming again is frequently stated in the New Testament. There are as many as fifty passages that deal with his return, and most of them are clearly, unmistakably, understood. Let us observe a sampling: "This same Jesus, who is taken up from you into heaven, shall so come in like manner as ye have seen him go into heaven" (Acts 1:11). "If I go and prepare a place for you, I will come again, and receive you unto myself; that where I am, there ye may be also" (John 14:3). "For this we say unto you by the word of the Lord, that we who are alive and remain unto the coming of the Lord shall not prevent (precede) them which are asleep. For the Lord himself shall descend from heaven . . ." (1 Thessalonians 4:15-16). "Looking for that blessed hope and the glorious appearing of the great God and our Saviour Jesus Christ" (Titus 2:13). "But we know that, when he shall appear, we shall be like him; for we shall see him as he is" (1 John 3:2). There is no doubt about it, our Lord is coming back. Are we anxiously awaiting his return?

THE PURPOSE OF HIS RETURN

The reason for Jesus' return is put in very simple terms in the Bible — to reward the righteous and to punish the wicked. In describing the judgment scene, the Lord said: 'And these (the wicked) shall go away into everlasting punishment: but the righteous into life eternal" (Matt. 25:46). And Paul, in later years, said that God would "recompense tribulation to them that trouble you," but that he would give rest to you who are troubled, "when the Lord Jesus shall be revealed from heaven with his mighty angels, in flaming fire taking vengeance on them that know not God, and that obey not the gospel of our Lord Jesus Christ: who shall be punished with everlasting destruction from the presence of the Lord, and from the glory of his power" (2 Thess. 1:6-9). "Then shall the wicked be revealed, whom the Lord will consume with the spirit of his mouth, and shall destroy with the brightness of his coming" (2 Thess. 2:8). "Henceforth there is laid up for me a crown of righteousness, which the Lord, the righteous Judge, shall give to me at that day: and not to me only, but unto all of them also that love his appearing" (2 Tim. 4:8).

Edward Gibbon, the English historian, who wrote the

Decline And Fall of the Roman Empire, gave several reasons for the rapid growth and strength of the church in the first century. Among these reasons was the belief in immortality: 'When the promise of eternal happiness was proposed to mankind on the condition of adopting the faith and of observing the precepts of the gospel, it is no wonder that so advantageous an offer should have been accepted by great numbers of every religion, of every rank, and of every province in the Roman empire." But he further stated that "the most dreadful calamities were denounced against an unbelieving world." The Christian looks with happy anticipation to his return, for then shall the righteous (both those who are alive at his coming and those who are asleep) be caught up "to meet the Lord in the air: and so shall we ever be with the Lord" (1 Thess. 4:17).

WHAT WILL TRANSPIRE AT HIS COMING?

There are a number of things that will take place when Jesus comes again:

(1) *The resurrection of the dead.* "But every man in his own order: Christ the firstfruits; afterwards they that are Christ's at his coming" (1 Cor. 15:23).

2. *The body of the Christian will be changed.* "In a moment, in the twinkling of an eye, at the last trump: for the trumpet shall sound, and the dead shall be raised incorruptible, and we shall be changed. For this corruption must put on incorruption, and this mortal must put on immortality" (1 Cor. 15:52-53).

3. *All men will be judged.* "For we shall all stand before the judgment seat of Christ" (Rom. 14:10). ". . . the word that I have spoken, the same shall judge him in the last day" (Jno. 12:48). "For the hour is coming, in the which all that are in their graves shall hear his voice, and shall come forth; they that have done good unto the resurrection of life; and they that have done evil unto the resurrection of damnation" (Jno. 5:28-29). Look at the judgment scene in Matthew 25:41-46.

4. *The end will come.* ". . . afterwards they that are Christ's at his coming. Then cometh the end, when he shall have delivered up the kingdom to God, even the

Father; when he shall have put down all rule and all authority and power" (1 Cor. 15:23-24).

5. *Christians will be taken to heaven.* (See 1 Thess. 4:17; Jno. 14:2-3).

6. *Death will be destroyed.* There will be no more death. "Death is swallowed up in victory. O death where is thy sting? O grave, where is thy victory?" (1 Cor. 15: 54-55).

With this promise of the occurrence of all these wonderful events at his coming, we should look forward to that day with great joy.

WILL HIS KINGDOM BE ESTABLISHED THEN?

There are many theories taught in our time to the effect that when Jesus returns, he will set up his kingdom in Palestine and rule over the earth for a period of a thousand years. This doctrine, or any variation of it, is nowhere taught in the Bible. It is difficult to know how fictitious and fatuous ideas get started. Gibbon remarked upon this subject. "When the edifice of the church was almost completed the temporary support was laid aside" and the doctrine of Christ's reign on the earth was rejected by the church.

The theory of a thousand years' reign of Christ on earth after his second coming makes the church a spiritual contingent, or accident (not planned, happened by chance), deprecates the Son of God, lessens the value of the church, reflects upon the intelligence of God and belittles the price Jesus paid for our sins (Acts 20:28). It is a failure to understand or a refusal to accept that the church is a kingdom, that Christ is now King, that Christians are citizens in that kingdom and that the New Testament is that official register and guide for our lives.

There is no doubt about it, Jesus Christ is now King. He is King of kings and Lord of lords (1 Tim. 6:15). Jesus himself affirmed that during the period of regeneration (when men are born again), "when the Son of man shall sit upon the throne of his glory, ye (twelve apostles) also shall sit upon twelve thrones, judging the twelve tribes of Israel" (Matt. 19:28). Paul declared that when Jesus comes again, he will deliver the kingdom up to God (1 Cor. 15:24). Instead of "taking up" rule and authority and power, he will "put down" all of these. Then Paul makes the very strong statement: "For he must reign, till he hath put all enemies under his feet. The last enemy that shall be destroyed is death" (1 Cor. 15:25-26). There are two evident truths worthy of our consideration in these passages: (1) "He shall reign till . . ." The word "reign" in this passage means "to be king." Paul is saying, "Christ will be King till . . ." (2) The extent of that reign will reach to the resurrection, or until death is destroyed. But in this chapter Paul declares that death will be destroyed by the resurrection (verse 54). So, Christ is now King and will continue to be King until the resurrection. Jesus has all the attributes of a full-crowned king: (1) He has all authority (Matt. 28:18). (2) Everything is made subject to him (Eph. 1:22-23). (3) He has a name that is above every name (Eph. 1:21; Phil. 3:9-10). (4) He exercises the power to deliver men from darkness and translate them into his kingdom (Col. 1:13). (5) He is highly exalted "far above all principality, and power, and might, and dominion" (Eph. 1:21). He will continue in this position until he comes back to judge the world.

WHEN WILL HE RETURN?

No man knows. No prophecy indicates that time. No passage reveals that day. It is pure speculation to name a day, and one who presumes to do so is a false prophet. Peter informs us, with reference to it, "But the day of the Lord will come as a thief in the night" (1 Pet. 3:10). It will be the last day (Jno. 6:44). It will be the end of time (1 Cor. 15:24). We are admonished to "watch and be ready," to make that preparation to meet him in joy and peace at his coming. "For what is our hope, or joy, or crown of rejoicing? Are not even ye in the presence of our Lord Jesus Christ at his coming? (1 Thess. 2:19).

QUESTIONS

How can we be sure Jesus is coming again?

In simple terms, what is the reason for Christ's return?

Name six things that will transpire when Jesus returns.

246

When was (or will) Christ's kingdom be established?
What are the attributes of a king which Jesus possesses?
Just when will the Lord return?

51

She teaches the

BODILY RESURRECTION OF THE JUST AND UNJUST

By Clayton Winters

In Acts 23:6 we read: "But when Paul perceived that the one part were Sadducees, and the other part Pharisees, he cried out in the council, Men and brethren, I am a Pharisee, the son of a Pharisee: of the hope and resurrection of the dead I am called in question."

Paul here expressed a hope that has sustained man through the ages of time — that there is to be a resurrection from the dead. Job, from the agony of a decaying body, could cry, "If a man die, shall he live again? all the days of my appointed time will I wait, till my change come. Thou shalt call, and I will answer thee: thou wilt have a desire to the work of thine hands" (Job. 14:14-15). As his condition worsened his hope but deepened: "For I know that my redeemer liveth, and that he shall stand at the latter day upon the earth: And though after my skin worms destroy this body, yet in my flesh shall I see God" (Job 19:25-26).

When David was compassed by the wicked, lurking secretly as greedy lions of prey, his hope of a resurrection defied the temporal threat. "As for me, I will behold thy face in righteousness: I shall be satisfied, when I awake, with thy likeness" (Psalm 17:15).

In the New Testament Jesus held forth this hope in unmistakable terms: ". . . The dead shall hear the voice of the Son of God: and they that hear shall live" (John 3:25). Again, "Yet a little while, and the world seeth me no more; but ye see me: because I live, ye shall live also" (John 14:19). Such a hope sustained Martha in the tragic loss of her brother: "Martha saith unto him, I know that he shall rise again in the resurrection at the last day" (John 11:24); and Paul could affirm amidst increased persecution and imminent martyrdom, "For we know that if our earthly house of this tabernacle were dissolved, we have a building of God, an house not made with hands, eternal in the heavens. For in this we groan,earnestly desiring to be clothed upon with our house which is from heaven" (2 Corinthians 5:1-2).

A GENERAL RESURRECTION
OF BOTH RIGHTEOUS AND WICKED

While some would separate the resurrection of the righteous and the wicked by a thousand-year period, and others would say, ". . . There is no resurrection of the dead" (1 Cor. 15:12); nevertheless, the Scriptures affirm a general and simultaneous resurrection of both. Jesus taught, "Marvel not at this: for the hour is coming, in the which all that are in the graves shall hear his voice, and shall come forth; they that have done good, unto the resurrection of life; and they that have done evil, unto the resurrection of damnation" (John 5:28-29).

Further proof of a general rather than a separate resurrection of the just and unjust is seen from the fact that both classes will be raised and judged at Christ's second coming. The Christian dead will be raised to be with the Lord: "For this we say unto you by the word of the Lord, that we which are alive and remain unto the coming of the Lord shall not prevent them which are asleep. For the Lord himself shall descend from heaven with a shout, with the voice of the archangel, and with the trump of God: and the dead in Christ shall rise first: Then we which are alive and remain shall be caught up together with them in the clouds, to meet the Lord in the air: and so shall we ever be with the Lord" (1 Thess. 4:15-17). At this same coming the wicked will be raised to everlasting shame and contempt: "And to you who are troubled rest with us, when the Lord Jesus shall be revealed from heaven with his mighty angels, in flaming fire taking vengeance on them that know not God, and that obey not the gospel of our Lord Jesus Christ: Who shall be punished with everlasting destruction from the presence of the Lord and from the glory of his power; When he shall come to be glorified in his saints, and to be admired in all them that believe (because our testimony among you was believed) in that day" (2 Thess. 1:7-10).

As Jesus portrays the judgment scene at his second coming, let it be observed that all are present. "When the Son of man shall come in his glory, and all the holy angels with him, then shall he sit upon the throne of his glory: And before him shall be gathered all nations: and he shall separate them one from another, as a shepherd divideth his sheep from the goats" (Matt. 25:31-32). And thus we would conclude that the resurrection will be both general and simultaneous.

But two Scriptures are often used to differentiate between the resurrection of the righteous and the wicked. These are 1 Thessalonians 4:6 and Revelation 20:5-6. The Thessalonian passage most certainly says, "And the dead in Christ shall rise first." But the question is, first before what? It is not first before the wicked dead are raised, for that is no part of the context; but rather first before the saints who are still living are caught up to be with the Lord. That is, the living Christians will not precede the dead ones in their being united with the Lord. This is its true context, and to make it say more than that is to abuse Scripture.

Again it is certain that Revelation 20 mentions a first and second resurrection. But we must remember that this book is symbolic in nature (see Rev. 1:1), and must not be interpreted in such a way as to conflict with literal Scriptures dealing with the resurrection. Also it should be observed that, aside from its figurative nature, Revelation 20:4-5 does not even teach a *general* resurrection of the *righteous*, as some would lead us to believe. Rather it concerns only the "Souls of them that were beheaded for the witness of Jesus . . ." This is a chapter dealing with the blessed state of those martyred for the cause of

Christ, not a proof-text for separate resurrections for the righteous and wicked.

A BODILY RESURRECTION

There are some who presume to deny a bodily resurrection. Even Jesus' body, they say, was probably dissolved into some gaseous substance rather than being reunited with his spirit at that garden tomb.

But such a theory is in direct conflict with what the Bible presents as a resurrection. When Jesus took the hand of the dead daughter of Jairus, she arose (Mark 5:41-42). That was a bodily resurrection. Jesus approached the tomb of Lazarus: "And when he thus had spoken, he cried with a loud voice, Lazarus, come forth. And he that was dead came forth, bound hand and foot with graveclothes: and his face was bound about with a napkin. Jesus saith unto them, Loose him, and let him go" (John 11:43-44). That was a bodily resurrection. At the death of Jesus there was a great earthquake, "And the graves were opened; and many bodies of the saints which slept arose, and came out of the graves after his resurrection, and went into the holy city, and appeared unto many" (Matt. 27:52-53). That was a bodily resurrection.

To be sure our bodies will be changed and adapted to an eternal nature (1 Cor. 15:51-54). Of this change Paul wrote, "Who shall change our vile body, that it may be fashioned like unto his glorious body, according to the working whereby he is able to subdue all things unto himself" (Philippians 3:21). But it will still be *our body* that is resurrected and changed. And so Paul could exclaim, "And not only they but ourselves also, which have the firstfruits of the Spirit, even we ourselves groan within ourselves, waiting for the adoption, to wit, the redemption of our body" (Romans 8:23).

DEATH IS SWALLOWED UP IN VICTORY

By the resurrection of Jesus Christ we have been begotten again unto a lively hope (1 Peter 1:3). He has delivered us from the bondage to which we have been subjected by the fear of death (Heb. 2:15). And no matter what forces Satan may marshal against us, one day the heavens will resound with the shout of the redeemed, "O death, where is thy sting? O grave, where is thy victory?" (1 Cor. 15:55). "Hallelujah, We Shall Rise!"

QUESTIONS

Through what did Old Testament saints find hope and encouragement?

What proof is there of a general and simultaneous resurrection of the just and unjust?

Why do 1 Thessalonians 4:16 and Revelation 20:5-6 not teach separate resurrections of the righteous and the wicked?

What Biblical proof is there of a bodily resurrection?

Will there be any kind of changes in our bodies in the resurrected state?

52

She proclaims
HEAVEN FOR THE RIGHTEOUS
HELL FOR THE WICKED

By Reuel Lemmons

An eternal God has provided an eternal reward for the eternal soul of man. Death isn't the end of it all. Scarce have the clods closed over us until we will be ushered into an eternal day. There will be a resurrection of all the dead, both good and bad. Oblivion isn't the eternal destiny after graduation from the school of life.

Paul, in the fifteenth chapter of First Corinthians, explains in detail the nature of the resurrection. "As in Adam all die, so in Christ shall all be made alive," is his conclusion. When the resurrection takes place, the righteous, trailing clouds of glory shall fly to the outstretched arms of him who went to Calvary that they might go to heaven. The wicked, unable to sleep, will have to arise to meet a God they have spurned and a Jesus they have turned down.

The Bible is specific and plain on the subject of Judgment. There will be a judgment. None will be able to sleep through it and none will be absent. All of us will meet God in Judgment. Many passages of Scripture refer to the fact that the dead, both small and great; both rich and poor; both good and bad will face God in judgment. We may stay out of church if we want to. We can live as mean as the Devil as long as we live if we wish. But there is one rendevous we are all going to keep: we will meet God in Judgment (John 5:28-29).

In Matthew 25, Jesus gives us some specific information about what will take place when the Judgment day dawns. He says, "When the Son of man shall come in his glory, and all the holy angels with him, then shall he sit upon the throne of his glory: and before him shall be gathered all nations: and he shall separate them one from another, as a shepherd divideth his sheep from the goats: And he shall set the sheep on his right hand, but the goats on his left" (25:31-33). We have the same picture in the wording of that powerful hymn:

> "There's a great day coming,
> A great day coming,
> A great day coming, by and by —
> When the saints and the sinners
> shall be parted right and left —
> Are you ready for that day to come?"

That question ought to be seriously considered by all who read these lines. The same Bible that tells us about heaven also tells us about Hell. There is no way to take one out of the Bible and leave the other in.

And there is no third option. All who miss heaven will end up in Hell. There is no other place to go. The judgment of God is final, and there is no higher court to which we can appeal an unfavorable verdict.

It is very final — this judgment. There is no second chance. There is no purgatory that we can be prayed out of. There is no possibility that someone else can be baptized for us after we are dead and effect our escape from the pit. Whatever reward we receive in the judgment, we will always have. It is eternal in duration. This is all the more reason why we ought to make our calling and election sure while we have the chance to do so (2 Peter 1:10-11).

The entire book of Revelation is given over to picturing for us, from many viewpoints, the cardinal fact that the lost will be punished while the redeemed will be richly rewarded in glory. Hell is designated as the abode of the lost forever, and Heaven is named as the home of the righteous forever.

We do not like to think about Hell. None of us would

want to go there. If we had a chance to test the reality of Hell for five minutes we would all, if we had the opportunity, want to obey the gospel. Hell is described often in the Scriptures — always as a horrible place where worms don't die, and the fire is never quenched (Mark 9:48). Jesus put it this way in Matthew twenty-five; "Then shall he say also unto them on the left hand, Depart from me, ye cursed, into everlasting fire, prepared for the Devil and his angels:" (verse 41).

It would be an awful thing to be shut out from the presence of God forever. Here in this life we would surely not want to be banished to a place where God never shows his power or providence. It would be much worse to have to spend an eternity in a place where light never comes, and grace and love and mercy are unknown.

If we were born totally depraved, and incapable of being saved, we might well blame God; but we were not. We are free moral agents — capable of choosing to be lost or saved. If any of us are lost it will be because we chose to be lost. God has done all He can do. Jesus has done all he can do. The ball is in our court and the next move is ours. If we are lost it will be our fault and none other's.

How much more desirable it is to be saved eternally, and to live in heaven following judgment. We can, you know.

Limited as we are to the vehicle of human speech, it is completely impossible to adequately describe the glories and the joys of that celestial world. Eye has not seen; ear has not heard; nor has it entered into any man's heart what God has prepared for the redeemed (1 Cor. 2:9). About all we can say is that God will wipe away all tears from our eyes forever. There will be no more sorrow nor sickness, and the angel says, there shall not be any more death; for these former things shall have passed away (Rev. 21:4).

All the tongues of all the orators and the pens of all the poets cannot do justice to a description of heaven. Only God can prepare such a place, for only God is infinite and omnipotent. And only God is love.

Dear reader, you have read through this little book. You have given serious consideration to your soul. You are convinced of your present state: you are either lost or saved. You have the hope of heaven or you do not. May we urge you with all the power of persuasion that we have, to not risk another day outside of Christ. Life is fraught with too much danger and uncertainty for you to leave your soul uninsured. Today is the day of salvation. Be saved while you can.

QUESTIONS

Review the teaching of 1 Corinthians 15 concerning the resurrection.

Some teach two separate resurrections. Discuss this in light of John 5:28-29.

What does purgatory mean? What does the Bible say on the subject?

What are some of the figures used to describe hell?

Discuss the picture of heaven described in Revelation 21 and 22.